T0246818

FALL COLOR HIKES
WASHINGTON

FALL COLOR HIKES WASHINGTON

TAMI ASARS

MOUNTAINEERS
BOOKS

MOUNTAINEERS BOOKS is dedicated to the exploration, preservation, and enjoyment of outdoor and wilderness areas.

1001 SW Klickitat Way, Suite 201, Seattle, WA 98134
800-553-4453, www.mountaineersbooks.org

Printed in South Korea
Distributed in the United Kingdom by Cordee, www.cordee.co.uk
First edition, 2022

Copyeditor: Ali Shaw
Design and layout: Heidi Smets
Cartographer: Lohnes + Wright
All photographs by the author unless credited otherwise
Cover: *An enchanted area teeming with golden larches welcomes hikers to the high country near Carne Mountain (Hike 18).*
Frontispiece: *Larches sprinkle themselves across the broad slopes near Carne Mountain.*
Back cover: *Brilliant autumn foliage abounds on the Granite Mountain hike (Hike 31).*

The background maps for this book were produced using the online map viewer CalTopo. For more information, visit www.caltopo.com.

Library of Congress Control Number: 2022933079

Mountaineers Books titles may be purchased for corporate, educational, or other promotional sales, and our authors are available for a wide range of events. For information on special discounts or booking an author, contact our customer service at 800-553-4453 or mbooks@mountaineersbooks.org.

Printed on FSC®-certified materials

MIX
Paper | Supporting
responsible forestry
FSC® C140526

ISBN (paperback): 978-1-68051-305-9
ISBN (ebook): 978-1-68051-306-6

An independent nonprofit publisher since 1960

CONTENTS

Hikes Overview Map 8
Introduction: Autumn Landscapes 10
Guide to Fall Foliage Photography 27
How to Use This Book 31
Map Legend 35

HIKES

MOUNT BAKER

1. Yellow Aster Butte 39
2. Chain Lakes Loop 42
3. Lake Ann 47
4. Excelsior Peak (Damfino Lakes Trailhead) 50
5. Park Butte 53

NORTH CASCADES, METHOW VALLEY, AND MOUNTAIN LOOP HIGHWAY

6. Tatie Peak and Grasshopper Pass 57
7. Cutthroat Lake 61
8. Cutthroat Pass 64
9. Easy Pass 67
10. Blue Lake 69
11. Maple Pass Loop/Lake Ann 72
12. Crater Lakes 75
13. Eagle Lakes 78
14. Lake Twentytwo 81

SPOKANE

15. Riverside Park Loop 85
16. Finch Arboretum Loop 88
17. Iller Creek/Dishman Hills Conservation Area 91

STEVENS PASS, LEAVENWORTH, AND WENATCHEE

18. Carne Mountain 94
19. Little Giant Pass 97
20. West Cady Ridge 101
21. Evergreen Mountain Lookout 104
22. Lake Valhalla 107
23. Hope and Mig Lakes 110
24. Colchuck Lake 112
25. Clara and Marion Lakes 116

NORTH BEND, SNOQUALMIE PASS, AND TEANAWAY

26. Lake Ingalls 119
27. Iron Bear and Teanaway Ridge 124
28. Rachel Lake and Rampart Ridge 127
29. Snow Lake 131
30. Melakwa Lake 135
31. Granite Mountain 139
32. Mason, Rainbow, and Island Lakes 142
33. Oxbow Loop 147
34. Bare Mountain 150

OLYMPIC MOUNTAINS

35. Staircase Rapids Loop 154

YAKIMA, SELAH, AND TIETON

36. Umtanum Creek Canyon 158
37. Tieton River Nature Trail 161

MOUNT RAINIER

38. Goat Peak 166
39. Naches Peak Loop 170
40. Upper Palisades Lake 173
41. Shriner Peak 177
42. Sheep Lake and Sourdough Gap 180
43. Myrtle Falls and Golden Gate Loop 184

INDIAN HEAVEN WILDERNESS

44. East Crater Lakes Loop 188
45. Thomas, Blue, and Tombstone Lakes 192

SCENIC DRIVES

Scenic Drives Overview Map 198

1. Artist Point and Mount Baker 199
2. North Cascades Highway 202
3. Mountain Loop Highway 205
4. Stevens Pass, Tumwater Canyon, and Leavenworth 209
5. Seward Park and Washington Park Arboretum 212
6. Snoqualmie Pass, Teanaway Road, and Blewett Pass 216
7. White Pass Byway Loop 219
8. Stevens Canyon Road to Paradise 224

Acknowledgments 229
Resources 230
Index 234

Hikes Overview Map

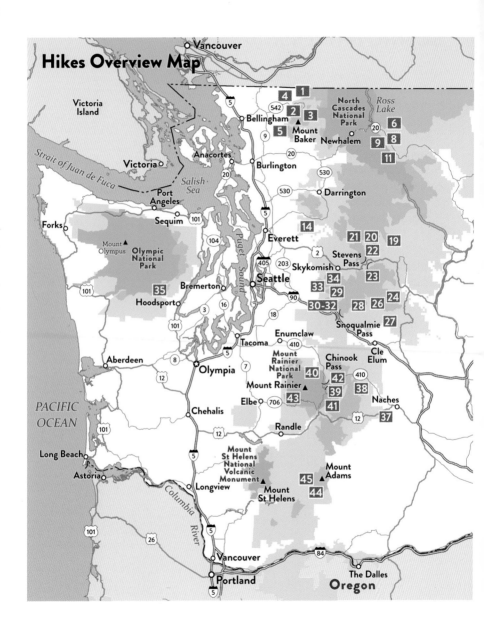

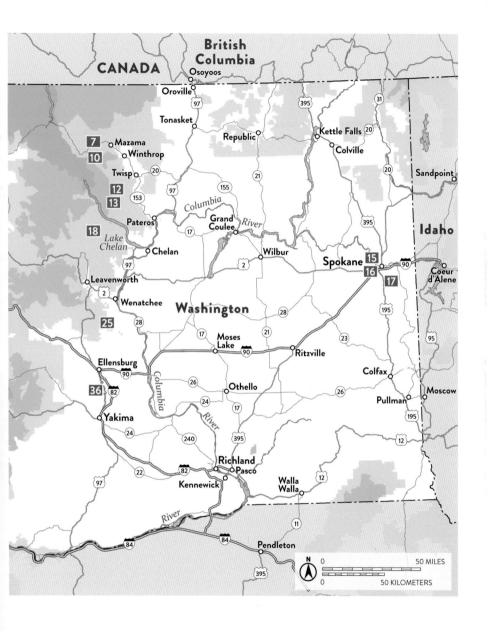

INTRODUCTION
AUTUMN LANDSCAPES

When you ask a longtime Pacific Northwest resident to name their favorite hiking season, the autumn time frame almost always makes the top of the list. Gone are the pesky mosquitoes waiting to pierce exposed skin, the balmy days laden with oppressive heat, and the consolidated piles of lingering winter snow in the high country. Instead, the landscape is changing colors, shedding layers, and preparing itself to dive headlong into winter's icy grip.

There is a tranquility that comes with watching nature accept the changes with peaceful submission, and lessons can be found in the crisp mornings, the smell of decaying earth, and the consistency of annual transformation that we watch from our front-row seats. But perhaps the most enticing reason to visit the backcountry in autumn is simply the eye-popping colors and the dustings of snow on the high, jagged peaks. Unequaled in saturation and brilliance are the red huckleberry bushes, the orange grasses, the rusty maples, and the golden larches framed against a bluebird sky.

Larches share the landscape with the fading seed pods of Western pasqueflower near Carne Mountain (Hike 18).

Scenic drives also offer a way to enjoy the changing seasons from camera-worthy turf as leaves drop and swirl with the gust from your passing vehicle. Even roadways seem inviting when framed by yellow maples or golden cottonwoods.

I've become as passionate about the mountains in the fall as I am about them in the summer wildflower season. Almost nothing can beat the sights and fragrances of a conglomeration of wildflowers during the summer, but the chilly air, the loamy soil, and the jewel-toned autumn vegetation presents a unique visual and olfactory experience that is present only with natural change.

A great horned owl stares at the author from the safety of its perch.

Of course, you'll want to share the colorful moments of your hike or drive with drool-worthy photos. When colors abound, the camera is happy—and when the camera is happy, the photographer is rewarded. In fact, to many, playing with a camera and getting the perfect shot is half the fun of a perfect fall day.

Being a Washington State native, I've grown up on these trails and am excited to share them with you, the like-minded folks who wander the hinterlands in search of something that makes your soul feel at rest. Within these pages are the blue-ribbon places to visit for fall splendor in Washington State.

In some parts of the state, such as the Spokane area and the Olympics, the reds, yellows, and oranges are tough to find amidst a sea of evergreens, but I've done my best to find at least a hike or two where maples, cottonwoods, or deciduous shrubbery dot the pathway and you can revel in the feelings of autumn.

When the mountains present us with one last peace offering to enjoy their hillsides before accessibility is limited, we gladly accept. May you meander to your heart's content discovering the many places that will lift your spirits, fill your camera, and top off your soul's cookie jar. Happy trails!

PUZZLING AND PERPLEXING PARKING PERMITS, PASSES, AND PARK PRICING

These days there are so many passes and regulations, it's often hard to know which one is which and what you'll need for where. Wouldn't it be great if there were just one giant pass that worked for every location? Sigh. Until that happens,

Color is alive on the slopes near Little Giant Pass (Hike 19).

we're left to unravel the pass-permit-paying conundrum. Perhaps this list will help:

Discover Pass

If you plan to play or park on land that belongs to the State of Washington, you'll need to get one of these passes. The pass comes in two versions, the annual pass and the day-use pass. The Discover Pass can be purchased at various vendor and retail locations across the state or online (see Resources). There are a handful of free days per year that are noted on the website as well. Oh, and by the way, if you want to be a cool kid, never call it a Discovery Pass. That's a rookie move.

Interagency Passes

As far as a utopian comprehensive pass goes, this one is as close as you can get. While it doesn't cover the Washington State recreational lands, which still require the Discover Pass, you can use it in lieu of the Northwest Forest Pass (see below) for federally operated recreational lands as well as national parks. The pass is actually a card, the same size as a credit card, which you show to the gate attendees at national parks or put on your dashboard when you park in pass-required areas. America the Beautiful is the name of the primary interagency pass, which is available to everyone for purchase. However, other versions (with a different physical design) are available at a discount or even free to various groups of people, such as senior citizens and those with permanent disabilities. Other qualifying groups include volunteers who offer 250 hours of service in one year on federally managed recreation sites, US military personnel and their dependents, and US fourth-grade students who go through Every Kid Outdoors. See the Resources section for websites.

Northwest Forest Pass

For developed Forest Service trailheads in Washington, such as those with designated parking areas, pit toilets, or picnic areas, you'll need either an Interagency Pass or the Northwest Forest Pass. The latter is available both online (see Resources) and at select retailers, and can be purchased as either an annual pass, good for one year from date of purchase, or a one-day pass.

National Park Fees and Passes

If you want to hike in a national park, but you aren't interested in purchasing an Interagency Pass, you'll need to pay an entrance fee that varies according to your mode of transportation (vehicle, motorcycle, bicycle, walking), either at the park or online (see Resources). If you find yourself frequently visiting one of those parks, you may want to consider purchasing an annual pass for that specific park.

Wilderness Use Permits

This one is less of a "permit" or "pass" and more of a form that the Forest Service requests you fill out if you are visiting a wilderness area. The information on it helps the Forest Service gauge the number of visitors using the area, which in turn helps them get grants and funding. It also helps them know how many people are out there if something unfortunate were to happen, such as a forest fire, during your trip.

It's the cheapest of the bunch because it's free and does not require any advanced planning to obtain. At some, but not all, trailheads in wilderness areas, you'll find a wooden box containing the permits (forms), which are carbon copies. If you see one, fill out the form with the relevant information about you and your trip, then attach one of the copies to your pack, and leave the other in the box's slot. As a side note, most of these boxes only have a stubby golf pencil, if you are lucky. Bring a pen from your glove box when you go to fill out the form, and consider donating it to the box when you're done. You'll alleviate the challenges for future hikers with that tiny bit of kindness, plus you'll win pay-it-forward points, which are super valuable when setting off for adventures.

Combat Parking

The showiest fall hikes, including many in this book, attract the masses. The seasonal window for these hikes is short, so understandably, me, you, and half the zoo are front and center for these impressive romps, and parking can get, well, downright ugly at times. Thanks to COVID-19, midweeks aren't always lighter than weekends anymore, and good weather makes crowds magically grow. Carpooling whenever possible will be much to your benefit.

Perhaps your best strategy is to schlep your sleepy hindquarters out of your warm bed before first light and get there before the day has warmed or become desirable. I've snapped my best sunrise pictures this way and found quiet solitude while most are still sitting at their kitchen tables pouring maple syrup on their pancakes. If that's usually you, you might try the afternoon game plan and get to the trailhead when most folks are hitting the summit or the middle of the hike. With luck, you'll be trading parking spots with the early birds. Just be sure to have that headlamp with fresh batteries along since darkness descends quickly at this time of year.

STAYING SAFE

A few simple tips can help you stay warm, dry, and safe as you venture out in the cooler months. Knowing them and being prepared might just save your life!

1. **Dress for the season:** When you left home, you might have done so under a sunny sky and calm winds, but mountains often make their own weather, and temperatures can drop very quickly, especially after sundown. I pack for cold weather by doing an assessment of garments, from my head right down to my toes—don't laugh; it works. Hat for my head, gaiter for my neck, warm jacket for my torso, gloves for my digits, etc. By covering your whole body mentally, you won't forget any of those easy-to-miss garments, and you'll be well prepared for the unexpected.

2. **Use shoe traction:** When fall imitates winter and snow covers the landscapes, it makes for beautiful photos but slippery trails, especially on the uphill. Invest in some shoe traction, such as Yaktrax or Kahtoola MICROspikes, which serve as tire chains or cleats for your shoes and help you get a better grip in slick conditions. I use mine not only in the fall but also in the winter months so that I don't have to stop hiking just because buzz-killing ice says so. Of course, if the snow falls in large quantities, you'll want to grab a pair of snowshoes and have some education on safely traveling in avalanche terrain before you set out for the hills.

3. **Light it up:** During cloudy days or the late fall time frame, it can be black as night by early evening, especially in the deep forests. Bring a headlamp with strong batteries and make a few mental notes about your surroundings as you wander.

4. **Let 'em know where you go:** Most folks know to let someone know where they are going and when they expect to return home, but why not take it one step further and email them a map or trail description? If you don't return home, at least they'll know where you likely were hiking.

5. **Carry a messaging device:** No, I don't mean the tiny telecommunication device (a.k.a. phone) in your pocket. Those are great, when service allows, but

Putting the sun to bed on Carne Mountain is a treat for the eyes and shampoo for the soul (Hike 18).

in many backcountry locations, reception is limited or not functional. Remote communication devices such as SPOT or Garmin inReach have recently flooded the market, making it easy and relatively affordable for casual hikers to send two-way texts and emergency communications when necessary. If you ever truly need it, it will be worth every penny. And if you don't truly need it, checking in to let family know you are running late is a courtesy that I'm sure they'd appreciate.

6. **Pack extra stuff:** You never really know when something unforeseen—like a twisted ankle or a navigational challenge—can eject you into a bad day or possibly a frigid night. I have cold-weather gear that lives in my day pack in the cold months. It contains a tiny sleeping bag that's only as big as a guinea pig, a small emergency bivy sac, an old lightweight jacket, and some extra granola bars. Of course, the other Ten Essentials (see sidebar) live in there too, but these other items are my what-ifs. I figure that overpacking for an emergency will prevent one from ever happening, right?

7. **Know north:** Paper maps and navigational compasses are so last season; however, they are still truly the only guaranteed things you'll have to navigate with that don't have a screen or a battery. Let's face it: although most of the hikes in this book are busy and well-marked, a snowstorm can be a game changer. It's not a bad idea to have the old-school navigation loot in tow.

8. **Dress like a Dorito:** Fall hiking coincides with hunting season, and it's not uncommon—especially on trails that are less frequented—to see camo-clad

A single vine maple leaf decorates the soil.

folks toting guns or bows. While this may be unnerving to those who don't hunt, rest assured most hunters are kind, sensitive to their intimidating appearance, and often chatty when they see hikers. During hunting season, which starts August 1 for various types of game in Washington State, it's wise to wear the color blaze orange on your person and also on your pooch. If you aren't a fan of looking like a mound of fake cheese, purchase a hat of this color and attach it with a carabiner to the outside of your pack. Or dress your pack in an orange safety vest by modifying it with some Velcro. It's probably best, though, to just suck it up and wear the ensemble, which is sure to bring out the jewel tones in your complexion.

9. **Be in the H$_2$O know:** Invisible to the human eye are parasites with names straight out of sci-fi productions (cryptosporidium, leptospirosis, giardia, etc.) that may hang out in backcountry water. Treating your water with either a filtration or a chemical method is highly recommended so you don't get beaver fever or accidentally ingest a bacteria cafeteria. Small tablets or filters are rather inexpensive and are a worthwhile addition to your hiking kit.

10. **Know what to do if you get into trouble:** If you get lost or injured and your return is delayed, your friends or family will probably be in touch with search and rescue. A few things can help your odds of returning home safely:

    ➤ **Remain calm:** As with all precarious situations, thoroughly assess the situation and don't panic. Do you see familiar landmarks? When was the last time you remember seeing the trail?

    ➤ **Gather downed firewood and make a small fire pit:** If it's getting dark, you need to keep warm overnight, so get ready to make a fire.

    ➤ **Stay put:** A fixed target is easier to find than a moving one, and if you keep moving, you may be doing yourself a disservice by expending much-needed calories.

    ➤ **Patch it up:** Stay current on basic first aid so you have knowledge of how to care for various backcountry injuries.

    ➤ **Carry a whistle:** Whistle blasts are much louder than yelling, and they require less effort, thus increasing your chances of getting help. A universal distress signal is three loud, short whistle blasts. When selecting a whistle, check its decibels—some are so loud, the manufacturer suggests ear plugs. If you really need one, that's your huckleberry.

COUNT TO TEN

Having the **Ten Essentials** on your hikes is important to your backcountry safety. They are:

1. Navigation (map and compass)
2. Sun protection (sunglasses and sunscreen)
3. Insulation (extra clothing)
4. Illumination (headlamp or flashlight)
5. First-aid supplies
6. Fire (firestarter, matches)
7. Repair kit and tools (knife)
8. Nutrition (extra food)
9. Hydration (extra water—for this one, I also have a small water filter in my kit)
10. Emergency shelter

I have mine in a small mesh stuff sack, which I move from my day hiking pack to my ski pack as the seasons change. That way, I don't have to walk around the house collecting every item each time I go out. I check the batteries in the electronics and the expiration dates on the food before I leave home.

WILDERNESS ETHICS— LEAVE NO TRACE

With the rapid population growth in the Pacific Northwest, it's more important now than ever to follow a few simple guidelines to save these places from overuse growing pains, which often result in restricted-use permits. In other words, leave no trace. The fine folks over at the Leave No Trace Center for Outdoor Ethics (www.lnt.org) have a detailed list of principles, which I've customized with a few extra tidbits:

1. **Plan ahead and prepare:** For these hikes, which you'll be driving to, this mostly means you need to think about how you'll park. With so many visitors on trails these days, parking gets full quickly, especially on weekends. But you figure you drove all

Fungi make fantastic photos as they pop up through decaying matter in late autumn.

Fall splendor adorns the trail's edges on Chain Lakes Loop (Hike 2).

this way, and well . . . shucks, you are determined! Let common sense prevail and don't be *that guy* who puts passing motorists in jeopardy as you open your car door into the lane of a major highway. Follow posted rules, pay attention to parking passes and permits, and if there are no more parking spots, *submit to the fact that you might need to find another hike*. Have a good plan B and be prepared to use it. This book is loaded with other equally beautiful trails that are waiting for you to explore. Leave no trace: park legally.

2. **Be considerate of other visitors:** Personally, I don't want to live in a world without Tom Petty either, but rocking out with your Bluetooth speaker pumping, or even at a low roar, is a buzzkill for those who actually came for a backcountry experience. Instead, purchase a pair of headphones with bone-conduction technology or transparency mode so that you can still hear the music while paying attention to your surroundings, or just hike with one ear bud. Or, you know, leave the rhythms for the car ride. The speakers in your Prius are better anyway. Leave no trace: rock out in the car.

3. **Respect wildlife:** We've all seen folks doing dangerous things simply in the name of a photo, like getting too close to a grumpy mountain goat. It's not worth the new followers and social media likes. Do not approach wildlife; they have limited time to get their fill of vegetation before a long, tough winter, and disturbing them disrupts their natural feeding patterns. Long lenses or good zooms are a great way to say you saw it without having to get close. Leave no

trace: avoid ending up on the nightly news.

4. **Dispose of waste properly:** Simply stomach turning is the experience of rounding a corner only to see a toilet paper wad sticking out from behind a tree. You just can't help but wonder what the potty squatter who left it was thinking. Invest in a small roll of pet waste bags and use them like a glove to pick up your used TP if nature calls. You won't have to touch it, and it won't be there for others to sneer at the rest of the season. Win-win. If you have code brown while on trail, bury that sucker at least 6 to 8 inches deep and 200 feet or more from water. Oh, and for the love of all things wild and crazy, please pack out that dog waste bag, especially since you went to the effort of picking up the waste. Double bag it, take it with you, and avoid leaving it trailside to "get later." We all know how easy it is to forget or misplace it.

A young mountain goat plays peek-a-boo from behind a subalpine larch tree near Lake Ingalls (Hike 26).

Leave no trace: follow the duty for your call of duty.

5. **Travel and camp on durable surfaces:** While it's tempting to sit on the grassy meadow and spread out your charcuterie, resist the urge. Instead, find a little patch of pumice, gravel, or downed trees to bust out lunch. As the saying goes, plants grow by the inch but die by the foot. Leave no trace: picnic on pumice.

6. **Leave what you find:** Although cutting a couple of red maple branches to tuck into the wreath on your front door is cheaper than going to the craft store, other hikers might miss those. Plus, the fabric ones last longer. The same goes for all the foliage. Leave no trace: mitts off the maples, Mickey.

7. **Minimize wildfire impacts:** Sadly, wildfires are destroying our backcountry more and more each summer, and while fire zones can have their own appeal, it's best not to contribute to their creation. Should you feel the need to spend the night in a warm glow or simply have a cookout, read up on the area's fire restrictions and be sure you are in a zone, and during a time frame, that they are permitted. When done, extinguish the flame thoroughly and break apart any fire rings you may have created. Then, head back to your car, fire up Spotify, and pull up Michael Martin Murphy and his passionate warbles on wildfire.

Smatterings of earth tones splash the boulders near Easy Pass (Hike 9).

A NOTE ABOUT SAFETY

Safety is an important concern in all outdoor activities. No guidebook can alert you to every hazard or anticipate the limitations of every reader. Therefore, the descriptions of roads, trails, routes, and natural features in this book are not representations that a particular place or excursion will be safe for your party. When you follow any of the routes described in this book, you assume responsibility for your own safety. Under normal conditions, such excursions require the usual attention to traffic, road and trail conditions, weather, terrain, the capabilities of your party, and other factors. Keeping informed on current conditions and exercising common sense are the keys to a safe, enjoyable outing.

—Mountaineers Books

Sure it's a horse in the song, but it's a whole new world for your playlist; you're welcome. Leave no trace: "She Ran Calling Wildfire."

8. **National park know-how:** Certain rules apply to national parks that don't necessarily apply elsewhere. Pets (service animals excepted) and bicycles have limited or no access on trails in Washington's national parks. Drones are a big no-no, dope (marijuana) is a nope, and stringent rules govern campfires and firearms. Study up on the park's official website and know what's allowed before you go. Leave no trace: get schooled on rules.

WHERE THE WILD THINGS ARE

Wild animals in the fall are generally moodier than those found in the spring and summer. Elk are grumpy due to mating season, bears are a bit more territorial about food sources prior to denning season, and Sasquatch is itchy as he tries to grow more hair for warmth in winter. A little understanding and the following information will help you avoid conflicts.

Bears

Washington State has a healthy black bear population; if you see a bear, it's most likely this species. But don't be fooled; they come in other colors, including brown, cinnamon, and rust.

In general, black bears are fairly shy animals, carrying on about their business while bobbing and weaving through the growing number of backcountry recreationalists. Seeing one is an honor and a treat, and most likely you'll walk away with a great story and a giddy mood. However, in the fall, bears are on a mission for survival. Autumn berries are ripe and packed with nutrients that bears need as they approach the cold weather, and if they find a patch, they will often claim

Black bears, like this one along Naches Peak Loop, work hard to pack on weight prior to hibernation (Hike 39).

it until they've exhausted the supply. Because berry bushes provide some of the most breathtaking fall colors, fall hikers are often sharing spaces with these amazing creatures. In places like Mount Rainier National Park, where bears are federally protected from hunting, they are much more conditioned to seeing people and will often be fairly close to a trail if berries are nearby.

While bear mace or spray can give you a little peace of mind, it can also cause some issues if it's misused. Watch a reliable YouTube video on its use to educate yourself so you know what to do should you get into the unfortunate situation of having to discharge the canister.

A bear biologist for Washington Department of Fish & Wildlife once told me that one of the best defenses for a bear conflict is a really loud whistle. With this intel, I now carry a Fox 40 Sonik Blast (120+ decibels) on my shoulder straps at the ready, but there are many brands and options available. Since it also can aid in rescue, it's just a good thing to have anyway.

Bear conflicts generally occur when a bear is startled, on a kill, protecting young, or any combination of those. Keep things bear-y peaceful by following a few simple guidelines:

> **Clap, sing, or shout:** Make noise, especially on blind corners or in high brush to help a bear know a human is nearby. Forget bear bells—they aren't a natural human sound. In fact, in one study done in Alaska, bears walked by the tester's blind without even acknowledging the bells. Researchers think the reason may be that the sound is similar to bird calls. Your voice is a much better tool, and it's free.

> **Walk in pairs or groups:** You naturally tend to make more noise with other people, so hike together if possible. It's more fun anyway, right?

> **Don't let kids wander off or run ahead:** Kids have a tendency to get out the wiggles by running, which can trigger prey drive instincts in animals and also make a grumpy bear grumpier. Keep your children with you and close by at all times, and educate them on the importance of good behavior in bear country.

> **Keep Fido on a leash:** Off-leash dogs can create quite an issue with bears.

- ➤ **No trailblazing:** While you might decide you want to channel your inner Lewis and Clark and go exploring, it's best to stick to the trails. Not only will you reduce your impact in the area, but you'll also generally minimize animal encounters.
- ➤ **Signs, signs, everywhere there's signs:** In the fall, trails are often muddy, which makes them great places to note bear tracks. Also, look for bear scat piles, which are generally large and filled with digested berries and other plant matter. Bears will often rip leaves and branches off huckleberry plants while eating, so keep your eyes open for disturbances in vegetation.
- ➤ **Dodge a bear's dinner:** Dead ahead! If you smell something dead, see birds circling above, or see a fresh carcass, leave the area immediately. You could be encroaching on a bear's idea of a delicious meal.
- ➤ **Avoid darkness:** In other words, hike during daylight hours when bears are least active, since this can decrease the chances of an encounter.
- ➤ **Tone down scents:** While eau de bacon is a lovely odor to waft from your kitchen on a Saturday morning, avoid wearing perfumes, lotions, or clothes that smell like this morning's breakfast and might be interesting to a bear.
- ➤ **Steer clear of headphones:** They keep you from hearing important clues around you. But if you must, in recent years bone-conduction or transparency-mode headphones have helped those who want to enjoy some jams to also hear the outside world a bit better.

Carpets of fall leaves surround a primitive boot path near Alta Mountain (Hike 28).

If you do get approached by a bear, remain calm, appear nonthreatening, and don't run. Avoid sudden movement. Bears instinctively want to chase something that offers pursuit. Identify yourself as human, speaking clearly and calmly. If it does not respond and walks toward you in a threatening manner, raise your voice, blow your whistle, and let it know you mean business. Don't try to climb a tree—black bears are very capable climbers.

Bears may show signs of agitation by popping their jaws, stomping their paws, swaying their heads, snorting, or clacking their teeth. Sometimes a bear may bluff charge in an attempt to threaten you, in which case standing your ground is even more important. Of course, if you brought some, have your bear spray's cap off and ready to deploy. Once the charge is over, find a tree to hide behind as you change your soiled drawers.

Thankfully, black bear attacks are extremely rare, but if a good day turns bad, it's good to know what to do. Bear spray is simply the best defense and should be used as the first option. If you forgot it at home, fight back, fight hard, and use any weapons such as rocks, sticks, trekking poles, or whatever you can find. If you get knocked down, punch and kick sensitive areas such as the eyes and nose. Once it's over, you'll have mad bragging rights.

It is believed that only a very small population of grizzly bears inhabit the state. Their habitats are in the North Cascades, where fewer than ten are thought to live, and the Selkirk Mountains, where populations are estimated at fifty to sixty. If you plan to hike in those areas, be sure to learn the appropriate behavior for interacting with grizzlies, which varies slightly from black bears, and keep your eyes and ears open.

Elk

During fall, the antlered ones tend to be a little grumpier than their normal, nonchalant selves because they are in a cycle called rut, also known as mating season. Rutting can make ungulates more aggressive since the males compete for the attention of the ladies in the herd and sometimes spar over who is bigger and better. Incidentally, this behavior can also be observed in humans at college parties, but I digress.

Common sense should prevail when watching wildlife, mainly: you and the mutt, away from the rut.

> **Keep your distance:** Resist the temptation to snap a close picture. Elk, in particular, are common in the backcountry in Washington and, if threatened or agitated, can turn on a dime with an unexpected charge.
> **Keep dogs on leashes:** This is especially critical if you hear an elk call, known as a bugle.

Bugling starts as a deep guttural echo, becomes a shrill, ear-piercing shriek some-times followed by grunts, and is nearly impossible to miss. If you haven't heard

Rutting elk are often agitated in fall. Be sure to observe and photograph them from a safe distance during encounters.

one, hop online and familiarize yourself with the odd sound, especially before you end up in the backcountry on blind corners.

When ticked off, elk may display a number of physical signs such as flaring their nostrils, holding their heads high, laying their ears back, or even occasionally beating the air with their hooves. If an elk becomes agitated or seems nervous, back away and seek shelter behind a large tree or sturdy obstacle. Elk tend to give chase for only a short distance before they've expended too much energy and abort their mission.

Mountain Goats

Biologists believe that Washington State has between 2400 and 3200 mountain goats roaming the mountain ranges. In the high country, it's not at all uncommon to see them on rocky hillsides or enjoying the grasses and greens of lofty meadows.

Occasionally, on highly populated backcountry trails, mountain goats become habituated and don't show any fear of people. While generally docile, they can be downright dangerous—after all, they have little knives growing out of

A nanny and her kid keep a watchful eye on the author as she focuses her long lens in their direction.

their heads and are freakishly strong. Sometimes, they are seeking your salt, otherwise known as your urine. These smart beasts have learned that people equal the minerals they crave and will wait around until someone delivers the goods. Here are some reminders for how to be safe in mountain goat country:

> **Piddle on pumice:** Urinate as far off-trail as you can, especially in heavily populated goat areas, such as Lake Ingalls. Goats will tear up vegetation to get at urine, so if possible, urinate on a hard surface, like a rock slab.

> **Stay back:** As with all wildlife, keep your distance and use your camera's zoom or your binoculars for a closer look.

Mountain Lions

For the most part, mountain lions steer clear of people, but if you do have an encounter, heeding these tips can help you live to tell the tale:

> **Get big:** Look them in the eye, make noise, wave your hands or poles above your head, and do all you can to look large.

> **Don't run:** Fleeing usually causes a lion to instinctively give chase.

> **If necessary, fight:** Attacks are extremely rare, but if you have to defend yourself, fight hard and fight dirty. Use bear spray if you brought it, and punch, kick, cut, and jab in vulnerable spots such as the eyes.

GUIDE TO FALL FOLIAGE PHOTOGRAPHY

Colorful fall foliage is stunning to the naked eye, but it also makes lovely souvenir pictures. Since it's all about the yellows, reds, and oranges, a few tips can get the oohs and ahhhs you seek as you showcase your outing.

Digital photography—with its instant results—is creating amateur photojournalists out of all of us, and some are having great success with gaining social media followers and, thus, sponsorships or ad revenues. Other people are creating their photos for wall art or to sell in digital ad campaigns or print media, while still others just enjoy sharing the images with friends and family. Whatever your purposes for creating fall masterpieces, learning the tricks of the trade can help.

Have fun, be creative, and remember, at the end of the day, the best memories are the ones stuck in the gray matter between your ears.

1. **Play with light:** Stand with your back to the sun and point forward for the best chance at illuminating the landscape in front of you. But sometimes, when the sun is low in the sky, it can be a focal point in the photo as the rays spread out through trees or onto the trail. To achieve this effect, point the camera directly at the sun using care not to overexpose the picture. Timing is everything with outdoor landscapes. If the lighting isn't optimal, crack open lunch and wait a bit to see if it changes, or plan your trip so that you arrive at your destination near sunset or sunrise, when colors are generally the most vibrant. Midday sun can be glaring, or it can be soft if clouds arrive—use what you've been given. If you don't have the luxury of a sunny day, reduce the amount of sky in the photo to avoid too much gray or blank space.

2. **Frame it up:** Get creative with your subject with a variety of framing ideas. For example, if you are shooting a tight group of larch trees, sometimes less is more. Perhaps focus on a wider aperture (f/2.8–f/5.6), which will soften the larches in the background, and make the foreground a simple close-up of a golden branch. Camera phones often have a portrait setting, which does the same thing automatically. Or look around for a knoll or peak to get height, then fit the whole scene in the frame. Play with vertical and horizontal options, and try natural borders, such as edges of standing trees, or downed logs in lakes.

3. **It's all in perspective:** Straight-on photos are often very pretty, but why not try something new? When you see something that catches your attention, such as a colorful cluster of huckleberries or mountain ash, shooting under or above it might allow you to get more of the background hillside or less of a gray sky. What about an awesome shot of dust coming off the back of trail shoes while in midstride through colorful low-growing foliage? Try perching yourself on a

When the sun is low enough in the sky, pointing your camera in its direction can have dramatically beautiful results.

hillside and shooting down too—sometimes stunning photos can be crafted using a bird's-eye viewpoint. Get creative!

4. **Capture moments with people:** When publications request photos with people, rarely do they request any of people walking away. Hiking shots are usually best if taken from the front or the side. This is tough to do if you are shy about asking, so jokingly announce to your hiking group in advance that you are the obnoxious paparazzi for the day. Stand above your crew on a hillside and shoot down at them walking along the brilliantly colored trail. Or capture the smiles from just below them as they perch on a colorful rocky outcropping near a stand of larches. Posed jumping shots are always fun too. Capture the joy of the day!

5. **Touch it up:** Photo-editing tools have created a virtual playground for pictures these days, with everything from old-timey filters to vignettes. In a world where literally everything can be added or taken away from digital photos, people tend to appreciate landscape pictures that look real instead of

overprocessed. Use care not to oversaturate colors in your pictures, which can make them look artificial in color. A tiny touch of the scale or slide on your photo-editing software goes a long way when you are playing with contrast, vibrancy, saturation, and exposure. The cropping tool can help narrow the subject in the photo so the eye goes to where it's intended. This tool is also useful to straighten the horizon. Your highlight and shadow tools can help you improve details when darkness creeps in or when lighting is really tough, such as in a shadowy lake basin surrounded by bright peaks.

6. **Play dot to dot:** While your photo might look spectacular digitally, print mediums often see things differently. Tiny colored dots otherwise known as pixels are ultimately responsible for the clarity of photos; in other words, the more DPI (dots per square inch) you have, the more vivid and clear the image and the better opportunity to enlarge it without losing clarity. Knowing whether or not you intend to use the photos in larger wall hangings or photo books, for example, will help you decide whether to take a camera that has the capabilities of creating higher-resolution images or to simply tuck your smartphone in your pocket. Most conventional cameras—whether you choose a point-and-shoot, a digital single-lens reflex (DSLR), or a mirrorless camera—have higher resolution capabilities and even the ability to shoot in raw format, which allows for more flexibility in post-processing. When looking to buy a conventional camera, research its specs for image quality, such as the size of the sensor, the quality of its optics, and the functionality of manual versus automatic settings.

Hop in front or to the side of friends and shoot them hiking toward you.

Using a tripod and a remote control on your camera can help prevent your shots from blurring in low light. No matter what your results, enjoy playing with the camera.

Plenty of smartphone cameras are quite comparable to conventional cameras in many of their abilities. Some enlargement for print is still possible depending on your phone's capability, and the user-friendly interface often autocorrects for lighting booboos and other rookie mistakes. What's more, most have unique settings like portrait mode, which adjusts depth of field and focuses on the subject in the foreground while blurring the backdrop. If you have time on your hands and want your socks blown off, do yourself a favor and search the internet for "mobile photography awards." It will astound you.

7. **Represent respect:** In every capture, if you look closely enough, there's an Easter egg of what was happening behind the shot. Steer clear of standing or walking on fragile alpine vegetation all in the name of getting closer to a goat or attempting a better subject angle. And, of course, avoid doing something risky and precarious (hand-feeding wildlife, balance-y poses on cliffs, etc.) just to get a shot. Everyone reading this book is smarter than that, but sometimes your camera just wants to do something against your better judgment, and they can be very strong willed. Lastly, respect the landscape and your gorgeous images by using discretion on the precise location when posting them online. Sure, these places aren't secrets, I mean, heck, I wrote a book on them, but with the internet having such a massive reach, one breathtaking photo can transform a quiet spot into Times Square on New Year's Eve. Keep curious minds at bay by tagging broad locations, such as #WashingtonState, #Cascades, or #PNW. I also recommend adding #tagresponsibly, which is an online campaign used in several states to help protect the wildlife and wild places. Using it means you are tight-lipped on exactly where you stood when the photo was shot and are committed to protecting wildlife, preventing overuse, and promoting LNT values.

No matter how you choose to capture your memories, a fall day out on the trail is sure to be one that will go down as an unforgettable, fantastic adventure.

HOW TO USE THIS BOOK

While most of this guide is self-explanatory, a few points might help clarify things, should you scratch your noggin in bewilderment. The hikes in this guidebook are ones that I personally enjoy when autumn arrives in the hills. The colors are almost always outstanding, and the ambiance screams of fall along these hikes' ridgelines and river valleys. For the most part, the hikes are organized from north to south and from east to west.

During one of my research hikes in the Mount Rainier area, I encountered a berry-grazing black bear who let me spend several minutes quietly and safely in his company as I composed photos with my long lens. There is tranquility in these wild places, especially as they wind down from their summer activity and prepare for their winter sleep. I hope you find this book useful in discovering your own adventures.

INFO BLOCKS

Each hike includes categories of information to help you plan your trip. Here's an overview and keys for what I cover in each:

> **Distance:** The distances are roundtrip, meaning the total mileage you can expect for the hike. I've done my best to get you to the most desired location for the time of year, while taking into consideration the distances and the limited daylight. Sometimes a hike will continue farther than, say, the summit or the viewpoint where the trail description ends, and I give an extended hike option. If your spirit carries you farther down the trail, it's up to you to do the math as you meander to your heart's content.

> **Elevation Gain:** The elevation gain is the total for the entire roundtrip hike. Sometimes, the high point is in the middle of the hike and you'll gain elevation on the way back as well as the way there. In cases of loops, elevation gain and loss occur throughout the whole hike and you'll find yourself climbing, sometimes, even near the end.

> **High Point:** The high point is the highest point on the entire journey and can occur almost anywhere along the trail, not necessarily at the desired viewpoint, beginning, or end. No matter where the official high point is, the end of the hike is usually when you *feel* the highest with those endorphins working in your favor!

> **Difficulty:** While I've tried to assess the difficulty of the hike through the eyes of the majority of hikers, I'm not going to get it right for every hiker, every time. This is, of course, because there are those among you who trail run, adventure race, lift weights, and think nothing of 4000 feet of elevation gain in a mere

four miles. Heck, you did that four times this week, right? If that's you . . . just assume everything in this book is easy.

For everyone else out there, I've done my best to make an educated guess on difficulty and am fully aware that sometimes, easy isn't necessarily easy if you haven't hiked in a while. One foot at a time gets you anywhere you want to go, even if your cheeks are as red as huckleberry leaves.

➤ **GPS:** GPSs, Global Positioning Systems, are amazing technology, but in the consumer market they are also somewhat limited in their abilities to be 100 percent precise. Take two GPSs down the same trail, and they will often give close but different readings. To give you the best data possible, I've taken two GPSs using identical datums down all the trails in this book, then compared the results with trusted paper maps to get the most accurate information I can. Sometimes the variables made my head swim in frustration, while other times, they were very similar. No matter the data, the true feather in your cap comes from walking the beautiful pathways of fall on your own muscle power. That's more brag-worthy than any digits!

Vine maple flaunt their neon leaves near Mason Lake (Hike 32).

> **Maps:** Carrying additional maps is never a bad idea. Green Trails Maps offer detailed, local maps that come from boots-on-the-ground gathered data. The maps contain points of interest, contour intervals, and important data, and for my work as a guidebook author, they prove invaluable. For most hikes in this book, I've included the Green Trails Maps' number; however, in cases such as the arboretums, I've pointed you to a website where you can view a specific map of the area. Green Trails Maps are found in many sporting or outdoor retailers throughout the Pacific Northwest and also online at www.mountaineersbooks.org.

> **Managing Agency:** This category outlines the specific ranger district, national park, or state office responsible for the hike you are about to take. Contacting the managing agency is not a bad idea if you are concerned about the condition of the trail, snowpack, or forest road accessibility. Conditions change quickly in the mountains, and these agencies often have the most current information.

> **Passes:** Since you often have to pay to play, this category lists the specific pass you need for each of the hikes in this book. These passes are generally available in person at outdoor or sporting goods retailers, or online through the site for the specific pass (see Puzzling and Perplexing Parking Permits, Passes, and Park Pricing in the introduction as well as the Resources section at the back of the book).

> **Dog-Friendly:** If our furry friends are allowed to join us based on land management rules, it will be noted here. Steeper hikes may challenge the smaller breeds, but most I've seen have moxie and gusto and will try their best . . . bless their little paws.

> **Kid-Friendly:** This is a tough category, because as we all know, kids vary so much with age and capability. For this book, I've assumed that most kids have smaller feet, less gumption, and shorter attention spans than their folks, thus the harder, longer hikes would likely not be a good fit. Then again, carrying the bitty babies in backpacks up challenging hikes might be a great workout for you and a refreshing outing for them. You ultimately know what they are capable of, but hopefully this category will guide you if you are unsure.

> **Amenities:** This category will tell you if you'll need to pop a squat behind a bush when you get there, or if the trailhead area has a pit toilet or other resources, such as picnic tables. I also note if I've discovered a primitive backcountry toilet along the route. These toilets aren't always pretty, but when ya gotta go . . . ya gotta go, and you'll likely be grateful it's there. Most are a small wooden box with a hole cut in the top for the seat and are hidden behind groves of trees out of eyesight from the trail. Usually, they have a wooden lid, which when opened yields a mass exodus of flies who are eager to escape, and you are directly in their line of fire, so stand back and repress the memory. Bring your own toilet paper, and avoid leaving any trash in the pit. Rangers and

The White Pass Byway Loop is a perfect way to see stunning fall colors from the warmth of your vehicle (Scenic Drive 7).

Map Legend

-------	Featured trail	**T**	Trailhead	**7**	Hike or scenic drive number
------	Other trail	**T**	Alternate trailhead	▲	Peak
·········	Unmaintained trail	**S**	Start of scenic drive	⌒	River or creek
→	Direction-of-travel arrow	**E**	End of scenic drive	⌒‖⌒	Falls
▬▬▬	Scenic drive	**P**	Parking	⬭	Water
▬▬▬	Highway	**R**	Restroom	⌂	Spring
▬▬▬	Paved road	▪	Point of interest	⛩	Lookout
= = = = =	Gravel road	▲	Campground or campsite	⌐¬	Park or forest boundary
(5) (90)	Interstate highway	**V**	Viewpoint	⌐¬	Wilderness boundary
(1) (11)	US highway	⛩	Picnic area	-•--•-	Powerline
(8) (89)	State route (SR)	) (	Pass	**N**	True north (magnetic north varies)
56 556	Forest road (FR)	] [	Bridge		

backcountry patrols are responsible for maintaining these beauties, and fishing out someone's freeze-dried meal packaging among piles of the unspeakable is truly a tough day at work. Ain't nobody got time for that.

> **Notes:** Look here for important information on topics such as rough trailhead roads, trailhead road closures, parking or crowding challenges, trail tread or river crossing difficulties, or other relevant communication. This category would be easy to pass over, but it's one of the most important in the information block.

> **Getting There:** Here's where you'll find basic driving directions to get you to the trailhead, usually starting from a somewhat nearby town. I also call out the number of parking spaces at the trailhead in the handful of instances where parking is especially limited.

SCENIC DRIVE DETAILS

Fall colors, of course, aren't reserved only for backcountry treks! Plenty of spectacular chromatic foliage is on display right from the window of your vehicle (with a heater and possibly a warm cup of coffee). With the comfort and luxury of wheels, you'll be able to explore more turf and see a wider variety of fall displays. In this section, I've done my best to get you to some of the most beautiful places where autumn peaks in all her glory, and I hope the approach I've taken will help you achieve the best journey possible.

- > **Roundtrip Distance from [City]:** This detail is designed to give you a best guess at the mileage you'll encounter on the trip from the closest town or city and back again. Of course, since there are several communities or towns en route, you may choose to start elsewhere and create your own mileage plan.
- > **Estimated Trip Duration:** Do you prefer to adventure the whole day or just a few hours? This detail will guide you to the length of time it will likely take to complete the drive. If you end up lollygagging with a picnic at a park or having a flight of cider at a small brewery, obviously you'll be having a fantastic day and you could throw timing to the wind. You do you.
- > **Communities with Services:** One of the best things about scenic drives is the chance to see towns or communities along the way and stop for a short walk or a bite to eat. Of course, you might need fuel or coffee too, so I've listed the towns along the route where you could fill up on both.
- > **Attractions:** This section is the "why should I go?" part of the information block. It gives you at-a-glance highlights and sweet spots you should expect to see as you drive the route.
- > **Passes for Stops and Entrances:** Sometimes parks, hikes, or leg-stretch destinations along the way require passes or permits. If so, I'll list the pass in this section to ensure that this, at least, will not be a surprise when you arrive at your destination.

Perhaps it's seeing larches on hillsides, watching farmers harvest their gardens, or getting up close to Mount Rainier that makes you grab your camera. Whatever it is, there's sure to be something for everyone as you explore Washington's scenic drives in autumn.

Opposite: A colorful carpet of foliage landscapes the trail's fringes near Little Giant Pass (Hike 19). Page 38: A light dusting of snow grazes the high country along Chain Lakes Loop (Hike 2).

HIKES

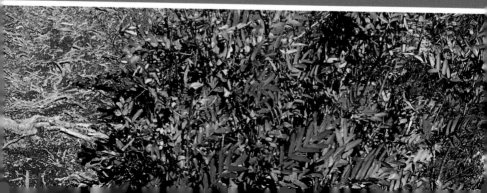

MOUNT BAKER

The northernmost volcano in Washington, Mount Baker boasts gorgeous glaciers, great views, and a wealth of playground opportunities, especially as the fall colors make their appearance. The tiny hamlet of Glacier is a good place to rent a cabin for a few days while you explore the vast backcountry without having to make the drive back to Bellingham, the closest big city.

Even though the area is fairly isolated, it's not unusual to have crowds coming from northwestern Washington as well as Canada to share in the immense beauty. As with all trails during fall, the time frame to enjoy the colors and barren trails before the snow sets in is short. Put on your happy face as you pass your fellow hikers, and do your best to get there in the early morning and on a weekday if possible. I've also had luck arriving later in the day with headlamp and warm jacket in tow, catching most folks on their way out as I walk in. If you choose this strategy, you may even get some good sunset colors. Truthfully, you'll see a lot of people no matter what, but solitude is traded for some amazing views, which makes it all worth it in the end.

1. YELLOW ASTER BUTTE

Distance: 8.6 miles
Elevation Gain: 2710 feet
High Point: 6150 feet
Difficulty: Hard
GPS: N 48°56.602', W 121°39.768'
Maps: Green Trails Maps No. 14: Mount Shuksan
Managing Agency: Mount Baker–Snoqualmie National Forest, Mount Baker Ranger District
Passes: Northwest Forest Pass or Interagency Pass
Dog-Friendly: Yes, on leash
Kid-Friendly: No
Amenities: Pit toilet at trailhead (but in poor condition)

Notes: Trail open to hikers only. Road may have potholes, but most passenger cars will make it. Bears frequent this area, so keep your eyes and ears open. This hike is extremely popular; avoid weekends if possible and have a backup plan if parking is unavailable. Use extra care when driving the narrow Twin Lakes Road and take note of opportunities to pull over if necessary to let a car pass.

Getting There: From Bellingham, drive 34 miles east on Mount Baker Highway (State Route 542) to the town of Glacier and the Glacier Public Service Center. From there, continue east on SR 542 for another 12.7 miles (46.7 miles from Bellingham) to Twin Lakes Road (Forest Road 3065) and turn left (northeast). (The Department of Transportation buildings are just prior to the turn.) Continue on the dirt and gravel road for 4.3 miles until a couple tight switchbacks deliver you to the trailhead located to the left of the road. Be certain your parked vehicle doesn't block the road.

You probably won't find any aster flowers that are yellow on this hike. In fact, if you see any holdovers from summertime, they are likely going to be violet in color. This butte was instead named after the Yellow Aster Complex, a large slab of felsic gneiss, or metamorphic rock, layered within the earth here. The stony surfaces of local peaks will definitely beg you to stop and gawk, but the splendid fall colors are the main course!

 Foliage: Bearberry, brackenfern, Cascade huckleberry, Cascade mountain ash, crowberry, pearly everlasting, rosy spirea, thimbleberry, vine maple, western moss heather

Right from the start, the colors of the hillside in front of you pull you like a magnet. You'll want to start snapping pictures before the hike even gets going, but just

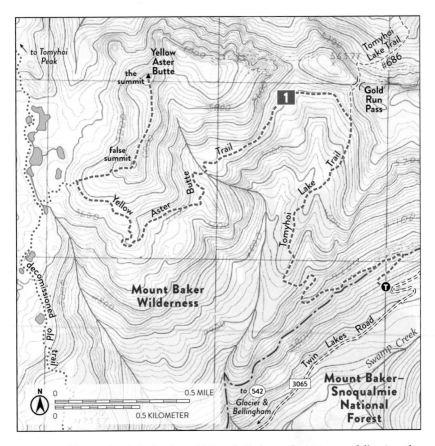

wait—you'll soon be right in the middle of all that color! You are following the Tomyhoi Lake Trail at this point, but you turn off it to reach Yellow Aster up ahead.

A forested climb kicks things off with a handful of steep switchbacks leading to a colorful avalanche swale almost immediately. Vine maples prefer moist soil with full sun, and this hillside provides a perfect opportunity for them to flourish. In fall, they exhibit brilliant tones of orange and red so bright that they look like a painting. Farther off, Winchester Mountain and the ridgeline to the northeast are stunning in the distance, as is Mount Baker now visible to the southwest. Mother Nature shows us that seasonal cycles can be beautiful as the dying thimbleberry leaves and brackenfern paint the hillside a yellowish hue. On the return trip, when Mount Baker is in your face and the lighting is slightly different, you'll want to take even more photos along this stretch.

Snow gathers on autumn foliage for a wintery scene in early fall.

At 0.5 mile, enter the Mount Baker Wilderness and continue your climb higher on the hillside, as you pop in and out of the trees. At 1.8 miles, arrive at a junction with the signed Yellow Aster Butte Trail and bear left (northwest) at the Y. The Tomyhoi Lake Trail continues north, a beautiful path for another day.

The Yellow Aster Butte Trail now follows a contour line around a forest cirque before reaching a basin, complete with a seasonal stream, below rocky summits. Rock hop across, and be on your way. This area has a tranquil feeling, and you might feel tempted to park yourself on a stony perch and soak in the lofty heights as they compare to your ant-sized human form.

But you didn't come all this way to just sit on a rock, so continue along the trail that now weaves in and out of evergreen groves complete with Cascade mountain ash trees displaying brilliant yellow- and orange-colored leaves and round, scarlet berries. These berries, which often linger well into winter, serve as an important food for birds and small rodents.

The trail becomes more airy and open, guiding you up and over rocky slabs mixed with meadows. Huckleberries steal the show here, lighting up the edges of the trail and distant hillsides with brilliant red foliage. Keep your eyes open for bears, especially during this time of year, since they count on getting the remaining remnants of nutrition on those bushes! Look to the southwest to see the pointy stone summit of Keep Kool Butte standing at attention, while distant jagged peaks make this landscape feel like a backcountry dream.

At 3.6 miles, arrive at an unsigned trail junction T. The left option heads downhill and visits a series of backcountry tarns, then connects to Forest Service Trail 699, the old approach to Yellow Aster Butte and current climbers route to Tomyhoi Peak.

At the T, turn right (east) uphill toward the summit of Yellow Aster, our goal. Give your quads and lungs a pep talk, since this steep pitch is not for the wimpy. Up you go, huffing and puffing, with views of neighboring peaks such as Tomyhoi and Damfino to take your mind off the grind. You'll reach a false summit in roughly 0.3 mile after the T, and the views—all the way to Canada—knock your socks off. A flat bench provides a great place to stop, snack, and swoon. But if weather conditions, daylight, and gumption are favorable, the true summit is gained by continuing along the trail another 0.4 mile. Head back when you just can't wait any longer for those Mount Baker vistas.

2. CHAIN LAKES LOOP

Distance: 6.6 miles
Elevation Gain: 1900 feet
High Point: 5395 feet
Difficulty: Moderate

GPS: N 48°50.798', W 121°41.607'
Maps: Green Trails Maps No. 14: Mount Shuksan

Managing Agency: Mount Baker–Snoqualmie National Forest, Mount Baker Ranger District
Passes: Northwest Forest Pass or Interagency Pass
Dog-Friendly: Yes, on leash
Kid-Friendly: Yes, experience dependent
Amenities: Pit toilet at trailhead, backcountry primitive toilet on route, picnic tables and backcountry camping options on route

Notes: Crowds abound; avoid weekends if possible. Use toilets instead of catholes. If that's not possible, human waste and paper must be packed out (not buried). Bears frequent this area—be bear aware. Muddy spots exist, especially after rain or snow—watch your step!

Getting There: There are two access points for this loop. The first, and my favorite, is from Artist Point. From Bellingham, drive 34 miles east on Mount Baker Highway (State Route 542) to the town of Glacier and the Glacier Public Service Center. Proceed another 23.5 miles to the end of the road, Artist Point parking lot.

Second access: Follow the above directions, but park at the Austin Pass picnic area 1.5 miles before Artist Point.

> While this hike is called Chain Lakes Loop, it utilizes several other trails in the area to make a full circle. You can enter at various places and go either direction, but my favorite is to start high, at Artist Point, and get the legs warmed up with a downhill before the climb, which falls in the middle. In autumn, this hike cannot be beat for beautiful colors! Dwarf bilberry, which grows on the subalpine slopes, is a short, woody variety that produces an azure-colored fruit that is sweet with almost an applelike finish. In fall, the leaves turn all the colors we love—yellow, red, orange, and burgundy—making photos from lofty viewpoints look like a watercolor canvas.

Foliage: Cascade huckleberry, Cascade mountain ash, dwarf bilberry, fireweed, oval-leaved huckleberry, pearly everlasting, rosy spirea, sedge

There are a couple trails that leave from the Artist Point parking lot, but we are looking for the well-signed Wild Goose Trail, which starts to the right of the pit toilets. Once you find it, start hiking east and cruise down the rocky incline for about 400 feet until you reach a crossing with the road you just drove up. Why did the hiker cross the road? To get to the trail on the other side. After the road crossing, the trail is a little hard to spot, so walk left (north) for a few feet, turn on your keen eyes, and voilà! Permanent cairns (stacked rocks) complete with an embedded picture of a wild goose in a triangular blaze reassure you that you have found the correct path.

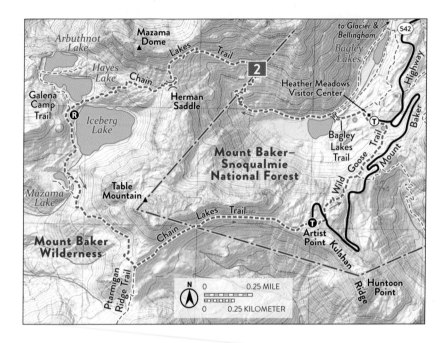

Down you go, with Mount Shuksan standing guard in the distance and the trail tread alternating between manmade steps, which are in need of repair in places, and rocky turf. In 0.6 mile from the trailhead, pass a signed junction for the Lake Ann Trail (Hike 3). Continue on the same trajectory downhill, with views opening up to Bagley Lakes basin and the northern hillside showcasing the continuation of our trail. Table Mountain's ridgeline off to the basin's left is a feast for the eyes and a place to look for grazing bears. Fireweed and Cascade huckleberry add some color to the foreground if you compose your photo with the plants on the lower third of the frame.

In roughly 1 mile from where you started, the trail delivers you to the parking lot for Austin Pass picnic area—the alternative starting point for this trail. Another toilet is here if nature is calling. A couple of peaceful lakes adjacent to the pavement tempt you to follow well-used trails near their edges, but most of these dead-end at picnic spots. Instead, walk on the pavement downhill until you reach a stone retaining wall, near the Heather Meadows Visitor Center. Give a nod to the Civilian Conservation Corps, which built the visitor center and the rocky wall in front of you in 1940 as part of a ski warming hut. Stop in and see the visitor center now or after your hike—it's a gem!

Follow a break in the rocky wall and a makeshift concrete-and-stone trail downhill until you reach the tree line and a sign noting Bagley Lakes Trail with an arrow

Winter takes an early hold of the high country while the last of the berry leaves showcase vibrant hues.

pointing left (southwest). Turn left here and continue—downhill —until at last you reach a sign, now pointed right (north), toward Chain Lakes Trail. A gorgeous stone bridge, with arches on its underside, guides you across the Bagley Lakes waterways until you reach a T on the other side. A second lake, also called Bagley Lakes, can be reached by turning right here, but for our loop's continuation, turn left (southwest).

The shoreline of the larger of the two Bagley Lakes is a vision in itself, with burgundy Cascade huckleberries and orange Cascade mountain ash near its edges. Sedge plants and dormant wildflower stalks add some tan to the mix, while red and white heather and subalpine fir offer a rich forest green for a mix of natural colors. Table Mountain in the background with the trail and its colorful edging in the foreground make a gorgeous autumn snapshot. Don't forget to ask your companions to model their hiking prowess, and grab a picture of them walking toward you without looking at you or your camera. Social media pic!

After cresting the shores of the lake, the trail continues its colorful march, mixing it up with a couple of talus fields, before ascending through a series of somewhat grueling switchbacks of various lengths. Thankfully you are in subalpine meadow bliss, so spectacular that even ultrafit hikers get winded from the exhilarating beauty. Behind you, Mount Shuksan steals the show, while the tranquil lake basin glows underneath the steep walls of scree from the crumbles of Table Mountain. Just ahead is Herman Saddle, our high point for the day, located almost 3.2 miles from where we started.

The descent after the saddle is a pleasant relief after the climb. Switchbacks give way to views of Iceberg Lake as well as Mount Baker's massive glacial face while dwarf bilberries cover the edges of the trail and make for stunning photos when they're in the foreground of your shots.

Hayes Lake comes into sight on the trail's right, as do a few viewpoints here and there, until you come to a rather confusing junction, 3.9 miles into the hike. A couple of game trails go off to either side of the main trail, and clearly, confused folks have gone every which direction, but if you just keep going downhill on the main trail you've been following, you'll be on the correct path. A short distance after that, the trail forks again. This time, you are near Hayes Lake. The main path leads to the left (southwest) while the right one heads toward Hayes Lake on a less frequented trail. A short 0.1 mile farther on, a sign for Galena Camp points the way to the right while our trail continues straight and slightly left (south). A backcountry toilet is found at this junction on a hairpin to the left here.

The main trail climbs a little bit now as it reaches the shores of Iceberg Lake, where bushes of yellow and orange Cascade mountain ash leaves and red berries complement the shoreline under the Table Mountain ridge. Snap away!

Thankfully the ascent is gentle, and again, the feasting of the eyeballs makes it feel a little less strenuous as you approach Mazama Lake to the trail's right and, soon, a sign pointing toward camping opportunities. Pikas, members of the rabbit family who look more like guinea pigs, say "meep" as you pass their rocky burrows along stretches of talus fields. Mount Baker seems to almost reach out and touch you while those fall colors still abound.

At 5.2 miles, reach the top of a tundra and alpine ridge and the official end of the climbing for the day. A trail junction with Ptarmigan Ridge comes up, but go left (northeast) to complete the loop. The scenery is far from over in the mountainous paradise, with Mount Shuksan back in view and stunning basins below. More burgundy Cascade huckleberries and yellowing sedge plants dot the meadows where scree fields and snow slides have not removed vegetation.

Reach the Artist Point parking area 1.3 miles after the top of the last climb, and celebrate your photos and your memories of an autumn day well spent!

3. LAKE ANN

Distance: 8.5 miles
Elevation Gain: 2120 feet
High Point: 4850 feet
Difficulty: Moderate
GPS: N 48°50.999', W 121°41.160'
Maps: Green Trails Maps No. 14: Mount Shuksan

Managing Agency: Mount Baker–Snoqualmie National Forest, Mount Baker Ranger District
Passes: Northwest Forest Pass or Interagency Pass
Dog-Friendly: Yes, on leash
Kid-Friendly: No
Amenities: Pit toilet available

Notes: Fall is a popular time for this hike, so avoid weekends if possible. Keep your eyes open for bears, as they frequent the area. Trail can be very muddy in the fall, so it's a good idea to pack a spare pair of "car shoes" for the ride home if you want to save your vehicle the dirt. The road to the trailhead is subject to seasonal closures with inclement weather. Double-check before you head out.

Getting There: From Bellingham, drive 34 miles east on Mount Baker Highway (State Route 542) to the town of Glacier and the Glacier Public Service Center. Proceed another 22.8 miles, passing the turnoff for Mount Baker Ski Area and enjoying the Heather Meadows area before locating the trailhead to the left.

The goal for this hike isn't necessarily the twinkling Lake Ann, but rather the views of Mount Shuksan, which are so grand, you'll nearly weep. Lake Ann, set in an alpine basin, is of course nothing to scoff at since it's located deep in the heart of Mount Baker Wilderness. The fragrance and colors of the bright, blue berries left over from bursting red bushes of Cascade huckleberry invite all the senses to partake in an experience that makes this one of the best places to enjoy fall.

 Foliage: Black alpine sedge, Cascade huckleberry, Cascade mountain ash, oval-leaved huckleberry, rosy spirea, sedge

You might think this is the easiest hike you've ever done when you get started, thanks to the fact that you are going downhill! Of course, what goes down must come up, so save your energy for this hill on the way back. For now, descend among mountain hemlocks and Pacific silver firs, stopping for the occasional views until you reach an open basin, in just over 1 mile. Here, a tranquil creeklet quietly bobs and weaves where you can rock hop across its reflective surface. This area in itself is grand and is the start of a few pops of color. Sedge plants love this sunshiny, wet basin and, in the fall, have orange tips on their stalks. Cascade mountain ash with

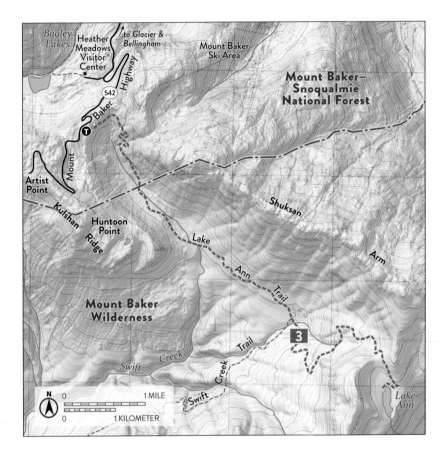

its yellow-orange leaves and red berries offers some height at the trail's edge, and a few bushes of Cascade huckleberry join the party with their burgundy leaves. With evergreens providing the spots of green and the shoulders of Mount Shuksan looking on, you could spend an hour just photographing this area alone—but wait, there's more!

At 1.5 miles from the trailhead, the trail crosses Swift Creek and ducks into a variety of conifers and Cascade huckleberry bushes before it pops out at another crossing of Swift Creek, roughly a mile later, and a junction with Swift Creek Trail to the right. You've reached the bottom of your descent for this stretch, and now it's time to climb.

The Lake Ann Trail ascends through meadows of Cascade huckleberries, Cascade mountain ash, rosy spirea, and sedge plants before it crosses a couple of large talus fields. Stop to swoon. Behind you to the southwest is the giant ice-cream cone of Mount Baker while the fall colors light up the hillsides in all directions. To the north, towering rocky spires of an unnamed ridgeline off the arms of Mount Shuksan cause you to stop and soak in even more outstanding views. While you gawk, look for black dots high on the ridges above you, then note if they are moving. On a recent hike I saw five bears on adjacent hillsides, but you might miss them if you aren't scanning. They are here for the lingering huckleberry bushes, and so are we!

At 1.5 miles after the Swift Creek Trail junction, 4 miles from the trailhead, the trail tread gets rockier, thanks to an alpine landscape, and reaches the top of a knoll where the climbing concludes and your quads get a much-needed break. A short distance farther, Lake Ann comes into view on the right side of the trail while Mount Shuksan, in your face, knocks your socks straight off. A well-traveled boot path leads to the sparkling shores of Lake Ann, while alternative trails lead to various views of Mount Shuksan and, eventually, a technical climbers trail. Wander and explore!

For the best photos of Mount Shuksan in autumn, set your aperture to small settings (f/8–f/16) so that the whole composition is in focus, and get low enough to capture the burgundy huckleberry leaves in your foreground with the glaciated giant in the back. Smartphone users may get a similar result by crouching low and shooting skyward with the berries in the foreground.

When you've gotten your magnificent shots, head back the way you came, happy and sassy.

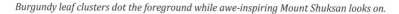
Burgundy leaf clusters dot the foreground while awe-inspiring Mount Shuksan looks on.

4. EXCELSIOR PEAK (DAMFINO LAKES TRAILHEAD)

Distance: 6.7 miles
Elevation Gain: 1630 feet
High Point: 5715 feet
Difficulty: Moderate
GPS: N 48°57.547', W 121°48.424'
Maps: Green Trails Maps No. 13: Mount Baker

Managing Agency: Mount Baker–Snoqualmie National Forest, Mount Baker Ranger District
Passes: Northwest Forest Pass or Interagency Pass
Dog-Friendly: Yes, on leash
Kid-Friendly: Yes, experience dependent
Amenities: Pit toilet at trailhead, primitive backcountry toilet on route

Notes: This drive is long, with rough potholes in places, but manageable for passenger cars if driven slowly. Boulders occasionally block access, so check online reports or call ranger station for updates.

Getting There: From Bellingham, drive 34 miles east on Mount Baker Highway (State Route 542) to the town of Glacier and the Glacier Public Service Center. Proceed another 1.8 miles and turn left (northwest) on the narrow and paved Canyon Creek Road (Forest Road 31). Follow this road for 7.5 miles until it changes to gravel. Pass through an open seasonal gate and continue straight. In a short distance, the road alternates between pavement, some of which is eroding, and gravel with occasional potholes. At 8.7 miles, continue straight on pavement and avoid side roads. At 9.2 miles, cross a creek on a paved bridge and in another 0.2 mile, cross another bridge. After the second bridge, bear right to stay on paved road. Big potholes and crumbling pavement follow, so take it slowly. At 11.7 miles bear left at a sign for "Damfino TH." At 12.7 miles cross another bridge over a creek. At 15.5 miles, go left at a sign marked with a hiker symbol and an arrow pointing left. At 16.9 miles, arrive at the Damfino Lakes Trailhead, with a pit toilet, a picnic area, and room for about fifteen to twenty vehicles.

While views here make this a gorgeous hike at any time of year, the fall makes this place come alive. Dwarf bilberry and Cascade huckleberry in dense patches on wide-open hillsides make a quilt of color when set against mountain heather and sedge plants. As with all the best fall trails, hike this one on a weekday and get here early if possible to enjoy the most solitude.

 Foliage: Cascade huckleberry, Cascade mountain ash, dwarf bilberry, oval-leaved huckleberry, rosy spirea, sedge

The trail starts off with a gentle, forested climb, then reaches the Canyon Ridge Trail junction heading off to the left (north) in 0.6 mile. Just beyond that, a

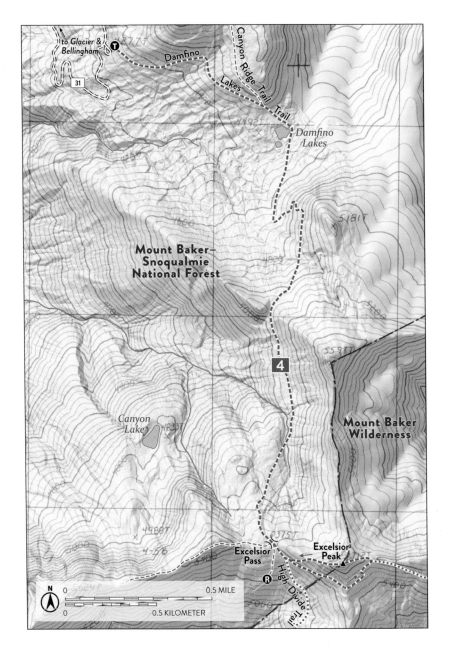

manmade wooden walkthrough barricade reminds cyclists that they aren't permitted here.

A short 0.2 mile after the barricade the trail turns into a fairly level wooden boardwalk on the edge of the first of the shallow, muddy Damfino Lakes, fringed by rosy spirea, Cascade mountain ash, Cascade huckleberry, and sedge. Watch your footing carefully, as the icy planks after a hard frost can have you doing an unexpected interpretive dance. The second lake/pond/swamp follows and is smaller than the first. If you've hiked a lot in the Northwest, you might be unimpressed by these lakes; however, they are quiet nooks, have colorful foliage on their edges, and offer a place for aquatic life to call home. If you are visiting in the morning, you might have better lighting for a couple photos in this area on your way back.

The trail climbs through hemlocks and firs until it traverses a large meadow under a ridgeline where views begin, and it's time to get excited for what's ahead. Near the trail's edges, Cascade mountain ash with its occasional reddish berry and orange leaves can make a colorful photo if framed against a blue sky or in the foreground of the distant peaks.

Solitude abounds amidst a kaleidoscope of colors near Excelsior Pass.

At 2.1 miles, a seasonal creek has you rock hopping over stones before climbing higher, now in the heart of vibrant pastoral landscapes. Viewpoints beg you to follow boot paths down to a couple of seasonal tarns, but save them for later if time permits. For now, continue ascending, with the views getting more and more grand until you reach the top of the ridgeline, known as Excelsior Pass, and—a short distance beyond—a junction with the High Divide Trail coming up steeply from the valley in front of you. The trail junction is a bit confusing, as a primitive trail heads off to a mountain to the right (west), while a signed, small trail here trots off into the forest for those in need of a backcountry toilet. The junction seems as if it's a three-way junction, but really there are only a couple of designated trails: left (southeast) or straight ahead (south). Go left to take the southeast option. This is the start of our Excelsior Peak loop.

After turning left, walk around the southern flanks of Excelsior Peak, traversing the meadows at its base. If you think you've seen everything this hike has to offer, just wait! Mount Baker's snowy summit rises above the forested, distant hinterlands while rugs of Cascade huckleberry, dwarf bilberry, various grasses, and decaying stalks of once showy wildflowers make a vision fit for a canvas. Follow the trail as it makes a horseshoe, turning back to the north now to offer views of Mount Shuksan and colors so vivid, you'll want to stay all day. Look for black bears in this area, since they are fond of these delicious, albeit now slightly overripe, berries.

In 0.4 mile after the High Divide Trail junction, gain the crest of the divide speckled with evergreens. The High Divide Trail continues to the right, but our adventure takes a different turn here. Look sharply to your left (west) for a faint game trail, which covers a steep, but breathtaking, 0.1 mile to the summit of the exposed Excelsior Peak. Take it in, friends—this is why we hike!

When the views have seeped into your pores, continue west, descending the game trail, until you complete the loop and reach the High Divide Trail. Go right (northwest) and back the way you came to complete a full, happy day.

5. PARK BUTTE

Distance: 8 miles
Elevation Gain: 2175 feet
High Point: 5450 feet
Difficulty: Moderate
GPS: N 48°42.427', W 121°48.778'
Maps: Green Trails Maps No. 45: Hamilton
Managing Agency: Mount Baker–Snoqualmie National Forest, Mount Baker Ranger District

Passes: Northwest Forest Pass or Interagency Pass
Dog-Friendly: Yes, on leash
Kid-Friendly: No
Amenities: Pit toilet at trailhead and backcountry primitive toilet on route

Notes: The views of Mount Baker, the blankets of color, and the old fire lookout built in 1932 entice you, me, and half the sea. Be sure to stay on the marked trails at all times, and plan to visit on a weekday if you can. Use the backcountry toilet instead of catholes when nature calls. If not, human waste and paper must be packed out (not buried).

Getting There: From Burlington, take exit 230 off I-5 and drive east on the North Cascades Highway (State Route 20) for 23 miles. Turn left (north) onto Baker Lake Road (after milepost 82) and travel for just over 12 miles. Turn left on Forest Road 12 and drive for 3.5 miles, then bear right (north) onto FR 13 (signed for Mount Baker National Recreation Area). In 5.2 miles, arrive at a large parking area with room for twenty-five to thirty cars.

> This hike is one of the most popular in the area, and for good reason; it offers a plethora of meadows featuring yellow and orange grasses as well as burgundy huckleberries. This area, when it's in peak fall coloration, looks like an autumn quilt. To be technical, wild huckleberries are members of the Vaccinium family, a fancy Latin word whose origin is unknown. Cascade huckleberry (*Vaccinium deliciosum*) grows in this area, as do several other varieties whose leaves turn a brilliant red. Between the evergreen heather shrubs, the tan and yellow fescues and sedge, and the showy huckleberry leaves, this area is a sight to behold!

Foliage: Alpine bentgrass, Cascade huckleberry, showy sedge, western fescue

Locate the trailhead to the west of the parking area, and almost immediately, come to a junction with the Scott Paul Trail to the right. Scott Paul is also a gorgeous place to visit, so put that on your must-hike list for a future date. For now, the trail shows mercy and eases you into a gentle walk through the fairly level Schriebers Meadow and the trickling waters of Sulfur Creek. The western fescue grasses and the remnants of wildflower stalks that wave in the breeze are straw colored in fall, making a pleasingly calm landscape. While these aren't the carpets of color you came for, photos in this area can be quite stunning when lighting is in your favor and the meadow is backlit and glowing. To achieve the best photo, point your camera toward the sun and get low enough that the rays are blocked by the foliage and not hitting your lens directly. If that's not possible and the sun is too high, position your hand or a lens hood just above and out of sight of the camera's lens to block the sun's rays. This shot is really more about luck in your lighting than anything else. If you are fortunate enough to have sun and soft lighting, you'll get the shot—otherwise, you'll walk away hitting delete, prepared to try again next time.

The trail begins climbing in and out of pockets of hemlocks and meadows until it reaches Rocky Creek, a moody flood zone thanks to the Easton Glacier sitting

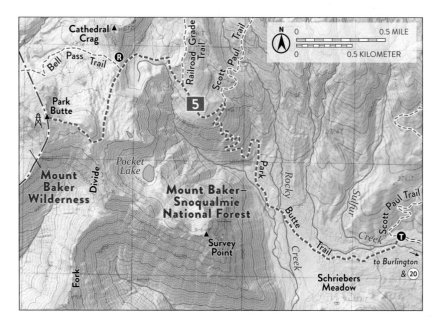

high on the mountain. As with most silty and debris-filled volcanic spillways, the trail gets rearranged as Mother Nature uses her water chisel to change the landscape each year. Some years, depending on the water's course, the Forest Service installs a bridge across the creek; otherwise, it's a rock hop. Follow the cairns and soon you'll be on the other side.

At roughly 2 miles from the trailhead, arrive at a trail junction with a connecting loop of the Scott Paul Trail and the beginning of the meadows you came to see! Thickets of hemlocks and cedars still try to steal the views, but soon enough, you are walking in a subalpine fall wonderland.

At 2.4 miles, reach a junction with the Railroad Grade Trail, which heads right (north) along the spine of the western moraine of the Easton Glacier. Here you have options. If you want wide-angle shots of the colorful landscapes through which you walk, this is a fantastic and highly recommended side trip. Embrace the trail steps and walk high into the rocky, sandy landscapes, keeping your eyes on the meadows to your left and the moraine to your right. You won't know which way to point your camera, so just turn in circles snapping away at the Easton Glacier and autumn tapestry of foliage, now underneath the rocky Cathedral Crag. Walk as far as you desire on this stretch of trail, then turn back the way you came until you once again reach the Park Butte Trail and continue right (west).

The Park Butte Trail envelops you in fall colors while displaying various tarns, some with reflections of Mount Baker—also called Koma Kulshan, or simply

Mount Baker is reflected in a small tarn.

Kulshan. The trail climbs a small, subalpine knoll to reach a junction with Bell Pass Trail heading to the right toward the Ridley Creek basin area and Mazama Park. If this trail looks suspiciously well traveled, it's because there is a backcountry toilet in this area. To use it, follow the Bell Pass Trail to the right (northwest) for a few yards, then look to the right where a small trail darts into the forest. Walk around the corner and you'll find the primitive potty box. That view—a fantastic place for a bathroom break! Don't put anything in the toilet that hasn't traveled through your body first.

Back on the Park Butte Trail, the way gets steeper now, but the views are so breathtaking, it's hard to know whether it's the grade or the views that cause you to gasp. Colorful hillsides are now backdropped by Mount Baker behind you, and in front of you and to the left are well-used trails leading to small tarns dotted with mysterious large boulders. On a calm day, a reflection photo of Mount Baker shot from the southern end of one of these still waters might be good enough to frame.

The final push rounds a small ridge and turns back to the west before reaching Park Butte Lookout and the splendid peak on which it stands. This peak was originally identified as a fire observation point in 1926, when forest personnel camped just below the summit and observed smoke by climbing a large tree on the peak's top. In 1932, the tree was partially removed; however, its roots remained and were used as anchors for the stairway of the constructed tower, a fourteen-by-fourteen-foot, four-sided structure. In World War II the lookout served as one of many posts for enemy plane spotting. The lookout is maintained by the Skagit Alpine Club, which works hard to keep the historical little structure in good shape.

If there are a lot of visitors, take turns at the lookout, since the rocky area on which it sits is small and steep in places. Picnics are best on the ridgeline below the peak or on the rocky edges of the reflective tarns. No matter where you take a break before your return trip, your eyes will be filled with surreal beauty.

Opposite: Larch trees steal the show on the way to Blue Lake (Hike 10).

NORTH CASCADES, METHOW VALLEY, AND MOUNTAIN LOOP HIGHWAY

If I had to pick a favorite area in this book with the most fall colors on display, it would be the North Cascades and Methow Valley. Larch groves display themselves with enthusiasm, turning a citrus golden color as they prepare to drop their needles, and showy crimson huckleberry bushes highlight the foreground of gorgeous lakes and spiky peaks. Because of the short season—and because so many folks file in to see nature in her party dress—these areas can, and do, get crowded. Visit in the wee morning hours, early afternoon, and on weekdays if possible to have a shot at some quiet time.

6. TATIE PEAK AND GRASSHOPPER PASS

Distance: 9.8 miles
Elevation Gain: 1750 feet
High Point: 6925 feet
Difficulty: Easy-moderate
GPS: N 48°42.125', W 120°40.401'

Maps: Green Trails Maps No. 50: Washington Pass
Managing Agency: Okanogan-Wenatchee National Forest, Methow Valley Ranger District

Passes: Northwest Forest Pass or Interagency Pass
Dog-Friendly: Yes, on leash

Kid-Friendly: Yes
Amenities: Pit toilets at nearby campgrounds

Notes: The road to Harts Pass is narrow with drop-offs and not for the faint of heart. In fact, it's the highest road in Washington and is arguably one of the most dangerous in at least one place. Take your time, especially on blind corners, and expect oncoming traffic. The road closes seasonally, and trailers are not permitted at any time. Be sure to bring plenty of water, as it's extremely limited in this area.

Getting There: From the community of Mazama, follow the paved Lost River Road toward Harts Pass. After the pavement ends at 6.8 miles, continue following this road, now named Forest Road 54, for 12 miles to Harts Pass. At FR 54-500, signed for Meadows Campground, turn left (south) and follow it for 2 miles to the road's end and the trailhead.

> As with so many hikes on this frequently sunny side of the Cascades, the theme of this one is amazing fall color, thanks to the gilded needles of subalpine larch trees. Because these hardy trees tolerate poor soil and will often multiply after fires or avalanches, they are perfectly suited for this climate and tend to grow in quaint groves along these sloping hillsides. And happily, this hike keeps you high on lofty traverses, which allow for aesthetically pleasing mountain views while keeping a relatively mellow grade. Win-win.

The open landscapes near Tatie Peak invite you to explore the majestic groves of larches.

Foliage: Bearded wheatgrass, Cascade huckleberry, dwarf bilberry, greenleaf fescue, grouse whortleberry, prairie June-grass, sheep fescue, subalpine larch, variable bentgrass

It's not often that you get to start a hike so high in Washington State, but here you are, already nearly in the clouds! Follow a game trail through the fire zone

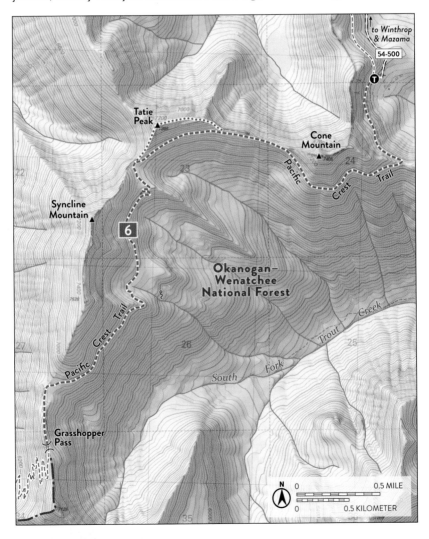

to reach the Pacific Crest Trail (PCT), and head left (south) on a gentle climb. The burn zone gives way to much more open landscapes until you reach a bit of a crescendo with the ridgeline at 0.75 mile.

Subalpine larches speckle the hillsides, standing out in the open, sucking in the sunshine, and taking their opportunity to gather moisture. In summertime, these apple-green trees provide nutrition for upland game birds, such as the blue grouse, and occasional nesting cavities for woodpeckers. This time of year, they are busy shedding needles and lightening their load. Evergreen trees such as firs or hemlocks may be able to grow through photosynthesis throughout the year, even in winter when the temperature varies. However, at these high elevations in the open landscapes, winter brings months of biting cold and strong winds, so larches hunker down, saving their energy for warmer days by dropping their needles. This strategy also helps them avoid getting heavy snow-laden limbs. Smart, right?

The trail now takes a turn back to the west and cruises just under the summit of Cone Mountain before gently gaining the ridgeline again where mountain views both to the north and the south are simply fabulous. Making a colorful mosaic at your feet are dwarf bilberry, grouse whortleberry, Cascade huckleberry, and various evergreen heather plants.

Folks with gumption and time on their hands may want to climb to the summit of Tatie Peak, located at 2.1 miles and found by following an unmarked but obvious boot path to the right (northwest) just before traversing underneath her peak. The views from the top are gorgeous—as are the views up ahead, so if you skip it, don't fret.

One of the best groves of larches is found before you reach another cirque shortly after passing under the shoulders of Tatie Peak. If you have little ones with you or your time is limited, this is a good turnaround spot.

Overcast days often bring beautiful cloud patterns, which make for good backdrops behind the yellow trees. Look for illumination on the trees as you wander along this ridge, and if you get good lighting, put your back to the sun and shoot toward the trees.

As the trail follows the rocky hillside traverse, it passes by another tall summit, Syncline Mountain. If you are low on water, your only real shot for it is located down a game trail to the PCT's left (east), a mile before Grasshopper Pass. This dribble is important for PCT thru-hikers, who often approach this area from the south in late summer and are frequently low on liquid by the time they arrive. With the popularity of this trail skyrocketing, the boot paths leading to the dribbles, along with the large open tent sites in the vicinity, are well established.

At 4.9 miles arrive at Grasshopper Pass, where all the things we've seen and loved so far meet together again in a breathtaking opus. Larch trees, abundant grasses, and huckleberries grow with supreme beauty, and views knock your shoes and socks off—laces included.

A spur trail takes off from the main one and leads to a rocky viewpoint to the south if your schedule and your feet agree to take the jaunt. This picnic spot will have you feeling gobsmacked with mountain layers and views. This is the happy place I go to mentally when I'm stuck in traffic or having a root canal. Feel free to make it yours too. You'll want to stay here all day, but eventually you'll have to head back the way you came.

7. CUTTHROAT LAKE

Distance: 4 miles
Elevation Gain: 420 feet
High Point: 4900 feet
Difficulty: Easy
GPS: N 48°33.379', W 120°39.289'
Maps: Green Trails Maps No. 50: Washington Pass

Managing Agency: Okanogan-Wenatchee National Forest, Methow Valley Ranger District
Passes: Northwest Forest Pass or Interagency Pass
Dog-Friendly: Yes, on leash
Kid-Friendly: Yes
Amenities: Pit toilet and picnic area at trailhead

Notes: State Route 20 closes seasonally, so double-check it's open before heading out. The trail reaches the Pacific Crest Trail on the top of Cutthroat Pass. Trail open to mountain bikes; no horses allowed at the lake.

Getting There: From Marblemount: Drive nearly 63 miles east on North Cascades Highway (SR 20), passing Rainy Pass and Washington Pass. In roughly 5 miles after Washington Pass, and shortly after a sharp hairpin turn (near milepost 167), turn left (west) onto a well-signed spur road for Cutthroat Lake and find a large, paved parking area.

From Winthrop: Drive west on North Cascades Highway (SR 20) for almost 27 miles. Turn right onto a well-signed spur road for Cutthroat Lake and find a large, paved parking area.

> Pack the kids, bring the dog, and enjoy fall along a gentle trail leading to a sparkling, large lake. The season is punctuated here with golden subalpine larch trees that pop up around the lake's shoreline and speckle the lofty peaks above the basin.

 Foliage: Cascade huckleberry, Sitka mountain ash, subalpine larch

In summer, this trail can be a dusty mess, but this time of year, it's usually tamped down by early hard frosts or the occasional light rain or snow. Before you really get your feet warmed up, cross the trail's namesake, Cutthroat Creek, on a sturdy bridge. If you are visiting in early morning, watch your step so you don't accidentally breakdance courtesy of an icy surface.

The gentleness of the trail grade continues as you hit a couple of sweeping switchbacks before traversing under a winter avalanche slope at about 1 mile.

Granite peaks dotted with larches shoot skyward, while the scene is mirrored in Cutthroat Lake's reflective waters.

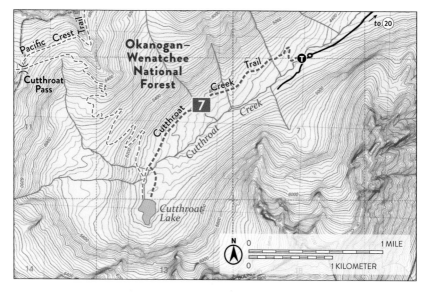

Huckleberry shrubs mottle the land, especially where the area is open to light or the soil has been disturbed by natural causes.

At 1.7 miles, a trail junction shows up via a signed tree. Stay left (south) to head to the lake, and you are almost there! Another sign reminds you that campfires and camping are not permitted within a half mile of the lake.

After the junction, a log bridge with no handrails crosses Cutthroat Creek. If it's icy, it's dicey! In fall, the creek is usually more of a trickle and is easily crossed with a rock hop, skip, and a jump, so if you find the log a bit intimidating, cross the cheater way. Continue following the main trail as it bobs and weaves through forest, crossing a log over a dry creek, until it arrives at Cutthroat Lake. Several unofficial spots around the lake provide views of the opposing shoreline, where golden larches are visible in clumps, tucked high into their alpine groves. Lighting for photos is tough in fall until around noon, when the sun illuminates the far southern end of the lake and lights the basin.

When you've had your fill, head back the way you came, or tack on a few more miles by extending your adventure.

EXTENDING YOUR TRIP

Retrace your steps back to the signed tree where you originally turned south to head to the lake. Follow the main trail to the left (southwest) and continue for 0.2 mile across a couple of wooden bridges before coming to a trail junction T. Turn left and cruise for less than 0.1 mile to the lake's northwestern shoreline, where a different view, perhaps with better lighting, greets you.

For another time, or maybe today if daylight is favorable, take a righthand turn (northwest) at the T to travel up to Cutthroat Pass (Hike 8), adding another 7.4 roundtrip miles and 1910 feet of elevation gain to your trip.

8. CUTTHROAT PASS

Distance: 10 miles
Elevation Gain: 2000 feet
High Point: 6800 feet
Difficulty: Moderate
GPS: N 48°31.084', W 120°43.988'
Maps: Green Trails Maps No. 50: Washington Pass

Managing Agency: Okanogan-Wenatchee National Forest, Methow Valley Ranger District
Passes: Northwest Forest Pass or Interagency Pass
Dog-Friendly: Yes, on leash
Kid-Friendly: No
Amenities: Pit toilet at trailhead

Notes: This hike is very popular, and parking can be challenging, especially on weekends. Arrive early or choose a weekday for slightly better parking opportunities. Use extreme caution parking on the side of the highway, and respect all no-parking signs. If snow or ice is along the trail, it's highly advisable to bring or wear shoe traction since hillsides in places are steep. State Route 20 closes seasonally, so double-check it's open before heading out.

Getting There: From Marblemount: Drive 51 miles east on North Cascades Highway (State Route 20) to Rainy Pass (near milepost 158). Turn left (north) onto a well-signed spur road for the Pacific Crest Trail North and find a large, paved parking area. From Winthrop: Follow North Cascades Highway (SR 20) west for 36 miles, reaching the signed Rainy Pass area. Turn right (north) into the parking area for Pacific Crest Trail North.

This whole area is steeped in subalpine larch trees with mountainous views so gorgeous, you might get misty. The native deciduous conifer lives happily at these high altitudes for upwards of four hundred years, some even longer than five hundred! If you see one with small purple cones, it's at least one hundred years old. If it has a large number of cones, it's likely over two hundred years. Word of this glorious, golden-treed paradise has spread, and folks flock here to see the resplendence. You won't be alone, but oh, will this landscape be a glorious sight!

 Foliage: Black alpine sedge, Cascade huckleberry, fireweed, fool's huckleberry, grouse whortleberry, Mertens' sedge, rosy spirea, Sitka mountain ash, subalpine larch

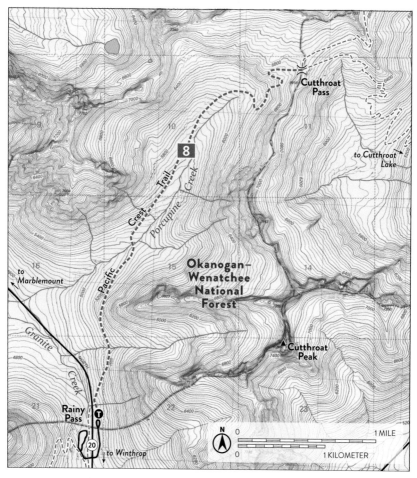

There are two ways to get to Cutthroat Pass: the way described here along the Pacific Crest Trail (PCT) or the Cutthroat Lake approach (Hike 7). Either approach is breathtaking, but having an opportunity to see some of Washington's brag-worthy scenery along the 2650-mile PCT is worth the climb. The trail starts out in a forest of evergreens such as western white pine, lodgepole pine, whitebark pine, and Pacific silver fir. The grade gently warms up your quads and seems respectful of your ascending efforts.

A seasonal creek greets you at 0.7 mile, along with another, Porcupine Creek, at 1.6 miles. Rock hop across quickly if the weather is warm, since a hornets' nest is often found in this area.

Hikers pick their way through snowy terrain amidst majestic mountains near Cutthroat Pass.

The climbing continues at the base of Porcupine Peak, gradually getting a little steeper just as the evergreens get thinner. Seasonal creeklets dribble and drip here and there, and at 3.5 miles, a sign with hiker and tent symbols points the way to sustainable camping in this delicate area. If you are ready for a break, it's a good place to stop and rest a minute.

If you haven't already taken out your camera, now is the time! Switchbacks help you get higher, while subalpine larches make your jaw drop in awe. These trees in their dormancy phases are striking visions of golden autumn perfection and proof that change can be beautiful. Proud mountains, such as Porcupine, Crooked Bum, Frisco, Corteo, and so many others dominate the horizon to the south, a grand sight to be sure. A standard lens will have a hard time capturing this: using a wide-angle lens or a panorama setting might work better.

From here, the larch march continues all the way to the pass, although they get sparser as you head higher into the vast subalpine landscapes. At your feet, various plants such as sedges and huckleberries offer shades of deep red, yellow, and orange, helping you compose colors a'plenty in each picture.

At 5 miles, reach the ridgeline, also known as Cutthroat Pass. To the southeast, Cutthroat Lake (Hike 7) twinkles in the basin below. Tan, bulbous boulders are scattered through the landscape and make wonderful, durable surfaces for you to spread out a picnic and sip hot chocolate. It's truly natural perfection! Head back the way you came, or if you have two cars, you could do a thru-hike ending at the Cutthroat Lake Trailhead (Hike 7).

9. EASY PASS

Distance: 7.3 miles
Elevation Gain: 2920 feet
High Point: 6515 feet
Difficulty: Hard
GPS: N 48°35.282', W 120°48.183'
Maps: Green Trails Maps No. 49: Mount Logan
Managing Agency: Okanogan-Wenatchee National Forest, Methow Valley Ranger District

Passes: Northwest Forest Pass or Interagency Pass
Dog-Friendly: Yes, on leash (with exception of the North Cascades National Park whose boundary is at the top of the hike)
Kid-Friendly: No
Amenities: Pit toilet and picnic table available at trailhead

Notes: State Route 20 closes seasonally, so double-check it's open before heading out.
Getting There: From Marblemount: Proceed east on North Cascades Highway (State Route 20) for approximately 45.5 miles to the well-signed Easy Pass Trailhead spur road to the right (southwest) side of the roadway. The trailhead is found in another 0.1 mile with parking for roughly ten cars.

From Winthrop: Proceed west on SR 20 for just over 42 miles, passing Rainy Pass. Turn left (southwest) on the well-signed Easy Pass Trailhead spur road and reach the trailhead 0.1 mile farther.

When the other trailheads near here are jam-packed, head over to Easy Pass for a less crowded option. The larches at the top are yellow and showy but not as prolific as they are on other local hikes; many are small, and the growing season is short. What this hike might lack in thick larch madness, it makes up for in spectacular colors and views on the way up, thanks to the mountain ash and huckleberries that blanket the hillsides. "Easy" does not describe the gentleness of the trail, since its arduous climbing will provide a solid, milkshake-earning workout. It's not quite as brutal as some heinie-kicking climbs in our state, but prepare for the grind.

 Foliage: Cascade azalea, Cascade huckleberry, fool's huckleberry, Sitka mountain ash, subalpine larch

If the intensity of the beginning of the hike remained consistent throughout the whole thing, the name Easy Pass would certainly be fitting. But don't let the

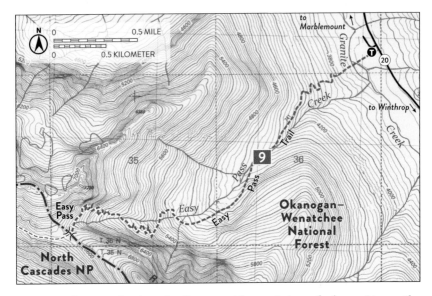

gentle stroll on wooden boardwalks set amidst sandy loam fool you. At 0.1 mile, arrive at a log bridge crossing the shallow Granite Creek. Toddle across using care, since the hand railings are a bit worn from use and weather. From here, the trail starts its upward trajectory through cedars and firs, steep in places but not horribly punishing. Several water crossings of Easy Pass Creek have you rock hopping as you cross, a good place for the pup to get a drink if he came along.

In 1.5 miles, the trail pops out of the forest in an open avalanche slope where views and color officially begin. Easy Pass is located in the saddle between Graybeard Peak to the left and New Morning Peak to the right, both impressive with pockets of year-round snow fields. If that doesn't tickle your fancy, you're sure to be impressed by the displays of gold, yellow, red, and orange mixed with green heather at your feet. Sitka mountain ash is the most vibrant of the plants in this area, with colors ranging from burgundy to neon orange and beyond! Its small, candy-apple-red berries grow in clusters and make the plant even more brilliant during this time of year. Add to that the crimson huckleberry leaves and the yellow Cascade azalea, and you have a gorgeous schematic fit for a postcard.

As you climb higher, don't forget to look behind you to the northeast for gorgeous views of rocky Methow Pinnacles, and be sure to keep your eyes out for mountain goats that like to frequent the rocky hillsides near here.

Tight switchbacks guide you farther up the open hillsides until the trail finally bursts out onto an exposed scree field with sparse vegetation and narrow footing in places. The larches are visible now, rewarding your efforts to get to your goal. At

Easy Pass, though not true to its name, is a good option for those seeking a less crowded hike.

last, at 3.5 miles, you arrive at a much gentler grade in a dispersed forest of subalpine larches. If you brought the pooch, this is your stopping point, since he's not allowed in the national park just ahead.

Lots of social trails crisscross the area, exploring the larches, but the main trail you've been following continues onward, reaching the signed boundary for North Cascades National Park and a resplendent basin with views of Arches Peak, Fisher Peak, and the impressive Fisher Creek valley far below your perch. The trail continues a very short distance before it descends on the other side, so you could always keep going, but most folks will want to turn around here, content with their accomplishment, eye candy, and up-close-and-personal romp with autumn. Twirl around a few times in the beautiful larches before heading back the way you came.

10. BLUE LAKE

Distance: 4.4 miles
Elevation Gain: 1050 feet
High Point: 6255 feet
Difficulty: Moderate
GPS: N 48°31.147', W 120°40.453'
Maps: Green Trails Maps No. 50: Washington Pass

Managing Agency: Okanogan-Wenatchee National Forest, Methow Valley Ranger District
Passes: Northwest Forest Pass or Interagency Pass
Dog-Friendly: Yes, on leash
Kid-Friendly: No
Amenities: Pit toilet at trailhead

Notes: This hike is very popular and parking can be challenging, especially on weekends. Be prepared with a plan for an alternative hike if the lot is full. Arrive early or choose a weekday for slightly better parking opportunities. State Route 20 closes seasonally, so double-check it's open before heading out.

Getting There: From Marblemount: Drive 54 miles east on North Cascades Highway (State Route 20), and turn right (south) onto a small road located between mile marker 161 and 152.

From Winthrop: Follow SR 20 west for 32 miles to find the Blue Lake Trailhead to the road's left (south).

It seems like a fall rite of passage to visit Blue Lake. It's not only the brilliant, golden subalpine larches wrappig you in their autumn splendor that take your breath away, but also the lake itself, which is a vision with a dusting of snow on the neighboring peaks. Mountain goats are locals here, so keep your eyes peeled and your dogs on a tight leash.

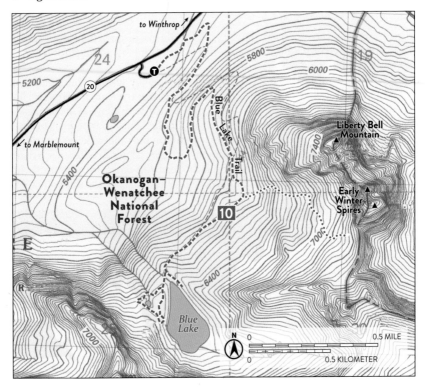

Foliage: Cascade huckleberry, Cascade mountain ash, fireweed, fool's huckleberry, grouse whortleberry, pearly everlasting, subalpine larch

Mountain hemlock, lodgepole pine, and western white pine greet you at the start, and because you are squarely on the eastern side of the Cascade Crest, the forest understory has an open feeling and springs to life with fall colors from Cascade huckleberry, pearly everlasting, and a variety of dormant perennials that offer an ecru hue in their final days.

The trail makes its way through an avalanche swale via long switchbacks, where sprawling views distract you from your huffing and puffing. Wildflowers thrive in the summer on these sunny slopes, and you might find a few stragglers hanging tightly to their seeds. Look for fireweed, a member of the evening primrose family, which stands three to six feet in height and in summer produces a gorgeous spike of numerous flowers atop one stem. This time of year, they go to seed, and their tops look like a tangle of finely spun silk fluff, each stalk capable of producing upwards of eighty thousand seeds.

At roughly 1.5 miles, the trail makes a southern trajectory and climbs high into your first cluster of golden subalpine larches framed against the jagged peaks of Liberty Bell, Early Winter Spire, and South Early Winter Spire, a rock climber's paradise. A boot-beaten trail shoots up to the east, serving as the unofficial and unmaintained climbers trail toward Liberty Bell. The burgundy ground cover of

The moist but well-drained rocky soils of the slopes near Blue Lake provide perfect habitat for larches.

Cascade huckleberry creeps into the heather, making this place feel magical, as if gnomes might just pop out from behind the bushes.

The climbing grade lessens as you continue through the enchanted golden trees. Give a look to the trail's right where Cutthroat Peak, Whistler Mountain, and various other peaks tower high above North Cascades Highway.

At roughly 2 miles, rock hop across Blue Lake's outlet, then take in an entirely different feast for your eyes—the lake and its southeastern neighbors, Posthole and Blue Lake Peaks. An old cabin, now in sad shape, is found tucked up on a hillside not far from the crossing.

The shoreline of the lake is one of the most scenic places in this area. On a still day, the subalpine larches reflect in the teal of the waters while the rugged peaks stand proud and tall high above. Cascade huckleberry bushes peek out from hillsides while the mustard-colored leaves of Cascade mountain ash reach out from the lake's edges. Photography is tough in this spot because the sun is often lower than the peaks, which stand at the lake's southern edge, so photos seem washed out. Take a few for memories, or wait until the day gets into the late afternoon hours and shoot with the lighting on the larches to the lake's eastern shore. Retrace your steps back to your car when you've had your fill.

11. MAPLE PASS LOOP/LAKE ANN

Distance: 7.3 miles
Elevation Gain: 2000 feet
High Point: 6850 feet
Difficulty: Moderate
GPS: N 48°30.973', W 120°44.124'
Maps: Green Trails Maps No. 49: Mount Logan

Managing Agency: Okanogan-Wenatchee National Forest, Methow Valley Ranger District
Passes: Northwest Forest Pass or Interagency Pass
Dog-Friendly: Yes, on leash
Kid-Friendly: No
Amenities: Pit toilet at trailhead

Notes: This hike is very popular and parking can be challenging, especially on weekends. Arrive early or choose a weekday for more solitude and parking opportunities. If parking is full, have a plan B for another local hike. If snow or ice is along the trail, it's highly advisable to bring or wear shoe traction, since hillsides in places are steep. State Route 20 closes seasonally, so double-check it's open before heading out.

Getting There: From Marblemount: Drive 45 miles east on North Cascades Highway (State Route 20), and turn right (west) onto a small road (Forest Road 600) located between mile marker 151 and 152. The trailhead, complete with a pit toilet, is in another 0.1 mile.

From Winthrop: Drive east on North Cascades Highway (SR 20) for 35 miles, then turn left (west) onto a short spur road (FR 600) containing the trailhead and parking area.

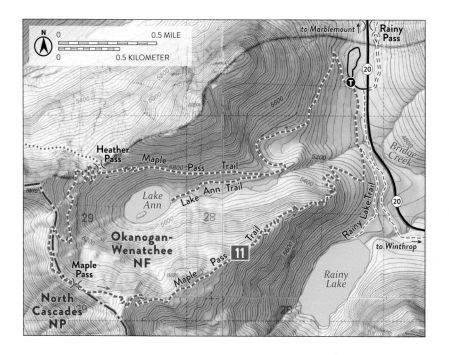

When you ask longtime residents about where to hike in Washington State in the fall, they almost always crow about Maple Pass Loop/Lake Ann, and for good reason. When this area puts on her charming display of golden larches and burgundy huckleberry bushes, she shows off her best features and dances for the camera. This Lake Ann is very different from the one in the Mount Baker area (Hike 3), since the slightly more arid climate invites less understory and, of course, more larches that thrive in the expansive shadeless areas of the eastern side of the Cascade Crest. The mystical jonquil coloration makes hiking here simply unforgettable.

 Foliage: Cascade huckleberry, dunhead sedge, fool's huckleberry, Mertens' sedge, showy sedge, subalpine larch

Since this is a loop, with the highest part being near the middle, going either direction requires a fair bit of effort to reach the crux. I prefer to start at the northern end, since it tends to be a bit gentler off the get-go and wakes your quads up a little more gradually.

Follow the paved parking area trail until you come to a righthand trail junction on a well-traveled path. Turn here, and moderately ascend into a forest of hemlock, pine, fir, and spruce. Up you go through a few patches of Cascade huckleberry and various decaying wildflower stalks left over from the warm summer.

At 1.3 miles, arrive at a trail junction and take the trail that heads off to the left to visit the twinkling, azure Lake Ann. Set in a rock-strewn cirque, it's absolutely worth the additional 0.8 mile out-and-back distance.

The loop continues climbing and arrives at open meadows high above Lake Ann. This subalpine wonderland is beyond breathtaking with panoramic views of rocky spires and towering peaks such as Crooked Bum, Black, Frisco, Rainy, Whistler, and others.

In just over 1 mile beyond the Lake Ann junction, the trail reaches Heather Pass, where boot-beaten paths meander in various directions. Due to the high number of visitors, the Forest Service has closed some of these game trails for restoration, so keep your eyes peeled for any small signs noting the closures. Subalpine larch trees join the pretty party, along with more Cascade huckleberry and

The trail is showy thanks to sunlight and a warm color palette near Maple Pass.

fool's huckleberry, all of which offer gorgeous deep-burgundy leaves to make fall photos with the golden larches a vision. If the sun is in front of you, as it often can be on this stretch, try shooting directly into it, with the trail in the center of the frame and the backlit larches on either side. Depending on the cloud cover or sun conditions, you may need to lighten the photo slightly in post-editing.

Continue through paradise, admiring the magnificent views. Tan stems of dormant perennials, along with the green foliage of red and white heather plants, mingle with the Cascade huckleberry and brilliant larches in hillsides of color fit for a crayon box. At 3.6 miles after the trailhead, arrive at Maple Pass, another lofty passageway through soaring peaks. Marinate in all this grandeur, and count your good fortune that you are able to visit places like this with the power of your own two feet!

The final climb delivers you to the top of a boulder-strewn knoll before it starts a steep, somewhat knee-aching descent through even more glorious larch trees. Say goodbye to Lake Ann in the basin below, and eventually arrive back in an evergreen forest before reaching the paved, ADA-accessible Rainy Lake Trail at 6.8 miles. Turn left (north) here, and do the happy dance for the final 0.5 mile to the parking lot where you started.

12. CRATER LAKES

Distance: 8.6 miles
Elevation Gain: 2420 feet
High Point: 6980 feet
Difficulty: Moderate-hard
GPS: N 48°13.203', W 120°16.088'
Maps: Green Trails Maps No. 115: Prince Creek

Managing Agency: Okanagan-Wenatchee National Forest, Methow Valley Ranger District
Passes: Northwest Forest Pass or Interagency Pass
Dog-Friendly: Yes, on leash
Kid-Friendly: No
Amenities: Pit toilet at trailhead

Notes: The road to Crater Lakes (and Eagle Lakes—Hike 13) is rough with lumps, bumps, and potholes, but passenger cars can make it.

Getting There: From the town of Carlton, head south on Methow Valley Highway (State Route 153) for 3.1 miles and turn right (west) on Gold Creek Loop Road. Restart your tripometer here, and in 1.6 miles, turn right on Gold Creek Road (signed for South Fork Gold Creek, Foggy Dew, and Crater Creek Camp). At 2.6 miles, stay straight, signed for Forest Road 4340. At 6.7 miles, the pavement ends, and shortly after, you bear slightly right at a fork. Proceed for 8.3 miles, then bear left at the road signed FR 300. From here follow a steep and rough road until it dead-ends at the trailhead and a large parking lot with room for about fifty cars, 13 miles from SR 153.

Sure, maybe this hike gets some heavy traffic during larch season, but it's not nearly the madhouse that you'll find at the more popular fall trailheads, and it's almost every bit as beautiful. The trail climbs, steeply at times, to a pair of shallow lakes safeguarded by spectacular golden trees with backdrops of fortress-like stony mountain faces—ya know, no big deal.

 Foliage: Cascade mountain ash, grouse whortleberry, dwarf bilberry, subalpine larch

The path starts off on the same trail that goes to Eagle Lakes (Hike 13) and is open to wheels, boots, and hooves. While horses and mountain bikes are allowed on Crater Creek Trail, the sometimes-steep and rocky-in-places terrain discourages most bikers from pedaling to the top.

At 0.7 mile, bear right (northwest) at a signed junction (the left goes to a horse ford) and cross a wooden bridge over Crater Creek.

Just 0.1 mile farther on, 0.8 mile into the hike, the trail reaches a signed four-way junction. Our trail, "Crater Creek Tr 416" according to a sign on a tree, is the first one to the right. A moderate climb begins here but lets up occasionally to give you a break.

With Cascade mountain ash stealing the show in yellows, the scene feels autumnesque even here. It makes a tranquil picture amongst the alder, Douglas-fir,

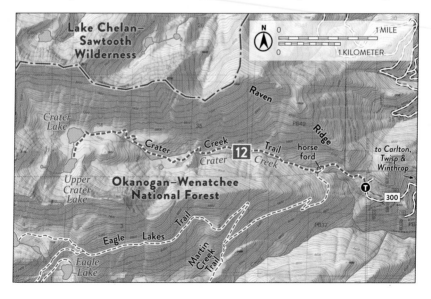

The enchanted upper Crater Lake is a vision in its autumn ensemble.

and Engelmann spruce trees, but you'll be more snap-happy when you see what's ahead, so avoid dawdling if time and daylight aren't on your side.

Crater Creek babbles and coos near the trail, offering a few spots for the pup to drink as you make your way up the valley. At just over 2 miles, the path climbs steeply through slabby rock and rewards you with views of golden larches across the valley to the trail's left. Another viewpoint shows up 1.5 miles past this one, also on the left (at 3.5 miles), and offers a perfect rocky perch for resting, gawking, and enjoying the moment.

The trail finally levels out at the first lake at 3.9 miles. A large camp with several downed logs makes a good place to drop the pack, explore the shoreline, and swoon at the views. Ringed around the lake's edges are brilliant yellow larches, their needles ready to hit the ground. Behind the lake, several impressive unnamed peaks stand at attention, their jagged summits intimidating the surrounding landscapes. The northern side of the lake has a few more campsites and might provide a more private picnic spot if you decide to make this your final destination. If not, enjoy, then continue onward for even more beauty at the upper lake.

Getting to the upper lake takes a little navigation since it isn't signed and there are plenty of side trails leading to the lower lake's shoreline but not the upper lake. With a little clever exploration, you'll get there. Follow the lower lake's eastern shoreline through the big camp, climbing over a large log or two, and then duck into the forest on a well-worn boot path. Stay to the east of the lower lake. If you pop out at the lower lake's shoreline, try again. The trail to the upper lake eventually makes its way south, climbing gently, until it delivers you front and center to the north end of the oblong upper lake, 0.4 mile beyond the lower lake and 4.3 miles from the trailhead.

Mount Bigelow steals the show while the larches enchantingly charm in the foreground. You can walk the lake's shoreline to the left or to the right, where even more views and a few campsites dot the region. So gorgeous and magical is this place, it almost seems like a fairy tale. Keep your eyes out for gnomes, just in case. If you see one, run—don't walk—back to your car the way you came. You might have eaten bad mushrooms.

13. EAGLE LAKES

Distance: 12.8 miles
Elevation Gain: 2550 feet
High Point: 7110 feet
Difficulty: Moderate-hard
GPS: N 48°13.203', W 120°16.088'
Maps: Green Trails Maps No. 115: Prince Creek

Managing Agency: Okanagan-Wenatchee National Forest, Methow Valley Ranger District
Passes: Northwest Forest Pass or Interagency Pass
Dog-Friendly: Yes, on leash
Kid-Friendly: No
Amenities: Pit toilet at trailhead and backcountry primitive toilet on route

Notes: The road to Eagle Lakes (and Crater Lakes—Hike 12) is rough with lumps, bumps, and potholes, but passenger cars can make it. The trail is multiuse and open to motorcycles, mountain bikes, and horses. Water is limited, so bring extra for the pups and the peoples, just in case the small seasonal creeks prior to the lake are dry.

Getting There: From the town of Carlton, head south on Methow Valley Highway (State Route 153) for 3.1 miles and turn right (west) on Gold Creek Loop Road. Restart your tripometer here, and in 1.6 miles, turn right on Gold Creek Road (signed for South Fork Gold Creek, Foggy Dew, and Crater Creek Camp). At 2.6 miles, stay straight, signed Forest Road 4340. At 6.7 miles, the pavement ends; shortly after bear slightly right at a fork. Proceed for 8.3 miles, then bear left at the road signed FR 300. From here follow the steep and rough road until it dead-ends at the trailhead and a large parking lot with room for about fifty cars, 13 miles from SR 153.

This is a well-loved, well-used trail and for good reason: it leads to a spectacular fall wonderland wrought with larches rimming mountain lakes. Motorcycles and mountain bikes are able to use most of the trail, save for the short distance to Upper Eagle Lake, the best destination of all, but don't let that discourage you from using your legs. The well-established trail is in good shape, aside from being a bit dusty, and makes a worthwhile autumn adventure.

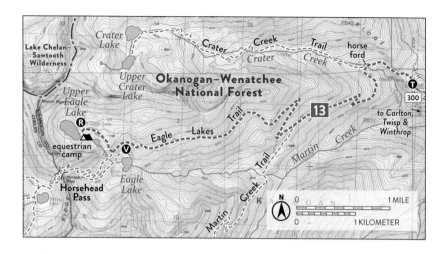

 Foliage: Cascade mountain ash, grouse whortleberry, dwarf bilberry, northwestern sedge, Scouler's willow, subalpine larch

When autumn comes to the mountains, this hike and its companion, Crater Lakes (Hike 12), with which it shares a trailhead, are must-dos. This one is longer than Crater Lakes, but its grade is less steep overall despite the elevation gain, making it a comfortable full-day exploring option.

Leaving the parking lot, the trail bobs and weaves through the woodlands and grassy knolls with views into the Okanogan-Wenatchee National Forest. At a signed junction at 0.7 mile, bear right (the left branch leads to a horse ford) and continue a short distance before crossing a sturdy wooden bridge over Crater Creek.

At roughly 0.8 mile, arrive at a well-signed four-way junction, one being the trail on which you are standing. To the immediate right is Crater Creek Trail. Our trail is the second right, Eagle Lakes Trail (signed for Eagle Lakes Trail 431), which takes you deeper into the valley. Keep your eyes and ears open for mountain bikes or the occasional dirt bike, which are free to cruise up this incline.

A moderate grade gets your heart pumping as the trail guides you in a westerly direction, throwing in a few switchbacks here and there to keep you on your toes. At 2.2 miles, and after nearly 900 feet of elevation gain, a signed junction to the left goes toward Martin Lakes (Martin Creek Trail), while our route continues straight.

Gorgeous subalpine larches show up on the hillsides across the valley at about 4 miles—a sneak preview of what's to come. In another mile, views of Eagle Lake, in the valley to the trail's left, start to peek through the forest, and at 5.5 miles,

Upper Eagle Lake showcases a mirror-like image of the golden larch trees in its jade waters.

a viewpoint just off the trail to the left, complete with a makeshift stone bench, invites you to stop for a moment.

At 5.7 miles, arrive at a signed junction with Upper Eagle Lake Trail 431.1. From here to Upper Eagle Lake wheels are not permitted, so if the *braaappps* have become a bit too annoying, you'll now have some reprieve. Turn right (northwest) and begin a gentle up-and-down final push to the granddaddy of fall lakes. When the larch trees are golden, so is the pathway . . . follow the yellow needle road!

An equestrian camp is located to the trail's left in 0.5 mile, followed by a signed trail to a box-style backcountry toilet to the trail's right. If you have to use the toilet, try to do it in between groups of hikers—the trees don't provide much privacy, and you might have a bit of stage fright if you don't time it well.

The lake is just beyond these other amenities and so is a primitive pathway guiding you to the left, toward groves of shimmering yellow conifers on the lake's southwestern shoreline. If the wind is still, there are plenty of opportunities for reflection photos at several shoreline spots along the way. To complement the yellow trees, the lake tends to have a teal tinge—a jaw-dropping sight and some serious soul shampoo. The best lighting for pictures during early to mid-October is before 11:00 AM, so do your best to get up with the chickens and get there early if photography is part of your goal.

Head back the way you came when you've marinated sufficiently in autumn's embrace.

EXTENDING YOUR TRIP

To make an even longer day of it, visit the lower Eagle Lake too. To do this, turn right (south) when you arrive back at the junction you took for Upper Eagle Lake Trail, and follow Eagle Lakes Trail for 0.6 mile farther along its pathway. Turn left (east) at a signed junction for Eagle Lake, and proceed for just shy of 1 mile downhill to its shoreline. Here an equestrian camp, several nice campsites, and a primitive backcountry toilet await. Views are pretty with larches here and there, but the hero of the trip is definitely the lake's upper companion. The roundtrip side adventure to lower Eagle Lake adds approximately 3 miles and 530 feet of elevation gain, so plan wisely with daylight and abilities to ensure you make it back in good time. When you retrace your steps, it will thankfully be almost all downhill once you reach the Upper Eagle Lake junction again.

For those who are super eager and have ample time, consider following Eagle Lakes Trail farther to the west for roughly 0.7 mile beyond the official turnoff to lower Eagle Lake and climbing up to Horsehead Pass, where even more views abound. Wherever you decide to call it a day, head back the way you came.

14. LAKE TWENTYTWO

Distance: 5.4 miles
Elevation Gain: 1350 feet
High Point: 2400 feet
Difficulty: Moderate
GPS: N 48°04.618', W 121°44.742'
Maps: Green Trails Maps No. 109: Granite Falls

Managing Agency: Mount Baker–Snoqualmie National Forest, Darrington Ranger District
Passes: Northwest Forest Pass or Interagency Pass
Dog-Friendly: Yes, on leash
Kid-Friendly: No
Amenities: Pit toilet and picnic area at trailhead

Notes: This is one of the most popular hikes in the area, and the parking area fills up quickly, especially on weekends. Park only in designated parking areas, and avoid parking on the highway or risk getting towed. As with all trailheads, but especially those along the Mountain Loop Highway, avoid leaving any valuables in your vehicle, as car prowls are especially high. Use caution on boardwalks on cold days—they can be icy.
Getting There: From Granite Falls, drive east on the Mountain Loop Highway for 11 miles to the Verlot Public Service Center. From there, continue east for 2 more miles until you see a sign for Lake Twentytwo and a short spur to the right (south) leading to the parking loop.

Fall colors on this trail are primarily limited to the areas around the lake where Cascade mountain ash, fool's huckleberry, oval-leaved huckleberry, and a plethora of grasses and ecru stalks of dormant wildflowers paint the hillsides and line the shoreline. But the lake isn't the only thing magnificent about this hike; the trail leading to it is a mossy, green wonderland populated with waterfalls, ferns, cedars, firs, and hemlocks. There is something for everyone who seeks a Northwest autumn hike.

 Foliage: Bigleaf maple, blue wildrye, Cascade mountain ash, fool's huckleberry, mountain hairgrass, oval-leaved huckleberry, pearly everlasting, rosy spirea, slender hairgrass, vine maple

From the start, you know this hike is special. The deep forest with healthy populations of evergreens such as Alaska cedar, Pacific silver fir, mountain hemlock, and western hemlock draws you in, and for this preserved magical place, the government is to thank. In 1947, due to a unique microclimate containing stands of virgin old-growth western red cedar and western hemlock as well as rare plants, this area was given permanent protection and set aside for study and education

Earth-toned foliage around Lake Twentytwo lends distinct fall color to the trail's edges.

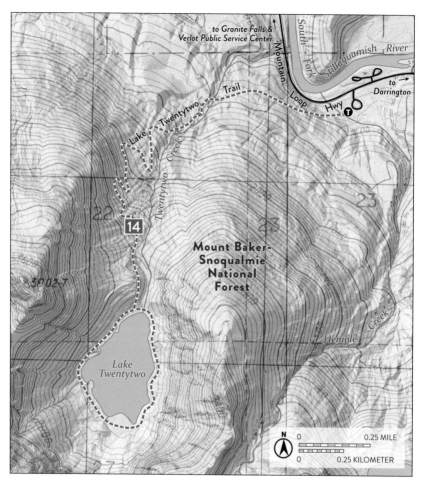

to Granite Falls &
Verlot Public Service Center

Trail

Lake Twentytwo

Twentytwo Creek

14

Mount Baker-
Snoqualmie
National
Forest

3002

Lake
Twentytwo

Hemple Creek

South Fork Mountain Loop Hwy

Stillaguamish River

to
Darrington

22   23   23

N   0   0.25 MILE
     0   0.25 KILOMETER

as a Research Natural Area (RNA). Some of the trees you'll see along your way are old giants!

The trail ascends steadily, climbing past waterfalls, dribbling creeks, and spectacular mossy cedar trees that beg you to stop and gawk. Bridges, trail stairs, and turnpikes in the trail attempt to keep your feet dry, but water somehow always finds its way to the path in this rainforest. At the base of the beautiful evergreens, ferns—such as deer, lady, maidenhair, and others—do their part to keep things oh-so-green everywhere you look.

At roughly 1.5 miles the trail crosses a talus slope where bigleaf maples, Cascade mountain ash, vine maple, and a few oval-leaved huckleberry bushes give you your first taste of fall colors. If the weather is clear, you might catch views of Liberty and Whitehorse Mountains to the north.

The trail reenters the forest and, before long, delivers you to the shoreline of the gorgeous Lake Twentytwo and her surrounding basin. Go right or left and make a loop around the lake to see this cirque in all its glory. Rugged peaks with sheer walls shoot skyward, while talus fields show off vine maples in shades of red. Fool's huckleberry, oval-leaved huckleberry, and rosy spirea also offer rich earth tones for your fall-color-seeking pleasure. The angle of the sun can make the light in this basin difficult to photograph this time of year, but during midday, if you happen to have sun or decent lighting, stand on the lake's western shoreline and try shooting the north side of the lake. You won't capture those giant peaks, but you will get some nice fall colors along with the tranquil teal water. The way you came is the way back, when you've finished feasting your eyes.

Opposite: *Modern engineering is to thank for the suspension bridge that carries hikers safely across the Spokane River in Riverside Park (Hike 15).*

SPOKANE

The east side of Washington State has some beautiful landscapes and scenic mountains, but finding fall foliage amidst the plethora of pine trees can be tricky. Even the most discerning eye will have to work a bit to pick out colors, but if you're lucky enough to live in Spokane, or happen to be visiting or passing through, these hikes will provide at least a few pops of color and give you that sweater-weather vibe.

15. RIVERSIDE PARK LOOP

Distance: 2.2 miles
Elevation Gain: 220 feet
High Point: 1715 feet
Difficulty: Easy
GPS: N 47°41.765', W 117°29.738'
Maps: Riverside State Park Overview Map (see Resources)

Managing Agency: Washington State Parks
Pass: Discover Passes
Dog-Friendly: Yes, on leash
Kid-Friendly: Yes
Amenities: Pit toilets, picnic tables, car camping area nearby

Notes: Riverside State Park is a very popular area, but parking is plentiful. Trail open to bicycles and horses.

Getting There: From I-90 in Spokane, take exit 280 and go north on Maple Street. Cross the Maple Street Bridge, then continue for 1 mile to N. Maxwell Street. Turn left (west) onto Maxwell for 0.3 mile until the road curves and becomes N. Pettet Drive. Continue on this road for 4.5 miles until the road (which becomes Aubrey L White Parkway) enters Riverside State Park, passes the campground, and arrives at the large paved parking area.

Tranquil water views and shimmering fall leaves are plentiful in Riverside Park.

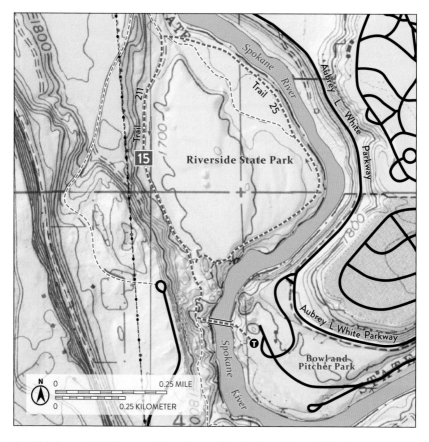

This beautiful hike provides plenty of peekaboo views of the Spokane River and, near its edges, the color. Also known as the Bowl and Pitcher Loop, you can customize this hike to be longer and see more of the river if you desire, or just stick to this shorter version. Grab the kids, the dogs, and a picnic basket and stroll through the pines while enjoying this frequently sunshine-filled hike.

 Foliage: Blue elderberry, narrowleaf willow, Woods' rose

From the parking area, follow the paved pathway as it meanders toward the river and crosses a spectacular cable suspension bridge. In the 1940s the Civilian Conservation Corps built the original 214-foot bridge that spanned the river, but in

1997, it was replaced with the one you see now. Despite modern engineering and improved safety measures, today's bridge was created to look and feel much like its predecessor. Take your time crossing it, and stop for photos pointing both up and down the banks, where willows provide a vibrant yellow foliage on the shoreline.

After the bridge, the trail climbs a small series of trail steps before coming to a junction near a covered picnic shelter, at nearly 0.2 mile. Turn right (north) here and follow the path as it passes through evergreens and arrives at another junction at 0.4 mile. Make a hard right (east) turn on this path, signed Trail 25.

The trail weaves its way through rocky outcroppings and viewpoints of the river, where more pleasant photos can be composed of the stone, the vegetation, and the river. At 0.9 mile, arrive at another junction and proceed straight (northwest) to remain on Trail 25. More viewpoints showcasing tranquil river scenes dotted with colors allow you more camera snaps and opportunities to take it in.

At 1.3 miles (0.4 mile past the last junction), turn left (west) and climb up a steep unsigned hill until you arrive at a road-turned-trail (Trail 211, but not signed as such). Turn left (south) and proceed straight ahead for 0.6 mile until you complete the loop. Continue, retracing your steps 0.2 mile to the covered picnic area, then turn left (east) across the bridge and toward your waiting car.

EXTENDING YOUR TRIP

If you want to spend more time in Riverside Park, check out the trails to the south of the junction near the covered picnic area, where a system of connected pathways winds itself along the river bends and throughout the peaceful park.

16. FINCH ARBORETUM LOOP

Distance: 1.2 miles
Elevation Gain: 20 feet
High Point: 2020 feet
Difficulty: Easy
GPS: N 47°38.608', W 117°27.741'
Maps: Finch Arboretum Self Guided Walking Tour (see Resources)

Managing Agency: City of Spokane Parks and Recreation Urban Forestry
Passes: None
Dog-Friendly: No, not permitted
Kid-Friendly: Yes
Amenities: Restrooms open through October 31, weather permitting

Notes: The arboretum is free to the public from dawn to dusk. Since you'll likely be walking in grass wet from either dew, snow, or rain, pack the waterproof footwear.
Getting There: From I-90 east in Spokane, take exit 277A. Continue on W. Garden Springs Road for 0.8 mile where it turns slightly right and becomes S. Rustle Street. In 0.1 mile farther, turn right (east) onto W. Sunset Boulevard. In 0.6 mile, turn right (southeast) toward S. F Street. Follow F Street a short distance as it winds around the

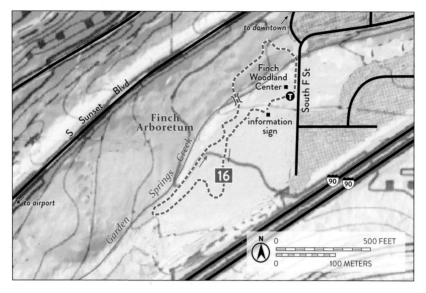

arboretum. Parking is in front of the Woodland Center, or at the end of the road, past the gate.

From Spokane heading west, follow I-90 and take exit 280A. Follow W. 4th Avenue for 0.4 mile, then turn left (southwest) onto W. Sunset Boulevard. In 0.1 mile, bear right to stay on Sunset Boulevard. In 1 mile, turn left (southeast) onto S. F Street. Follow F Street to the right as it winds around the arboretum. Parking is in front of the Woodland Center, or at the end of the road, past the gate.

Folks looking to stroll under large autumn-colored boughs will enjoy wandering through the arboretum's delightful deciduous trees. There is freeway noise aplenty, but if you imagine it's just a waterfall, or put some soft music on your headphones, you might just be transported far away from a busy downtown. This place is all about the leaf saunter or the picnic spot, not a workout, as grassy lawns take the place of trails.

 Foliage: Ash, beech, cherry, elm, hawthorn, maple, oak, willow

Start by following the path toward the information sign where you can find details about the arboretum. Next head along the grassy lawn southwest toward the beech, ash, and willow tree areas, where small tree signs identify their species. Pictures, especially when the sun is out and low in the sky, can be gorgeous if you

A quaint pedestrian bridge across Garden Springs Creek makes a wonderful place for photos.

angle the camera slightly upward and capture sunrays through the trees. Other shots, including portraits of folks hiding under the large limbs, work well here too.

Continue exploring as you make a big loop by visiting the oak, hawthorn, maple, and cherry trees before finding a small, picturesque bridge crossing Garden Springs Creek. On the southeast side of the creek, a rather compact red birch tree drips with yellowed leaves and dark branches, making an ideal place for a tranquil landscape photo.

Slowly make your way back to your vehicle when you've enjoyed the autumn visions.

17. ILLER CREEK/DISHMAN HILLS CONSERVATION AREA

Distance: 5.1 miles
Elevation Gain: 1250 feet
High Point: 3135 feet
Difficulty: Moderate
GPS: N 47°36.103', W 117°16.909'
Maps: USGS Spokane SE, Dishman Hills Conservation Area Trail Map—Iller Creek Unit (see Resources)

Managing Agency: Spokane County
Passes: None
Dog-Friendly: Yes, on leash
Kid-Friendly: Yes
Amenities: Honey bucket

Notes: Open from dawn to 10:00 PM unless otherwise posted. This hike description is from the northern trailhead; a second trailhead is available at Stevens Creek to the south.

Getting There: From Spokane, travel eastbound on I-90 to exit 285/E. Appleway Boulevard/Sprague Avenue. In 2 miles, turn right (south) onto S. Dishman Mica Road. At 4.3 miles, turn right (southwest) onto Schafer Road. At 5.2 miles, turn right (west) onto E. 44th Avenue. At 5.4 miles, turn left (south) onto S. Farr Road, and at 5.7 miles, turn right (west) onto E. Holman Road. Follow Holman Road for 0.7 mile (to 6.4 miles on the tripometer) to find the trailhead and the parking area along the road's right.

This hike isn't likely to be bursting with vibrant color—in fact, most of the tones of fall in this area are rather muted. Despite that, fall is everywhere you look, from a smattering of leaves on the ground to the rattling dried foliage above your head, just waiting for the next big gust of wind. What's more, this hike features rich views of the Spokane Valley, pastoral landscapes, and plenty of perches to kick back and relax. If you get lucky and hike on a warmish day, it's the perfect place to spend the afternoon marinating in the season.

Foliage: Black hawthorn, blue elderberry, oceanspray, water birch

Follow the well-signed trail as it leads beyond the sign and comes immediately to the first junction. Since this is a loop, you could go either way, but going right (south) at the Y gets the rather mundane part of this hike out of the way first and also is a bit flatter off the get-go. Proceed through crunchy water birch leaves

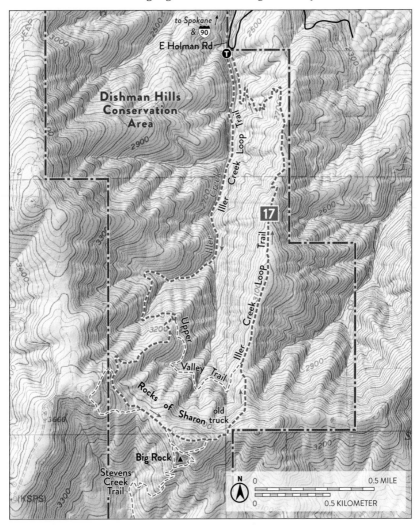

at your feet, staying straight at all the game trail junctions. At 0.3 mile, to the trail's right, reach a bench with a bit of a backward lean. It's seen some better days but is available should you need a prop for something like fixing your shoe or grabbing something from your pack.

Remain on the main trail, ignoring all the smaller, unsigned boot paths; you'll cross a water dribble at 1 mile. The climbing is steeper here, but stay with it—it will soon be a bit easier.

After passing two more creeklets, arrive at another signed junction located at 1.6 miles. To the left is Upper Valley Trail, which cuts across the valley, while to the right (southwest) is the continuation of our trail, Iller Creek Loop. Evergreens mix with oceanspray, water birch, and the occasional blue elderberry as you continue climbing and top the ridgeline.

At 2.2 miles, a signed trail junction goes downhill to the right, but our journey bears left (southeast). You are now on the stunning spine of the climb, and

Leaves crunch under your feet as you wander in a subdued version of fall.

the rocky towers, including Rocks of Sharon and Big Rock, are worth a look. Rock climbers use them too, so if you hear clinking and clacking up high, it's probably the rope warriors. Behind you now are large metal media towers for local Spokane stations, a stark contrast to the natural rocks and viewpoints to your right.

A number of picnic and lookout spots show up over the next half mile as you work your way up and around the ridge. A short hill climb is followed by the start of the descent, just as an odd abandoned vehicle is found to the trail's left; Mother Nature is trying to make sure it disappears under plant debris, but it has secrets to tell and won't go until it's ready.

At 3.2 miles, stay straight (north) at the signed Upper Valley Trail and continue your pleasant downhill. The trail switches back to the west and reaches a curious, well-used, unsigned junction, 4.8 miles from where you started. Turn left (south) here and follow the trail for another 0.3 mile until you once again reach the trailhead to complete your loop.

Next page: *A smattering of autumn guides your feet as you travel near Little Giant Pass (Hike 19).*

STEVENS PASS, LEAVENWORTH, AND WENATCHEE

The lush Central Cascades are filled with beautiful carpets of hillside colors and hidden nooks and crannies to explore. As with so many fall hikes, the roads to the trailheads and sometimes the trails themselves can be rough and tough, with a lot of climbing and bumps. Go slowly and take your time as you make your way. The reward will be worth it all!

18. CARNE MOUNTAIN

Distance: 8 miles
Elevation Gain: 3620 feet
High Point: 7085 feet
Difficulty: Hard
GPS: N 48°04.976', W 120°50.097'
Maps: Green Trails Maps No. 113: Holden

Managing Agency: Okanogan-Wenatchee National Forest, Wenatchee River Ranger District
Passes: None
Dog-Friendly: Yes, on leash
Kid-Friendly: No
Amenities: None

Notes: Parts of this hike can be muddy and slick after early snow or a lot of rain. The trail tread is steep and primitive in places, and plant roots are tripping hazards at times. Use extra care with footing. High-clearance vehicle highly recommended for trailhead access.

Getting There: From the junction of US Highway 2 and State Route 207, also known as Coles Corner, follow SR 207 northeast toward Lake Wenatchee. In 4.3 miles from US 2, bear right (north) on Chiwawa Loop Road. At 4.8 miles, bear right (northeast) to stay on Chiwawa Loop Road. At 5.6 miles, turn left (north) on Chiwawa River Road, signed for Chiwawa Valley. In a short distance this road turns to Forest Road 62, also called Forest Road 6200 on some maps. Stay on FR 62, avoiding all side roads including signed camps and trailheads, until the pavement ends 16.7 miles from US 2. Continue on the unpaved FR 62 for 11.2 more miles (27.9 miles from US 2), passing several campgrounds, some with pit toilets, before arriving at a sign to the right pointing toward Phelps Creek Trailhead (FR 6211). Turn right (north) and the bumping really begins! This road has a reputation for being the worst around here, with deep ruts and erosion issues, but most high-clearance vehicles, along with some strategic driving, can get you there. In 2.3 more miles (30.2 miles), arrive at the end of the road with parking for roughly fifteen to twenty vehicles.

Carne Mountain is all about larches and big vistas—a reward for the grunting you'll have to do to reach your goal. As members of the pine family, larches cleverly blend in as just one of the gang in the summertime, sporting beautiful green needles and not really getting much attention, but come autumn, it's game on. Unlike their ever-green cousins, deciduous larches siphon nutrients from their needles to store in their trunks, leading to a splendid gold coloration as the needles die. The ability to drop their needles makes these trees much better suited for colder, harsher climates, where heapings of snow could break limbs. What's more, the regeneration of needles makes them more resilient to fires and insects. Enjoy the Einsteins of the forest, then reach the view-soaked top of Carne. It's about as perfect as a day gets during autumn in the Cascades. Get you some!

 Foliage: Cascade huckleberry, Cascade mountain ash, Geyer's sedge, quaking aspen, Scouler's willow, Sitka mountain ash, western larch

Almost immediately, the trail crosses a seasonal tributary to Phelps Creek—a fine place to hydrate the pup if you brought her.

A gentle grade serves as a good warm-up as you saunter along Phelps Creek Trail for 0.2 mile, until you reach a signed junction for Carne Mountain Trail 1508. Bear right (northeast) here and begin ascending the steep grade. Embrace the

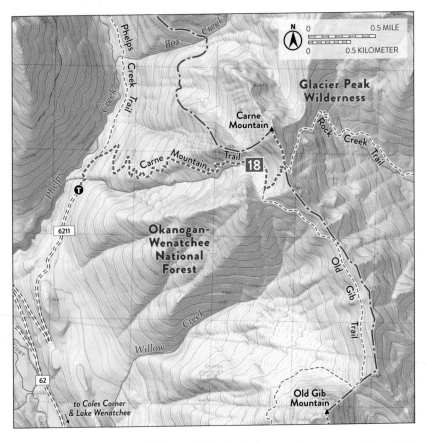

pace; it's not a race. Thankfully, switchbacks help ease the steepness to get you higher and higher. In places, the woody roots on the trail's edge try to get attention by hazardously sticking out, so watch your footing and stop for views. Narrow tread and the occasional blowdown keep you on your toes too.

In just over 2 miles of forested climbing, you enter a more open area, where you spot your first grove of yellow larches amongst a rocky cliff face to the southeast. This is only the appetizer—just wait until you taste the main course!

At 2.9 miles, the trail reaches a level basin, where some dribbles from a seasonal creek add ambiance to the peaceful grassy meadow. The trail appears to be guiding you like a red carpet into groves of brilliant larches just ahead on slopes. This is what you came for—get out the camera! In most cases, if you turn your back to the sun, the lighting will be in your favor to contrast the golden trees against a bluebird sky. However, on cloudy days, fill the frame primarily with the trees to avoid the washed-out sky. Don't forget to get some macros, or close-up pictures, of the larch needles.

After a short reprieve from the climbing, it starts again, although this time, you are stopping frequently to snap photos of those stunning trees at all angles, so it doesn't feel as steep. At 3.4 miles arrive at a signed junction for the Old Gib Trail to the right, and Rock Creek Trail to the left. Head left (northeast), now technically on Rock Creek Trail, although some maps don't show it as such, and continue climbing. Soon you'll reach the Glacier Peak Wilderness boundary noted by a signed tree to the trail's left.

The grind continues, and 0.3 mile after the junction (3.7 miles from the

Hikers enjoy a sunny fall hike through a thicket of glittering larches.

trailhead), the path reaches the ridgeline where a couple of unsigned trails veer off. Immediately to the right is a spur up to where an old lookout used to stand until it was destroyed in the 1960s. Straight ahead and going down the other side of the ridge is Rock Creek Trail, which you've been following up to this point (also called Carne High Traverse or Leroy Creek High Route on some maps). Our trail, the spur to the summit of Carne, goes left (north) and continues up the spine of the mountain for another 0.3 mile until it reaches the glorious rocky top, with views that will make you purr. Enjoy every drop of this breathtaking landscape before heading back the way you came.

19. LITTLE GIANT PASS

Distance: 10 miles
Elevation Gain: 4340 feet
High Point: 6420 feet
Difficulty: Hard
GPS: N 48°01.550', W 120°49.716'
Maps: Green Trails Maps No. 113: Holden

Managing Agency: Okanogan-Wenatchee National Forest, Wenatchee River Ranger District
Passes: None
Dog-Friendly: No, not permitted
Kid-Friendly: No
Amenities: None

Notes: This hike requires a wet wade across the Chiwawa River, which can be high and hazardous at times. Read current reports and/or contact the ranger station before you go. The road is rough, but passenger cars can make it by going slowly. High-clearance vehicle recommended.

Getting There: From the junction of US Highway 2 and State Route 207, also known as Coles Corner, follow SR 207 northeast toward Lake Wenatchee. In 4.3 miles from US 2, bear right (north) on Chiwawa Loop Road. At 4.8 miles, bear right (northeast) to stay on Chiwawa Loop Road. At 5.6 miles, turn left (north) on Chiwawa River Road, signed for Chiwawa Valley. In a short distance this road turns into Forest Road 62, also called Forest Road 6200 on some maps. Stay on FR 62, avoiding all side roads including signed camps and trailheads, until the pavement ends 16.7 miles from US 2. Continue on unpaved FR 62 roughly 24.9 miles, passing several campgrounds, some with pit toilets, before arriving at the well-signed trailhead to the road's left. There is parking for about five or six cars; if it's full, park along the road if there is room and it's safe to do so.

This trail can be broken down into three sections: the forest climb, the fire zone/rocky area, and the subalpine meadows near the top. While the whole trail is pretty, the colorful meadows at the top are so scenic, you might feel oddly euphoric when you arrive. Getting to those meadows, however, is really tough, and this hike will kick most people's heinies, including those who are in great shape and are used to hard challenges. For one, it starts off with a shoes-soaking, swift-river crossing then proceeds with a climb so steep in places that you'll be dreading the knee-creaking return. Groan, grunt, toot, cry, and do whatever else is needed to make it to this ridgeline in fall. The tapestry of fall colors blankets the hillsides in all visible spots in the meadows, while the distant snow-laden peaks of Fortress, Chiwawa, and Phelps stand guard to the north. What's more, on the other side of Little Giant Pass lies a secret hidden valley that very few have ever seen. The deep valley is dwarfed by even more snowy, jagged peaks, including the elusive Glacier Peak, one of Washington's more secretive volcanoes. Your soul will feel rested despite your body feeling sore. Don't miss it!

 Foliage: Cascade huckleberry, dwarf bilberry, Sitka mountain ash, subalpine larch

You might want to just wear your water shoes upon leaving your vehicle and tie your hiking shoes to your pack, since the first challenge, a crossing of the Chiwawa River, comes up almost immediately.

The wading can be challenging, as the water level fluctuates from mid-calf in the late summer to knee-high or mid-quad at times in the fall. If there happens to be a

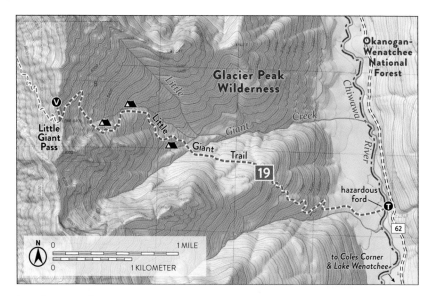

lot of snow melt, or recent rains, it can even be higher, although in fall, it's almost always crossable. As with all water crossings, unbuckle your pack and make sure each foot is well planted before taking the next step. If you have trekking poles, ensure you have three points of contact between poles and feet before progressing. Whatever you do, you'll be aching to get across quickly, since that water is frigid and you will be wincing from the numb ache on your extremities by the time you get to the other side. Doesn't this hike sound fun? Trust me, it's gorgeous and worth this effort.

Once across . . . deep breath. You are now in Glacier Peak Wilderness. Find a log to regroup, dry off, and change shoes, using extra care to make sure you don't have sand between your toes that might cause blisters, like an oyster makes a pearl.

Once you've done that, face the next obstacle: finding the trail. The shoreline gets eroded each year, and folks often do laps trying to find the path. It's almost exactly straight ahead, if not slightly to the right, of where you crossed. Sometimes there are rock cairns to follow, but if not, keep looking and I promise you'll find it—the trail itself is obvious once you get up from the shoreline. Years ago, this flat area was known as Maple Creek Campground, although now all evidence of such a place is gone.

The climb makes its way through the evergreen forest, with devilsclub, Cascade huckleberry, and Nootka rose populating the understory. Just after 2 miles of climbing, the hillside gets much steeper, making you shake your head at who on earth built this squirrely track. The answer? Sheepherders looking for the fastest way to take their livestock uphill to grazing lands. Huff and puff up the slope, then find reprieve after cresting a small ridge.

At almost 3 miles, a colorful hillside to the trail's right gives you a sneak peek of what's ahead. Shortly after that—and rather unexpectedly—the trail descends to a rock-hop crossing of Little Giant Creek, where a couple of small campsites await tents, or in our case, sit pads for weary day hikers.

After leaving the creek, the type 2 fun really begins (and by "type 2 fun," I mean a lung and quad workout like no other). You got this . . . simply place one foot at a time. The trail climbs steeply through an old fire zone laden with overgrown brush, which you might have to whack with your poles. Thankfully the brilliant colors of huckleberry and ash take your mind off your breathing for a minute or two. Red-tailed hawks occasionally squawk in the sky while chipmunks scamper around the trail's edges.

At 3.7 miles, the trail climbs a steep, rocky outcropping through rock cairns until it delivers you to a small ravine where Cascade and dwarf huckleberries grow in droves. If your timing is good, there will still be plenty of berries to eat for a little sugar boost to get you to the top. In roughly 0.5 mile from the rocky outcropping (about 4.2 miles overall), a small camp to the trail's right offers a place to rest and conveniently puts you close to water if you need to filter a little for the bottles.

The carpets of color are breathtaking as you continue, with burgundy huckleberry bushes, yellowed grasses, orange ash, and deep-green conifers. This is what you've worked so hard for, and it only gets better! To the north, rugged snowy peaks show off and beg for attention, while to the north and west, Carne Mountain (Hike 18), Old Gib, Saska, and others stand proudly. If you feel lightheaded, it could be from the views and not just the grind!

Erupting in color, Little Giant Pass is one of the hardest but most rewarding of fall hikes.

At 4.9 miles from the trailhead, reach the ridgeline and prepare to drop your jaw. In front of you is the huge, bold Clark Mountain, and slightly hidden to its right is Glacier Peak, the fourth-tallest peak in Washington. Under their mighty towers is the deep, verdant Napeequa River valley, a feast for the eyes and a rest for the soul. This is a place for wildlife to graze and frolic and for native plants and aquatic life to thrive, a truly wild place to witness. The word *Napeequa* is a Salishan word meaning "white water," and this place probably got its name because the water that flows here heavily in the spring is almost all white, thanks to the glacial silt. The trail continues into the valley, but our goal is almost accomplished.

Better views of the valley and the peaks can be seen by following a boot-beaten path to the right (north) toward Little Giant for under 0.1 mile, where a ledge perch has enough room for a couple of people to sit and enjoy. Pick your footing carefully, as it's narrow and precarious in places. A couple of subalpine larch trees sprinkle Little Giant's shoulders, adding to the glory. Once you've let this place seep into your pores, wander back the way you came with a renewed soul.

20. WEST CADY RIDGE

Distance: 7.6 miles
Elevation Gain: 2250 feet
High Point: 4845 feet
Difficulty: Moderate
GPS: N 47°55.586', W 121°16.639'
Maps: Green Trails Maps No. 143: Monte Cristo and No. 144: Benchmark Mountain

Managing Agency: Mount Baker–Snoqualmie National Forest, Skykomish Ranger District
Passes: Northwest Forest Pass or Interagency Pass
Dog-Friendly: Yes, on leash
Kid-Friendly: No
Amenities: Pit toilet

Notes: The road to the trailhead is rough, though passenger cars can make by going slowly. High-clearance vehicle highly recommended.

Getting There: From Everett, follow US Highway 2 east for 49 miles. At 1 mile past Skykomish, turn left (northeast) onto Beckler Road (Forest Road 65). At 6.9 miles after leaving US 2, the pavement ends. In 0.1 mile, go straight (north) to stay on FR 65, which crosses a one-lane bridge. At 12.8 miles from US 2, reach a five-way intersection. Take the second left (west), signed for FR 63. After another 2.4 miles (15.2 miles from US 2), cross a bridge over the North Fork Skykomish River, then immediately take the next right, signed for FR 63 with an arrow. Proceed for 2 miles on FR 63, then stay right (east) at a Y signed FR 6300 with an arrow. Find the trailhead at the road's end in 2.5 miles (19.7 miles from US 2). This trailhead also serves the Quartz Creek and North Fork Skykomish Trails. The West Cady Ridge Trail is located to the parking area's right (east).

Sometimes you need a hike without crowds, where solitude can be found in the quiet forest, burgundy meadows, and scenic mountain views. If you really need to get away from it all, this is one of those tranquil hikes, especially on a weekday. The forest is pretty, welcoming, and deep, but the ridge at the top is the official prize for your efforts, with outstanding scarlet-colored huckleberry meadows and sweeping views of Glacier Peak and neighboring mountains.

 Foliage: Cascade huckleberry, dwarf bilberry, Sitka mountain ash

Western red cedars, Douglas-firs, and hemlocks stand proudly as you duck into the forest and begin your hike in this typical Northwest forest. In just 0.3 mile, a sturdy wooden bridge guides you over the North Fork Skykomish River, where, below you, the water cascades into a rocky slot canyon and purrs with a relaxing white noise. Enter the Wild Sky Wilderness, which is announced via a tree sign, just after crossing the bridge.

West Cady Ridge is abundant in vistas and bountiful in berries.

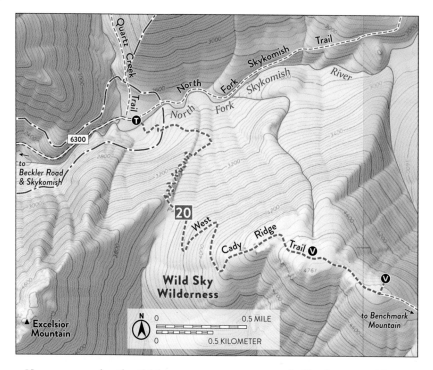

Up you go under the thick evergreen canopy, past half a dozen trickles and creeklets as you climb higher and higher. This is stunning in its own right, but in just shy of 3 miles, the forest passes the baton to the lush meadows you came to see.

Turn around and glance to the northwest where the towering Monte Cristo, Kyes, and Columbia Peaks dominate the skyline with their glaciers and snowfields. At your feet, ruby huckleberries decorate the trail's edges, while persimmon-colored Sitka mountain ash with its bright-red berries gives height and dimension to the landscape. Frame pleasing fall photos of the trail edged with fall colors and the distant peaks looming in the background.

At 3.8 miles, the trail flattens out some and comes to the top of a small rise. To the left (north) is a spur trail to a viewpoint of Glacier Peak, Portal Peak, June Mountain, and others—a great goal for the day. Nibble the remaining huckleberries now, or pick some for a tasty snack on the way home after you retrace your steps.

EXTENDING YOUR TRIP

If you have more energy and time, you could extend your hike by wandering farther up the ridge to Benchmark Mountain, adding 6.8 miles roundtrip and 1460 feet of elevation gain. Views just keep getting better and better the higher you go!

21. EVERGREEN MOUNTAIN LOOKOUT

Distance: 3 miles
Elevation Gain: 1380 feet
High Point: 5587 feet
Difficulty: Moderate
GPS: N 47°49.582', W 121°16.618'
Maps: Green Trails Map No. 143: Monte Cristo

Managing Agency: Mount Baker–Snoqualmie National Forest, Skykomish Ranger District
Passes: Northwest Forest Pass or Interagency Pass
Dog-Friendly: Yes, on leash
Kid-Friendly: Yes
Amenities: Primitive backcountry toilet along trail

Notes: The road getting to the trailhead is extremely rough and long—expect to drive for at least 75 minutes after leaving US Highway 2. High-clearance vehicles are recommended. This road has washed out previously, so double-check its accessibility before you go. Parking is limited; be prepared wih a plan B if you get there and it's full.
Getting There: From Everett, follow US 2 east for 49 miles. At 1 mile past Skykomish, turn left (northeast) onto Beckler Road (Forest Road 65). At 6.9 miles after leaving US Highway 2, the pavement ends. In 0.1 mile farther, go straight (north) to stay on FR 65, which crosses a one-lane bridge. At 12.8 miles from US 2, reach a five-way intersection. Turn right (east) onto the road marked for 6550 Evergreen Lookout. In 1 more mile, go left (southeast) at an unsigned Y onto FR 6554. In 0.1 mile, the road is signed FR 6554, confirming you are on the right track. At 1.9 miles from the Y (15.7 miles from US 2), go through an opened gate and cross over Evergreen Creek on a single-lane bridge. Follow the road to its dead end at the trailhead and a turnaround area in another 7 miles (22.7 miles from US 2). There is parking for five to seven vehicles.

> Driving out to this hike, you might think, *Where in the world is this author taking me?* But those who stay the course and put in the effort, especially on a sunny day, will be more than rewarded with delightful views of Glacier Peak, hillsides of crimson huckleberry bushes, and a historical lookout tower located front and center in Wild Sky Wilderness.

 Foliage: Cascade huckleberry, dwarf bilberry, Sitka mountain ash

The relatively new trailhead sign for Evergreen Lookout Trail 1056, complete with information on the lookout itself, welcomes hikers. To its left (north) is the trail itself. The steep grade makes you stop to catch your breath, or slow your pace, as you climb the slope. Thanks to the Evergreen Mountain Burn set by loggers in

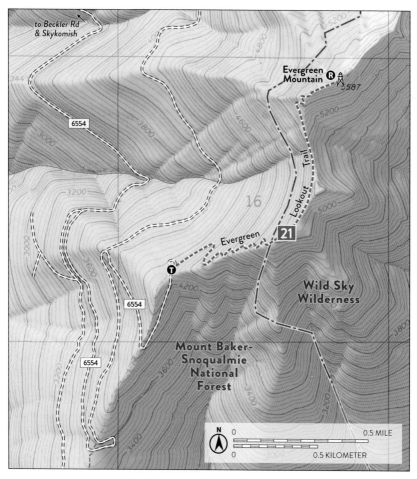

to Beckler Rd
& Skykomish

Evergreen
Mountain Ⓡ 🗼
5587

6554

16

Lookout Trail

Evergreen 21

Wild Sky
Wilderness

6554

Mount Baker-
Snoqualmie
National
Forest

6554

N   0   0.5 MILE
    0   0.5 KILOMETER

1967, you have plenty of wide-open views of the shoulders of Evergreen Mountain, to both the northeast and the southeast. Keep your eyes open for dots of black on these slopes—bears occasionally hit this area to nibble on the last of the berries before winter.

The lookout is not in view yet, but the trail is short, which leads to curiosity about where the little structure is located. You'll get there very soon!

At 0.4 mile, zigzag up a series of meadowy switchbacks before entering a forest containing the boundary of Wild Sky Wilderness.

The climbing continues, letting up with only a few gentle steps here and there. Huff and puff . . . you got this . . . you are almost there. The views get even more

A short, steep hike leads to the weathered wood of the Evergreen Mountain Lookout.

grand the higher you go, especially as you pop out of the trees and gain the barren slopes. Hey, there's the tower, on the hill up there! Huckleberries, primarily of the Cascade mountain variety, grow hardily on the slopes as you continue higher and higher, grunting on the last grueling bit, until, at 1.5 miles, you find yourself standing at the classic L-4-style, fourteen-by-fourteen-foot lookout tower.

Glacier Peak, to the north, stands proudly along with all of its buddies—Portal Peak, Silica Mountain, Johnson Mountain, Benchmark Mountain, and so many others. Spin in circles to see even more, including Mount Fernow, Mount Daniel, Terrace Mountain, Sunrise Mountain, and the lot. This view is epic. What's more, you'll find a primitive backcountry toilet by continuing along the trail beyond the tower and taking a sharp turn to the left (west) down a short spur trail.

The tower itself is pretty cool too! Originally built in 1935, this historic cabin stood strong, staffed by fire personnel until the 1980s. Like so many of Washington's lookout towers, it was used as an Aircraft Warning Service Station during World War II. In 1990, it underwent a restoration and was nominated for the National Register of Historic Places. Today, it is part of the lookout-and-cabin-rental program, with active rental opportunities from August to October, conditions permitting. For rental information check www.recreation.gov or contact the Skykomish Ranger District. You might want to stay here forever and bask in this view, but when you are done, it's thankfully a short walk back, all downhill, the same way you came.

22. LAKE VALHALLA

Distance: 6.4 miles
Elevation Gain: 1450 feet
High Point: 5100 feet
Difficulty: Moderate
GPS: N 47°48.139', W 121°04.634'
Maps: Green Trails Maps No. 144:
Benchmark Mountain

Managing Agency: Mount Baker–
Snoqualmie National Forest, Skykomish
Ranger District
Passes: Northwest Forest Pass or
Interagency Pass
Dog-Friendly: Yes, on leash
Kid-Friendly: Yes, experience dependent
Amenities: Primitive backcountry toilet
along trail

Notes: There are two trails to Lake Valhalla. The trailhead for the longer approach is located across from Stevens Pass Ski Area, while the shorter option, coming from the Smithbrook Trailhead, is the one described here.

Getting There: From Stevens Pass Ski Area, head east on US Highway 2 for 4 miles. Shortly after the divided highway begins, turn left (northwest), crossing the westbound lanes, onto Forest Road 6700 (also referred to as Smithbrook or Rainy Creek Road). Immediately cross over a small bridge with a sign noting the Smithbrook Trailhead. Continue for almost 3 miles to the parking lot on the left.

Thanks to its proximity to both the western and eastern sides of the Cascade Crest, this hike has a wide variety of huckleberries as well as Sitka mountain ash, vine maple, and at least two varieties of spirea. To the layperson, that means you'll see plenty of fall colors both in the open areas along the forested trail and at the lake. But be forewarned—the lake is stunning, and you might be tempted to stay all day! Watch the clock so you don't run out of daylight, or be sure to bring a good headlamp.

 Foliage: Blue wildrye, Cascade huckleberry, fool's huckleberry, narrow-leaved cotton-grass, oval-leaved huckleberry, rosy spirea, sedge, shinyleaf spirea, Sitka mountain ash, vine maple

The Smithbrook Trail fools you at first by keeping you rather level as it wanders past the babbling Smithbrook Creek. But soon it starts climbing and, at 0.4 mile, reaches the Henry M. Jackson Wilderness. Switchbacks guide you through fir, spruce, hemlock, and the occasional Alaska cedar before leveling out near a large boulder field to the trail's right. The climbing resumes, slightly less steeply now, and at 1.2 miles the trail reaches a junction with the Pacific Crest Trail (PCT) at what's known as Union Gap. Turn left (southwest) and continue your hike.

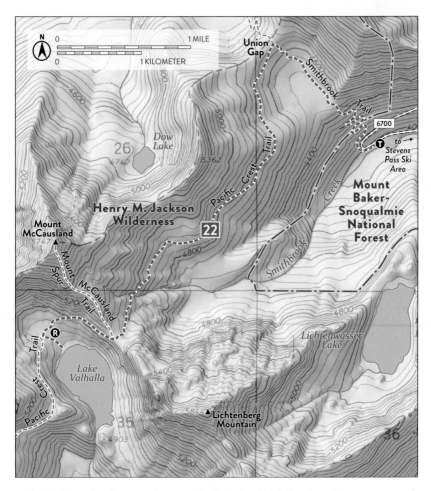

Huckleberry bushes growing at waist height offer fall coloration as you march onward and enjoy their burgundy leaves. Sitka mountain ash in orange, yellow, and red dot the pathway's edges, adding to autumn's party. Thankfully, the trail grade is rather gentle, and you can enjoy the colors and views of the Smithbrook Creek basin and distant peaks without too much fancy footwork.

At 2.7 miles, the trail crests a small pass, where a well-used but unsigned game trail to the right leads to Mount McCausland. Taking this detour is a steep, huffy-puffy, 1-mile roundtrip, brushy adventure, so unless daylight and gumption are on your side, you might want to save this one for another time. Instead, continue onward with glimpses of Lake Valhalla starting to appear to the trail's left.

Autumn's colors flourish on the lapping shores of Lake Valhalla.

At 3.1 miles, look for a sign pointing down toward a day-use area and a back-country primitive toilet spur trail. (It's easy to miss! If you get to a large meadow with dribbling creeks, you've gone too far.) Turn left (southeast) and follow the well-worn boot path to the lake's northwestern shoreline. From this vista, the pointy stone summit of the proud Lichtenberg Mountain is prominent to the east with two types of huckleberries, Cascade mountain and oval-leaved, carpeting its slopes. On bright days, this area has good lighting at midday, making for dreamy photos with enough time to grab a snack and head back to your car before dark. Stay alert: camp robbers, a.k.a. Canada jays (or gray jays), have learned some bad manners and will swipe your sandwich right out of your hand if you aren't paying attention. Resist their sweet faces and subtle noises—they need to learn to forage, especially since winter is coming!

When you've enjoyed this magical landscape, head back the way you came.

23. HOPE AND MIG LAKES

Distance: 5 miles
Elevation Gain: 1520 feet
High Point: 4645 feet
Difficulty: Moderate
GPS: N 47°42.768', W 121°06.445'
Maps: Green Trails Maps No. 176:
Stevens Pass

Managing Agency: Mount Baker–
Snoqualmie National Forest, Skykomish
Ranger District
Passes: Northwest Forest Pass or
Interagency Pass
Dog-Friendly: Yes, on leash
Kid-Friendly: Yes
Amenities: Primitive backcountry toilet
along trail

Notes: This trail can only be approached from the eastbound lanes of US Highway 2. If you are coming from the east, turn around in Skykomish and follow the directions below. Use caution when parking on the narrow spur road, as it can be tight and crowded. If parking near the trailhead is full, head down to Forest Road 6095 and park on its shoulders.

The Hope and Mig Lakes area boasts copious amounts of vibrant shrubbery: a vision in fall.

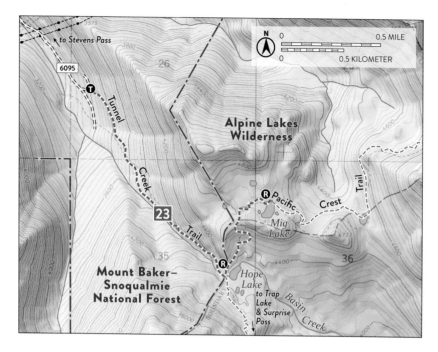

Getting There: From the town of Skykomish, follow US 2 east for 12 miles. On a hairpin turn, turn right (east) onto the easy-to-miss, unpaved FR6095. Use extreme caution turning off the highway. Continue for 1.2 miles and bear left onto a dead-end spur road. Locate the well-signed trailhead to the road's right.

> If you are in search of good huckleberry colors without too much distance, this is a good selection. Two shallow lakes set along the Pacific Crest Trail provide a great place to see fall colors, as the quantities of bushes near the shorelines and in the neighboring meadows are plentiful. What's more, the mosquitoes are long gone! Win-win.

 Foliage: Cascade huckleberry, fool's huckleberry, oval-leaved huckleberry, rosy spirea, Sitka mountain ash, vine maple

The trail kicks off with a gradual climb up Tunnel Creek Trail, which in 0.3 mile arrives at a viewpoint of a neighboring ravine to the trail's right. It's pretty, but fall isn't showing up too much yet, so keep 'er rollin'. Several creeklets drip down from the hill above the trail and necessitate rock hops but, thankfully, not wet feet. Mud in places gets slippery after rain, so use caution as you continue your uphill trudge.

Just after 1 mile the trail crosses a scree field where a few vine maples burst into gorgeous colors of yellow, coral, and red. Continue onward, steeply at times, until you reach the Alpine Lakes Wilderness, noted by a tree sign 1.4 miles from where you started. Immediately after, reach a junction with the north- and southbound Pacific Crest Trail (PCT). A primitive toilet can be found via a short trail to the left (north) while straight in front of you is tranquil Hope Lake.

Cascade huckleberries and Sitka mountain ash in reds, oranges, and yellows populate the shoreline while evergreens look on from behind. A primitive trail leads to campsites on the lake's eastern shoreline, where vibrant-red patches of bushes make for a fine reflection photo on a calm day.

Head north along the PCT, wandering through more autumn-sprinkled meadows with little puncheon bridges and a somewhat narrow trail. After 0.8 mile on the PCT (approximately 2.2 miles from the starting point, depending on how many extra steps you put in at the Hope Lake stop), arrive at the western shore of Mig Lake, where crimson huckleberry bushes, orange Sitka mountain ash, and yellow-tinged fool's huckleberry bushes crowd social trails that eventually lead to a large camping area at the north end. A primitive backcountry toilet is located here if nature calls.

When you are done, head back the way you came.

EXTENDING YOUR TRIP

When you get back to the Tunnel Creek Trail junction (the way you came), continue south on the PCT, climbing for a visit to the breathtaking Trap Lake and Surprise Pass. Just be sure you have enough daylight to retrace your steps, since this hike will add an extra 8 miles roundtrip with roughly an extra 1850 feet of elevation gain.

24. COLCHUCK LAKE

Distance: 8.5 miles
Elevation Gain: 2280 feet
High Point: 5580 feet
Difficulty: Hard
GPS: N 47°31.662', W 120°49.259'
Maps: Green Trails Maps No. 209S: The Enchantments

Managing Agency: Okanogan-Wenatchee National Forest, Wenatchee River Ranger District
Passes: Northwest Forest Pass or Interagency Pass
Dog-Friendly: No, not permitted
Kid-Friendly: No
Amenities: Pit toilet at trailhead and backcountry toilet along trail

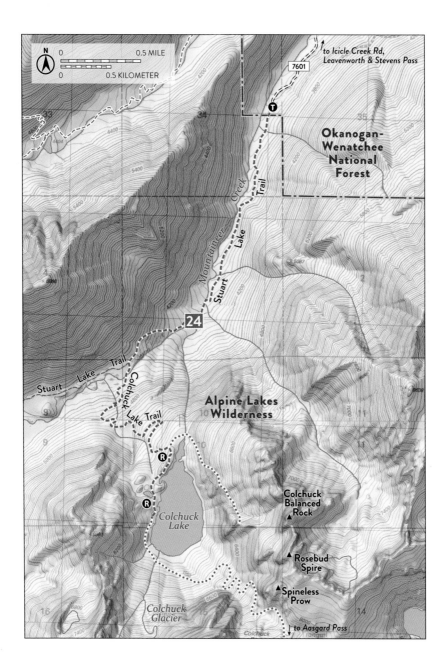

Notes: Camping firmly regulated by permit only from May 15 to October 31. Dogs/pets, horses/stock, drones, and campfires are not allowed. Due to the extreme popularity of the area and limited parking, it's best to plan your trip early on a weekday. No-parking signage has recently been installed and is strictly enforced.

Getting There: From the far western edge of Leavenworth on US Highway 2, near the Union 76 gas station, turn south onto Icicle Road (also known as Icicle Creek Road) and follow it for 8.4 miles. Turn left onto Eightmile Road (Forest Road 7601) and continue on the bumpy gravel road for 3.8 miles to the parking area and trailhead.

To state the obvious, Colchuck Lake, set within the Alpine Lakes Wilderness, will steal your heart and maybe your soul. You'll work your hindquarters off in an effort to reach it, but boy oh boy, when you do, you are in for an autumn treat! The dramatic alpine cirque is punctuated by the jade-colored lake, the gilded subalpine larch trees, and often, fresh snow on the highest peaks. You'll feel like you've been transported directly into a Hollywood movie where a green screen displays scenery that is so dreamlike, it couldn't possibly be real. Oh, but it is. There's a reason this hike is so popular, and you're about to find out what it is.

 Foliage: Cascade huckleberry, Cascade mountain ash, fireweed, grouse whortleberry, subalpine larch

The trail begins on Stuart Lake Trail 1599, slightly confusing for those going to Colchuck, but rest assured it goes there as well as Lake Stuart. Off you go on a gentle trail grade through firs and pines with the babbling Mountaineer Creek providing your soundtrack.

After 1.7 miles, cross over the picturesque Mountaineer Creek, where tumbling water makes for an eye-catching sight as it powerfully shapes the stones all around its edges. Have a stern meeting with your quads at this point because they are about to get a good workout.

Ascend a series of switchbacks through large boulders, and give a nod to the creative trail building that gets you around them. Just when your heart starts pumping, views of the deep valley below you as well as the surrounding peaks above you take your mind off the grind. Here and there, sparse fall foliage, such as Cascade huckleberry and Cascade mountain ash, does its best to remind you of the colorful season.

At 2.5 miles arrive at a trail junction where straight ahead (east), or slightly to the right depending on where you stand, is the continuation of Stuart Lake Trail, the one we've been following. Our trail, now Colchuck Lake Trail 1599A, goes left (south) and continues doing the boulder dance, throwing in some large roots, ledges, and views for good measure.

The steepness amplifies on the final push, then just as you are ready for a break, you reach the top of the climb, roughly 3.8 miles from where you started, and descend to the lake.

You are standing in unquestionably one of the most scenic locations in all of the Cascade Mountains. In front of you are the sharp teeth of Dragontail Peak and other grand Enchantments peaks with a foreground of teal-green lake. Ahead of you, between the two most prominent peaks, is a summit known as Aasgard Pass, a steep, grueling, and often hazardous climb that leads to the Upper Enchantments.

Evergreens populate the mountain's shoulders, sprinkled with a smattering of golden subalpine larches. Head right to a rocky shoreline perch, spread out a picnic, and take it all in. A primitive backcountry toilet is located just a few steps beyond the rocky shoreline on a small, signed trail.

The word *Colchuck* is a Chinook Jargon, or pidgin trading language, word for "cold water." For fun, stick your hand in it. I dare you. Even in summer, it makes me shiver.

Photography can be tricky due to the low path of the sun in autumn and the large peaks in the shadows. For some of the best photo opportunities, follow a boot path around to the right (west) side of the lake until you reach a small tarn, separate from the lake. Above that, on a sloping hillside, glorious larch trees abound. An unnamed rocky summit proudly sticks its nose into the air in the background, giving this shot a rugged, alpine feeling. Around noon in early to mid-October, if you stand on the northeastern side of the tarn, the sun lights up the twinkling golden needles in this spot, and the calm jade water catches their reflection. Add

An eye-popping blast of fall is reflected in the still, emerald waters near Colchuck Lake.

snow to the equation and you've set yourself up for a lot of great photos and an autumn hike you won't soon forget!

When you are finished exploring the lake's shore, carefully retrace the route to your starting point, taking your time and going easy on your knees.

25. CLARA AND MARION LAKES

Distance: 3.2 miles
Elevation Gain: 990 feet
High Point: 5490 feet
Difficulty: Easy-moderate
GPS: N 47°17.651', W 120°23.925'
Maps: Green Trails Maps No. 211S: Wenatchee/Mission Ridge

Managing Agency: Okanogan-Wenatchee National Forest, Wenatchee River Ranger District
Passes: None
Dog-Friendly: Yes, on leash
Kid-Friendly: Yes
Amenities: None

Notes: If you end up on this hike late in the season, it makes an enjoyable beginner snowshoe outing. In most years, because of drier conditions, the larch trees tend to turn a bit later than others elsewhere. Check trip reports or shoot for later in the season if you want to ensure the golden coloration. If you have a GPS on your smartphone and you are busy driving, just set the guidance for Mission Ridge Ski Area.

Getting There: From Wenatchee, follow signs leading to Mission Ridge Ski Area by turning south onto State Route 285 and following it for 4.5 miles until its junction with the

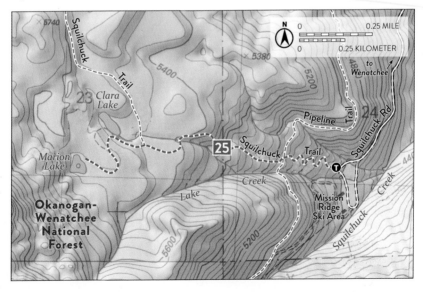

Tall western larch trees grow hardily along the rocky shoreline of the shallow Clara Lake.

Columbia River Bridge and East Wenatchee. Don't cross the bridge, but rather continue south on Mission Street. In 0.9 mile, Mission Street becomes Squilchuck Road. Follow Squilchuck to its end, 11 miles farther, and find a large parking area to the road's left, just before the entrance to Mission Ridge Ski Area. The trailhead is across the road.

If you are looking for an easier hike, where you don't have to spend the whole day hiking to see larch trees, this might just be the right one for you. While it doesn't have sweeping mountain views, it does have those appealing golden trees that grace the shoreline of two shallow lakes. It's a good one for folks who might want to combine a hiking trip with other activities, like window shopping in Leavenworth or taking a scenic drive up Tumwater Canyon. Or you could spend the whole day at the lakes with a picnic and a hammock—your call!

 Foliage: Blue elderberry, fireweed, oceanspray, Scouler's willow, western larch, Woods' rose

From the trailhead, the climbing feels challenging, and in places it certainly is, but for the most part, it's a gradual ascent. Blowdowns throughout the years, thankfully cleared, line the trail's edges. Usually in fall, the Mission Ridge staff is getting the resort ready for the snowfall, and you can hear a variety of manmade noises until you climb deeper into the forest and leave it behind.

At 0.4 mile, cross over the signed Pipeline Trail and continue straight ahead (west). The trail you are following is called the Squilchuck Trail, though the signs pointing that direction only mention the lakes. The trail splits in several spots where hikers have created social trails, so pick your path—they all lead back to the main trail.

Cross a tributary of Lake Creek at 0.9 mile and breathe a little easier with a gentler grade. Larches mixed in with spruces, pines, and firs lightly populate the landscape while you continue making your way west toward the lakes.

At 1.2 miles, arrive at a Y junction, sometimes signed, sometimes not. Go left (west) here. The right branch is a continuation of Squilchuck Trail, while the other heads toward our destination.

A short 0.1 mile farther, find yourself at the shoreline of the larger and more scenic of the two lakes, Clara. The teardrop-shaped lake has a pleasant shoreline trail with spots to sit, nibble a snack, and enjoy the scenery. Along its shoreline, blue elderberry, Woods' rose, and fireweed offer some color in the foreground while larch trees on the lake's edges stand proud with golden needles. Pikas, rock-dwelling members of the rabbit family, sound an alarming "eeep" as they guard the scree piles to the lake's northern and western sides.

To get to Marion Lake, continue following the main trail left around the bulb of Clara's teardrop and to the southwest over a rocky knoll. Don't get pulled to the left where a boot path 0.2 mile from Clara Lake leads southward away from our destination. Instead, continue a westbound trajectory on a well-worn pathway until you reach the shores of the very shallow, and sometimes hardly there, Marion Lake. Even if the lake is only a puddle, the larches around it are beautiful and you came this far, so why not check it out? Then retrace your steps back to the trailhead.

Opposite: A creeklet trickles through Headlight basin as Mount Stuart supervises (Hike 26).

NORTH BEND, SNOQUALMIE PASS, AND TEANAWAY

Along the I-90 corridor and not far from the towns of North Bend and Cle Elum are a handful of spectacular fall hikes waiting for your admiration. Some of them are well-loved and, therefore, crowded during autumn's finest displays. Put on your crown of patience and know that soon this area will sleep under a blanket of quiet snow. Until then, mentally embrace the folks who, like us, are just trying to get a little fresh air in their lungs and vistas in their eyes.

26. LAKE INGALLS

Distance: 9 miles
Elevation Gain: 2580 feet
High Point: 6500 feet
Difficulty: Hard
GPS: N 47°25.105', W 120°56.265'
Maps: Green Trails Maps No. 209: Mount Stuart

Managing Agency: Okanogan-Wenatchee National Forest, Cle Elum Ranger District
Passes: Northwest Forest Pass or Interagency Pass
Dog-Friendly: No, not permitted
Kid-Friendly: No
Amenities: Pit toilet at trailhead

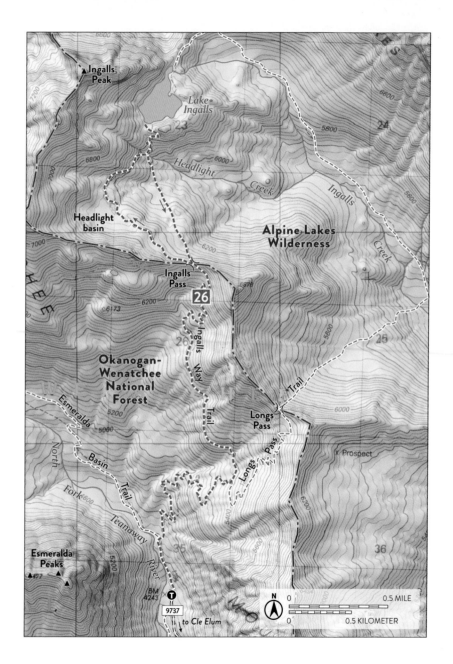

Ingalls
Peak

Lake
Ingalls

23

24

Headlight
Creek

Ingalls

Headlight
basin

6200

Alpine Lakes
Wilderness

Creek

Ingalls
Pass

26

26

Ingalls Way

6173

6200

5978

5600

25

Okanogan-
Wenatchee
National
Forest

Trail

Trail

6000

Esmeralda

Longs
Pass

5200

Longs Pass

North

Basin

Prospect

Fork

Trail

6200

36

Teanaway

Esmeralda
Peaks

5200

River

BM
4243

T

9737

to Cle Elum

N

0   0.5 MILE

0   0.5 KILOMETER

Notes: Rough road, but passenger cars can make it by going slowly. This hike is extremely popular, and parking fills up quickly. Hike on weekdays if possible, and arrive early. Respect the "Parking This Side Only" signs if the parking lot is full and you are forced to park on the road. Mountain goats live in the area and can be aggressive—give them space. Minor rock scrambling is required to reach Lake Ingalls, and navigation can be challenging. Shoe traction highly recommended in icy or snowy conditions, as steep hillsides may become hazardous.

Getting There: From I-90 near Cle Elum, take exit 85 and head northeast. After a short distance, bear right (southeast) onto State Route 10, which yields onto SR 970. Follow SR 970 for almost 7 miles, then turn left (north) on Teanaway Road. Drive 13 miles on this paved road, watching for free-range cattle, until it ends in a gravel fork. Bear right here (northeast), signed for Beverly Campground/Esmeralda Basin Trail 1394 and Forest Road 9737. In 1.3 miles, stay left (northwest) at a signed fork for Beverly Campground. In 6.6 miles, bear right (northeast) at another fork, this time signed Trail 1394. In 1.7 miles farther, find a large parking area and trailhead at the end of the road.

> Going to Lake Ingalls in the fall is a mandatory seasonal rite of passage. It's as if Mother Nature herself blessed it by lining up spectacular views of Mount Stuart, golden groves of subalpine larch trees, trickling waterways through meadows, a twinkling azure lake, and strong, healthy mountain goats. You'll work for the rewarding views, but once you've visited, the bar for autumn hiking will be set at a whole new level.

 Foliage: Cascade huckleberry, grouse whortleberry, red elderberry, sedge, subalpine larch

The trail kicks off by following an old road-turned-trail adjacent to the bubbling and churning North Fork Teanaway River. This is Esmeralda Basin Trail, which you will follow for a short distance before turning off.

At 0.4 mile, turn right (northeast) at a trail junction signed for Ingalls Way and begin climbing a series of pleasantly graded switchbacks under pines, firs, and hemlocks. (Dogs are officially off limits on Ingalls Way Trail, so if you brought the fur baby, you'll have to change plans here, perhaps returning to the earlier junction and heading to the Esmeralda River basin instead.)

As you climb on Ingalls Way Trail, autumn shows up along the trail's edges with the burgundy leaves of Cascade huckleberry and grouse whortleberry as well as the sand-colored stalks of dormant wildflowers now gone to seed and ready to bed down for winter.

At 1.4 miles arrive at a trail junction for Longs Pass Trail. Stay left (north) here, just as our path opens up with fewer trees and gorgeous views of Esmeralda Peaks to the west and Fortune Creek Pass near Fortune Peak to the north. After the

Mountain goats carry on their mission of finding nutrients and minerals underneath a gilded forest.

Longs Pass junction, the trail traverses several exposed, sandy, and somewhat loose-soiled hillsides where you'll want to watch your footing carefully, especially in snowy or icy conditions.

The route continues steeply at times through rocky outcroppings, groves of trees, and seasonal water runoffs until you get near the top of the climb, where the first of many gorgeous, glinting subalpine larch trees greets you. At roughly 3 miles, you gain the ridgeline, officially the Alpine Lakes Wilderness boundary: stop and behold magical views of vast landscapes. Mount Stuart towers like a fortress directly in front of you while groves of subalpine larch trees interspersed with their evergreen cousins grow bountifully on what is known as Headlight basin. If you are spent, you are short on time, or the path is snowy, you might be happy calling this the end of the hike and perching yourself here to enjoy the splendor. But if not, carry on!

There are two trails, an upper and a lower, that lead to Lake Ingalls, which is not visible from this ridge. The trails make a big loop, with Lake Ingalls at the northern end, so why not take one in each direction to be sure you've seen it all? But be forewarned: both trails are somewhat tricky to find and follow, and neither is signed. The most followed, and hence worn, is the upper trail found by turning left (northwest) just after the pass instead of going straight down. Here, the upper trail bobs and weaves in and out of rocks, then traverses a flat area laden with magical stands of golden subalpine larches, meadows with heather and huckleberry, crystal-clear tarns, and dribbling creeks. You'll feel like you fell face-first into a fantastical fairy tale. Mountain goats love this area and fancy nibbling on the larch needles. They seem tame, as they are used to people, and even appear to pose at times. But the sharp pointy bits on their heads are dead giveaways that approaching them is a bad idea! Keep your distance and recognize that it's still a photographer's dream come true on so many levels. If possible, get to this area before noon for the best lighting on sunny days.

Subalpine larch trees have long lives averaging around five hundred years. Some even live for a thousand years or more—oh, what they have witnessed! Because they live so long, they are in no hurry to increase their height or width, and growth is very slow. Their deliberate sloth-like tendencies allow their roots to extend out and down, keeping them deeply anchored against high winds and heavy snows. Seeing them grow in this rocky environment makes you appreciate their tolerance for the cold, snowy, stormy climates where they've rooted. Greet these hardy ones as you pass—they're tougher than a five-dollar steak.

Continue traversing the basin before you see the upper trail connect, very unassumingly, with the lower trail; the two trails hold hands for the final stretch northbound to Lake Ingalls. Several paths over the years have taken hikers up and over boulders and rocky pockets to reach the lake, so if you are following something that looks even somewhat traveled, it's probably correct. Use extreme caution on footing in this area and look for cairns, or rock stacks, which lead the way. At this point, you'll be questioning if you are on the right trajectory since you still can't see the lake, but if you are headed north or northeast and are climbing up rocks, you are likely going the right way. A small rocky ridgeline gives way to the lake beneath you. There it is!

When you've enjoyed the lakeshore, head back the way you came, but this time follow the lower trail through the basin and back toward the trailhead for a change of scenery.

27. IRON BEAR AND TEANAWAY RIDGE

Distance: 6.5 miles
Elevation Gain: 1930 feet
High Point: 5520 feet
Difficulty: Moderate
GPS: N 47°21.349', W 120°43.053'
Maps: Green Trails Maps No. 209: Mount Stuart and No. 210: Liberty

Managing Agency: Okanogan-Wenatchee National Forest, Cle Elum Ranger District
Passes: None
Dog-Friendly: Yes, on leash
Kid-Friendly: Yes
Amenities: None

Notes: The dirt road has occasional potholes and a water crossing. This trail is multiuse and open to motorcycles, mountain bikes, and horses, although traffic is light. Thanks to the drier climate, mud is generally minimal on this trail.

There are two approaches to this hike's destination. The one described here, off US Highway 97, is shorter, requires the least amount of dirt road driving, and does not require a parking pass. The other trailhead has a pit toilet, requires a Northwest Forest Pass or an Interagency Pass, and is a slightly rougher and longer road approach.

Getting There: From I-90 near Cle Elum, take exit 85 and head northeast. In a short distance, bear right (southeast) onto State Route 10, which yields onto SR 970. Eventually SR 970 turns north and becomes US 97. Keep your eyes open for mile marker 158, and shortly after it, 18.7 miles from merging onto SR 970, turn left (north) onto Forest Road 9714, signed for Iron Bear Creek Trail 1351. Follow the dirt road, which has a few ruts and bumps, for roughly 3 miles to find several makeshift parking areas and one designated parking lot near the trailhead. A car ford of Iron Creek is necessary just prior to the trailhead, so if you are worried about your passenger car scraping the watery bottom, park just before it, rock hop, and walk a short distance up the roadway. A tree sign here points cars (or feet if you didn't drive the ford) to the signed trailhead.

To get to the alternative trailhead, follow SR 970 north from Cle Elum for roughly 7 miles. Turn left (north) on the paved Teanaway Road and follow it 12.5 miles to its end. Bear right (northeast) on FR 9737, now dirt. Continue 1.3 miles to the first right fork (northeast) onto FR 9703, signed for Trail 1351. Follow this road for 3.3 miles to the road's end, where you'll reach Miller Peak Trail 1379.

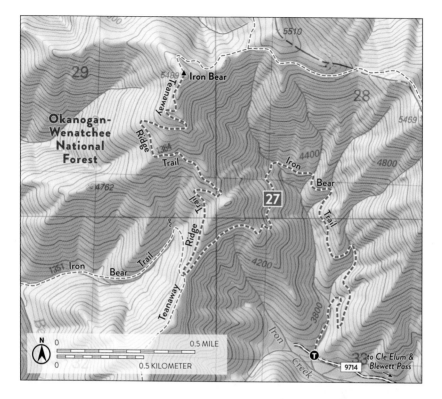

So, you want to see larches, you say? This is the hike for you. Sure, there are other places to see them, but the ease of the grade, the wide-open ridgelines, and the overall ambiance of this hike make it one of the best around, perfect for a fall day of exploring.

Foliage: Cascade mountain ash, dwarf bilberry, grouse whortleberry, oceanspray, pearly everlasting, Scouler's willow, serviceberry, western larch

Pretty much immediately, the trail comes to a rock hop with Iron Creek where, with a little bit of grace, you can get across with dry feet. From there, a moderate climbing grade wakes up the quads and heart as you bob and weave through the ponderosas, white pines, and firs. The crisp autumn air fills your lungs as you anticipate the upcoming views. Larches start showing up on neighboring hillsides, and at 1 mile, you hop your way over yet another crossing of Iron Creek.

The trail now heads west and wanders up a rock-laden slope with more views of brilliant golden larches until it reaches the top of a ridge at 1.6 miles. A signed four-way intersection points out where the Iron Bear Trail continues straight ahead, and to the right and left is Teanaway Ridge Trail. Turn right (north) here and continue climbing up, up, and away.

Now that you're on the ridgeline, Mount Adams and Mount Rainier begin to show off their summits to the southwest. Larches in nearly all directions steal the show from their evergreen cousins and give us that true taste of autumn. These glorious deciduous conifers grow here thanks to the drier climate of the eastern

A row of western larch trees display their yellowed needles under Teanaway Ridge.

side of the Cascade Crest, where they thrive in open, somewhat dry, sunny land-scapes. Photography can be amazing here late in the day if the sun is backlighting the trees. You'll likely need a tripod for the best results since you'll be losing a lot of light as the day gets on.

The trail continues climbing on a moderate grade with viewpoints so pictur-esque, your camera won't know how to stay in your pocket.

In places, concrete erosion-prevention blocks give the trail a durable surface where switchbacks or steps might get eroded with motorized use.

At just over 3 miles, the trail breaks out into rocky outcroppings with peekaboo views of Miller and Navajo Peaks as well as the tippy, snowy top of Mount Stu-art, the second-highest nonvolcanic peak in the state. Roughly 0.2 mile beyond the start of the rocky area, reach an unsigned trail junction. Directly to the left (west) is a well-traveled short spur leading to the rocky summit of Iron Bear, our destination. The top will spin your head with its swoon-worthy vista, along with plenty of places to sit and enjoy a snack. For most, this makes for a perfect day where views abound and endorphins flow like water. Turning back here, retracing your steps to your vehicle, and seeing the larches in different lighting is about as pleasant as fall gets.

EXTENDING YOUR TRIP

Those with more gumption or time to burn may want to continue hiking, follow-ing Teanaway Ridge Trail to County Line Trail. Perhaps an off-trail romp to the top of the wide-open, trail-less Jester Mountain (which will add an additional 1.3 miles roundtrip with 515 feet elevation gain) might suit your fancy too, or you could continue even farther north to the well-traveled Miller Peak. Going to Miller Peak is a giant day, putting you at an additional roundtrip distance of 9.1 miles with approximately 3300 feet of extra elevation gain. There are other hikes and even loops you can do in this area, but whatever you choose, remember that fall comes with an early call time, thanks to sundown. A headlamp is your friend!

28. RACHEL LAKE AND RAMPART RIDGE

Distance: 10.6 miles
Elevation Gain: 2200 feet
High Point: 4650
Difficulty: Hard
GPS: N 47°24.049', W 121°17.015'
Maps: Green Trails Maps No. 207: Snoqualmie Pass

Managing Agency: Okanogan-Wenatchee National Forest, Cle Elum Ranger District
Passes: Northwest Forest Pass or Interagency Pass
Dog-Friendly: Yes, on leash
Kid-Friendly: No
Amenities: Pit toilet at trailhead and backcountry toilet along the trail

Notes: The narrow road to the hike is gravel and can have potholes. Parking can be challenging on weekends, so arrive early.

Getting There: From I-90 between Snoqualmie Pass and Cle Elum, take exit 62 and turn north on Kachess Lake Road/Stampede Pass Road. Stay on this road, passing Kachess Campground. In 0.3 mile beyond the campground (5.6 miles from I-90), bear right (north) onto Forest Road 4930, signed for Rachel Lake. Follow signs for Rachel Lake until the road dead-ends in a parking loop for the trailhead, just over 9 miles from the freeway.

This hike is like a brilliant, big mosaic in the sense that there is so much to see, you'll have to choose where you focus. This route takes you not just to Rachel Lake but also to Rampart Lakes, Lila Lake, and Alta Mountain if you choose. You might want to go up to Rachel Lake on one visit and then on the next, pick another destination. Seeing them all in one day is possible for those who are strong, and physically fit, start early, and have a good headlamp for the way down. This is not an easy hike even to the first destination, Rachel Lake, as most of the elevation gain comes in one long, grueling mile; however, once you get there, it's a pleasant touch of fall. Go beyond Rachel Lake to Rampart Ridge and visit the nearby lakes, or chug up Alta Mountain and you'll be blasted in meadows of fall colors from nearly every variety of huckleberry found in the Pacific Northwest as well as Sitka and Cascade mountain ash. Add some sapphire coloration with the lake and the sky, and it's possible to get an award-winning fall photo.

 Foliage: Cascade huckleberry, Cascade mountain ash, fescue, fireweed, fool's huckleberry, oval-leaved huckleberry, red elderberry, rosy spirea, Sitka mountain ash, vine maple

From the parking area, locate the trailhead, complete with informational signage, to the north. The first bit of trail happily guides you along the bubbling Box Canyon Creek and seems moderate enough, popping in and out of evergreens, streamside trickles, and brushy meadows. But at 2.7 miles, the climbing takes off and *boy howdy*, does it ever. Roots, rocks, mud bogs, rocky slabs, and water drips cause you to scramble at times with both your hands and your feet as you shoot skyward with giant steps and complaining muscles. It's not a picnic, but hang in there! Boot paths from confused hikers go in a lot of different directions, but most arrive back at the main trail or are blocked off by logs or sticks in an effort to help you stick to the right way.

Roughly 0.5 mile before you reach the lake (3.5 miles from the trailhead), the trail mercifully levels out and rock hops under a scenic waterfall—a welcome break for your eyes and your quads. The last little push to Rachel Lake is nearly straight

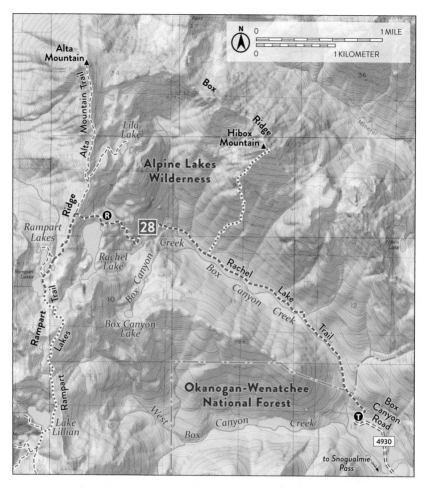

up, so you arrive with a sweat-soaked brow and a tired body; good thing this place is so amazing! A signed trail leading to a primitive backcountry toilet is located to the trail's right just before the lake. Be sure to pay attention to this flat area and make a mental note that you'll want to come back here after you visit Rachel Lake, since it's where you'll find the main trail leading to Rampart Ridge, Rampart Lakes, Lila Lake, and Alta Mountain.

Several campsites and rocky outcroppings at Rachel Lake offer places to plunk down and rest for a few minutes. Oval-leaved and Cascade huckleberries grow around the eastern shoreline, while vine maples give off color from the scree fields to the west. Fall has fallen here for sure, and if you've run out of steam you

Lila Lake and her surrounding basin are straight out of a fairy tale in fall months.

can just call it a day at Rachel Lake and give yourself accolades when you retrace your steps back to your car. You will have covered roughly 8 miles (roundtrip) of hiking and 1650 feet of elevation gain—nothing to scoff at! But, if you really want to see fall explode, push on because it gets even better.

The main trail can be hard to find once you've visited Rachel Lake, so if you are confused, head back the way you came and look to the left (north) for a narrow, well-traveled trail. For Rampart Ridge and more lakes, go northwest on the narrower main trail, circling just above the lake's northern edge before climbing up a steep prominence. Views back from where you came reveal Box Canyon Creek drainage, Hibox Mountain, and other impressive distant peaks while Rachel Lake sits quietly in the basin below you. The hillside you are climbing as well as the lakes, ridges, and mountains above you are in full autumn display, and what a vision it is! Huckleberries make hillsides of spectacular crimson, burgundy, and scarlet colors, while Sitka and Cascade mountain ash plants grow a bit taller and bring orange-colored leaves and candy-apple-red berries to the color extravaganza.

Hoary marmots love this area, and this time of year they are on a mission to fatten up for winter. As true hibernators, they spend the winter months with body temperature and body functions limited, sleeping in the same underground burrow where they live during the summer. In the fall their hoary-tinged, or gray, coats are as grand and showy as you'll ever see them.

At 0.3 mile after Rachel Lake, reach a T-shaped trail junction. Go left (south) here to reach Rampart Lakes and Rampart Ridge in about 1 mile. Thankfully, the path is gentle, compared with what you've just climbed. Boot paths go in nearly every direction around lakes, tarns, and connecting waterways which are framed nicely with the gorgeous fall shrubs and jagged mountains enticing you to take their photos. When you've explored long enough, head back to your wheels.

EXTENDING YOUR TRIP

If you go right (north) at the T, you can visit either Alta Mountain or Lila Lake or both. From this spot, a roundtrip visit to Alta Mountain takes you 2.6 miles (1300 feet of elevation gain), Lila Lake 1.6 (615 feet of elevation gain), and both 3.6 (1915 feet). You could shorten those distances and still see the beauty by not going quite to the summit of Alta or by looking over Lila Lake from the unofficial viewpoints. To see Alta Mountain, go right at the T and stay on the main trail for 0.3 mile until you reach a well-used but unsigned and tricky-to-notice trail veering to the left. The trail starts a stout climb up a meadowed ridge filled with huckleberry, Cascade mountain ash, heather, vine maple, and views of neighboring peaks so beautiful, it will make you want to stake it, claim it, and call it home. It steepens as it climbs and becomes a knife edge that is exposed and rocky, so if you feel uncomfortable, stop, take in the spectacular scenery, and turn back when your nerves have had enough. Brave souls will carry on to the summit using fancy footwork and extra moxie. Lila Lake twinkles in the basin below you with high granite peaks around her deep-blue water. If you want to visit both, head back the way you came until you reach the junction on the main trail, then go left (northwest) to Lila Lake's shores.

29. SNOW LAKE

Distance: 6.8 miles
Elevation Gain: 1650 feet
High Point: 4400 feet
Difficulty: Moderate
GPS: N 47°26.723', W 121°25.408'
Maps: Green Trails Maps No. 207: Snoqualmie

Managing Agency: Mount Baker–Snoqualmie National Forest, Snoqualmie Ranger District
Passes: Northwest Forest Pass or Interagency Pass
Dog-Friendly: Yes, on leash
Kid-Friendly: Yes, experience dependent
Amenities: Pit toilet at trailhead and backcountry toilet along trail

Notes: On the weekends, this trail is like Walmart on Black Friday, but thankfully the parking area is usually large enough to contain the masses that arrive before ten in the morning. Hike midweek to avoid the crowds, or start your hike very early. This area is prone to avalanche hazards, so if heavy snow is in the area, check the avalanche forecast before heading out or avoid this trail.

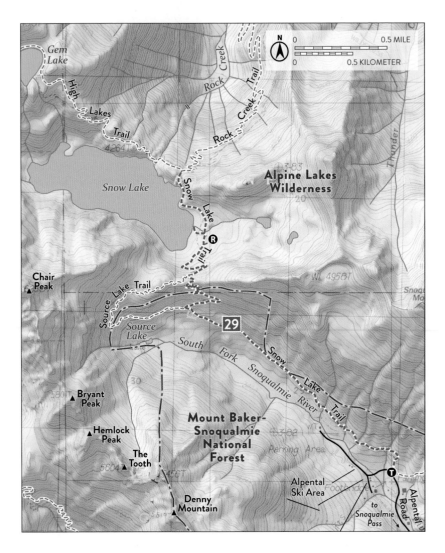

Getting There: From North Bend head eastbound on I-90 and take exit 52 near Summit at Snoqualmie. Turn left (north) and cross under the freeway. Stay right (north) at a junction with Forest Road 58 and follow the road known as Erste Strasse as it winds northbound, passing homes and condominiums until you arrive at a large parking area for Alpental Ski Area to your left (west) in 1.6 miles from I-90.

While Snow Lake is one of the busiest hikes along the I-90 corridor, it's also one of the most scenic, especially in autumn. Crimson vine maples framed against bright blue sky or gray talus fields give life to the hillsides on the way to your destination, while at the lake itself the various burgundy huckleberries mix with green heather to complement the understory. The giant cobalt lake is swathed in peaceful places to picnic, rest the soul, and enjoy the autumn sights before winter hides this grandeur under a blanket of white.

 Foliage: Cascade huckleberry, fool's huckleberry, oval-leaved huckleberry, Sitka mountain ash, vine maple

The trail to Snow Lake is really a pleasant ramble that gains gentle elevation, at least for the first 1.7 miles, save for a few well-constructed, steep trail steps right off the get-go. Views of the Alpental ski resort to the trail's left are colorful, and you can almost imagine the place ripping with skiers in a couple short months. As you make your way northwest, the trail mixes evergreen forest, talus fields, and brushy avalanche swales while also crossing a few late-season trickles.

At 1.7 miles, our trail takes a hard right (east) at a junction with the Source Lake Trail. You'll be tempted to go straight and visit Source Lake because the trail grade is gentle compared to the Snow Lake Trail, which is now in for a climb. Thankfully, the switchbacks leading through vegetated talus slopes offer inspiring views of Chair Peak to the trail's west. You haven't traveled that far from your vehicle, but it feels like you are worlds away from civilization, thanks to the rugged topography.

Up you go, now enjoying views of the orange leaves and red bulbous berries of the Sitka mountain ash and the red vine maples that grow with ease on this light-soaked hillside. Sitka mountain ash is part of the rose family, and its berries are an important food source for birds. The berries can be eaten by humans too, but they are extremely tart and usually only gathered for jams or pies. Here's a fun fact: they are actually sweeter after the first frost. As a common-sense reminder, don't attempt to eat any berries unless you have a positive identification—some things in nature aren't always on your side.

The last bit of climbing on the hillside is the steepest and most grueling. Grunt, moan, scowl—do whatever you need to do to grind up it, until you reach the flat saddle at the top of the ridgeline and catch your breath. It feels longer than the 0.7 mile it's been from the Source Lake Trail junction, thanks to the beads of sweat clinging to your eyebrows. At least it was beautiful. Speaking of beautiful . . . on to the lake!

From the saddle, the trail descends into the lake basin through more talus and scree fields. Watch your footing carefully even though the lake is so scenic: you could easily do a triple toe loop if you're too distracted. Little members of the rabbit family—pikas—squeak and carry on in the boulders. Before you know it,

Sitka mountain ash contributes a fall palette to the panoramic vistas near Snow Lake.

you are walking through scarlet huckleberry leaves mixed in with evergreen shrubs along the lake's shore. A primitive backcountry toilet and designated camping spots are found in the area via well-signed boot paths.

The best views and places to park your heinie are found on rocky outcroppings just above the lake's eastern shoreline where, if you point the camera in the right direction, you can capture the lake, Chair Peak, and a pop of autumn color thanks to the Cascade huckleberries. The afternoon makes for tough shadows, so try to grab this shot before noon. Head back the way you came before you turn into a pumpkin.

EXTENDING YOUR TRIP

If the clock and the get-up-and-go are on your side, you may want to extend your hike approximately 2.8 miles roundtrip and 1400 feet in elevation to Gem Lake. To do so, follow the Snow Lake Trail around the lake's northeastern side and continue west, passing a junction for Rock Creek Trail. The trail we are following is now called High Lakes Trail and climbs in a northwestern direction, beyond most of the crowds and into even more huckleberries and gorgeous autumn colors, until it reaches the much smaller but extremely peaceful shores of Gem Lake. Keep your eyes peeled for sooty grouse, which are masters at flapping, fluttering, and startling you as you unexpectedly walk by them in their camouflaged coats. Even farther beyond Gem Lake are Upper and Lower Wildcat Lakes, but routefinding is much more difficult, so if you decide to visit them, be sure you are armed with good maps, routefinding skills, and plenty of daylight.

30. MELAKWA LAKE

Distance: 8.5 miles
Elevation Gain: 2750 feet
High Point: 4600 feet
Difficulty: Hard
GPS: N 47°24.860', W 121°26.364'
Maps: Green Trails Maps No. 207: Snoqualmie Pass

Managing Agency: Mount Baker–Snoqualmie National Forest, Snoqualmie Ranger District
Passes: Northwest Forest Pass or Interagency Pass
Dog-Friendly: Yes, on leash
Kid-Friendly: Yes, to Denny Creek
Amenities: Pit toilet at trailhead and backcountry toilet along trail

Notes: The road to the trailhead closes seasonally; double-check with the ranger station if you are visiting late in the fall. Use extreme caution around the trail's edges near waterfall overlooks, especially in icy conditions. The bridge over Denny Creek is washed out, but most years in the fall, you can rock hop with dry shoes.

Getting There: From I-90 east near North Bend, take exit 47 and turn left (north), crossing over the freeway (those coming from westbound, go right (north) off the exit). Go right (southeast) at the T onto Forest Road 58. In another 0.2 mile, turn left (east) to remain on FR 58. Continue on FR 58, passing Denny Creek Campground, until you reach a large parking area to the road's right, roughly 2.5 miles from the T. Note: The old trailhead used to be located to the left before the new parking area was built, but the spur road leading to it is now closed. The trailhead for Franklin Falls Trail is also located near here, along with a pit toilet and ADA parking.

If FR 58 is closed from exit 47, you may still be able to get to the trailhead by taking exit 52. Turn north (going under the freeway if coming from the eastbound lanes) and proceed 0.2 mile until you reach a fork in the road with FR 58. Head west (slightly left, parallel to the interstate) on FR 58 and follow it as it winds around for just under 1 mile. The trailhead will be on your left.

Fall in the Alpine Lakes Wilderness is an enchanted time. Not only are the endemic Sitka mountain ash shrubs in full yellow, orange, and red coloration at the rugged Melakwa Lake's edges, but the vine maples light up the path with crimson colors along the way. If it's colors you enjoy but scenery you seek, this is the hike for you—a breathtaking mountain lake, a 142-foot waterfall, and rugged mountains for gawking. But it isn't easy. The trail tread requires tricky footwork over talus fields and a tough huff-and-puff as it climbs up tight switchbacks near Hemlock Pass. Just take it one foot at a time with a lot of breathing and rests, and you'll get there. When you do… you'll revel in both your accomplishment and the sights.

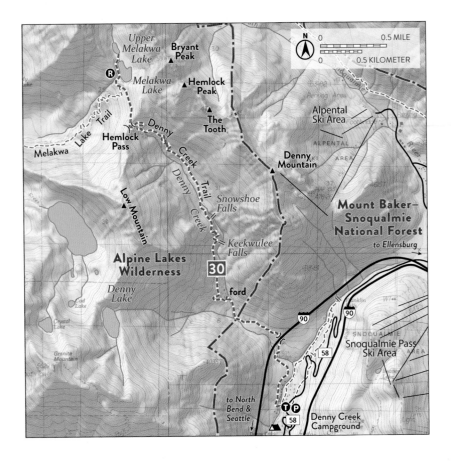

Foliage: Cascade huckleberry, devilsclub, fireweed, Menzies' spirea, oval-leaved huckleberry, pearly everlasting, service-berry, Sitka mountain ash, thimbleberry, vine maple

Follow the trail from the large parking area through the forest, across the road, and over toward the Franklin Falls Trailhead. One last pit toilet awaits if you forgot to use the one at the parking area. From here, walk around the gate at the car bridge, cross over the river, and continue up the road, passing several vacation cabins, until you reach the official trailhead for Denny Creek Trail. The pit toilet here has been locked for years but still stands tall and willing as if to mock your bladder.

From the very start the trail dives into a healthy old-growth forest, complete with large hemlocks, western sword fern, yellowing devilsclub, moss, and green for days. It would be completely idyllic were it not for the constant hum of free-way traffic. At 0.3 mile, cross a narrow but well-crafted wooden bridge spanning a forested stretch of Denny Creek, where you get your first true taste of fall with Cascade huckleberries and vine maples in crimson coloration near the creek's edges. Other plants, such as devilsclub and thimbleberry, are in the throes of their dormancy transition and offer yellow-tinged leaves. A slow shutter or motion blur of the water and foliage makes for a lovely photo.

At about 1 mile, the trail crosses far under a large freeway overpass, which can be a little unnerving when you look up and see large semi trucks. Carry on—soon you'll forget you are anywhere near civilization. At 1.3 miles, arrive at a crossing with Denny Creek where the bridge is washed out. In autumn, the water level is usually low enough that you can teeter-totter across on rocks without wet shoes. On sunny, warm days this bank is lined with people basking in the shallow pools and enjoying the mini waterslides over the smooth granite stone. If you brought the wee ones, this might be your final destination for the day. If not, keep on trudging.

After the creek crossing, the route gains elevation under a forest canopy until it breaks out onto a talus field that is steep at times as it climbs a ravine. Because of the rocky slope and winter snow slides, evergreens are small or scarce and the sunlight infiltrates the hillsides where plants like vine maple, thimbleberry, goatsbeard, slide alder, brackenfern, and salmonberry have taken over. Ecru stalks of wildflowers, such as red columbine, scarlet paintbrush, Sitka valerian, and tiger lily flop over at the end of their season. Watch your foot placement carefully as you ascend the precarious rocks, especially since now the gorgeous Keekwulee Falls is coming into view via a gorge on Denny Creek to the trail's right. The word *Keekwulee* translates from Chinook Jargon, a pidgin trading language, to "to fall down." Use care in this spot, since the viewpoints come very close to the edges of the cliff straight down to the creek. The waterfall's total height is 171 feet, with two dropping tiers; the first one you are seeing is 142 feet. To the trail's right, the jagged mountain darting into the heavens is known as The Tooth, a popular technical alpine rock climbing area usually approached from near Snow Lake on its northeastern side. What a vision!

Your climbing continues until you find some reprieve for your lungs at just over 2 miles. I like to call this area the false pass, because your brain is excited about getting close to the top, although it's still another 1.8 miles to the actual top, known as Hemlock Pass. For now, rock hop across Denny Creek again, take a deep breath, and continue ascending through talus fields with even more vine maples reaching out to greet you in various shades of red. The climbing gets even steeper at this point with what feels like endless switchbacks on tricky footing. This uphill grunt challenges even the fittest of hikers. Stick with it—the reward is coming!

At 3.8 miles, reach the thank-goodness-it's-flat Hemlock Pass and pause to catch your breath. You are getting very close to the lake, so if you can, save that snack for a few minutes longer.

Awe-inspiring views of rugged mountain glory greet hikers along the shorelines of Melakwa Lake.

In 0.3 mile after descending Hemlock Pass (4.1 total mileage), bear right (north) toward the signed Melakwa Lake at a trail junction. The signed Melakwa Lake Trail 1011 heads west and down toward Pratt Lake, which would be fun another day. For now, continue on toward Melakwa Lake. A little bitty climb follows and then boom—here you are!

At the lake's outlet, cross a log jam that looks intimidating but is quite stable, then reach the day-use area, complete with a primitive backcountry toilet immediately afterward. On the lake's shoreline, Sitka mountain ash radiates with yellow and orange leaves sporting clumps of bulbous red berries, while the lake twinkles in jade. On the opposite shoreline, Cascade mountain and oval-leaved huckleberries carpet the area in shades of merlot under groves of evergreens.

If you still have pep in your step, follow a boot-beaten trail over boulders from the day-use area around the left (western) side of the lake until you reach Melakwa's northern outlet. Walk north and discover Upper Melakwa Lake only 0.2 mile from its big sibling. Quiet campsites with rocks for picnics are found on the lake's eastern shore. Watch the time so you have plenty of light for the pumice prancing required as you make your way back the way you came.

31. GRANITE MOUNTAIN

Distance: 8.5 miles
Elevation Gain: 3800 feet
High Point: 5629 feet
Difficulty: Hard
GPS: N 47°23.870', W 121°29.196'
Maps: Green Trails Maps No. 207: Snoqualmie Pass

Managing Agency: Mount Baker–Snoqualmie National Forest, Snoqualmie Ranger District
Passes: Northwest Forest Pass or Interagency Pass
Dog-Friendly: Yes, on leash
Kid-Friendly: No
Amenities: Pit toilet at trailhead

Notes: As with all I-90 corridor hikes, this one is crowded and parking fills up quickly, especially on weekends. Arrive early or avoid weekends. Car prowls are frequent in this area—take valuables with you. Avalanches occur frequently over the trail due to the slope's pitch, so if heavy snow has recently fallen, check the avalanche danger or simply avoid this hike.

Getting There: From North Bend, drive east on I-90 and take exit 47. At the stop sign, turn left (north) and proceed over the freeway. When the road becomes a T, turn left (west) and follow it a short distance to the Pratt Lake Trailhead. The parking area is limited to roughly thirty-five to forty cars and fills up quickly; however, roadside parking is permitted.

If you've hiked Mount Si and thought it was steep and grueling, just wait until you grind up Granite Mountain! The climb is a heinie shaker, but every calf-cramping, quad-stinging, lung-straining step will be worth the effort when you experience the sweeping views of Mount Rainier and the Alpine Lakes Wilderness, not to mention the brilliant, autumn foliage. The classic L-4-style lookout tower on the top of this peak is even more reason to get to the summit and explore the rocky viewpoint.

 Foliage: Beargrass, Cascade huckleberry, dwarf bilberry, fireweed, goatsbeard, pearly everlasting, red elderberry, rosy spirea, Sitka mountain ash, vine maple

From the get-go, the trail—at this point called Pratt Lake Trail—welcomes you with evergreens such as western red cedar, western and mountain hemlock, and Douglas-fir heavy with thick bark and draping moss, a testament to the Northwest climate. In just over 0.5 mile, a switchback guides you near a brushy avalanche chute and offers a sneak preview of what's ahead before heading back into the forest. Dribbling creeklets dance down hillsides high above, reminding you to hydrate before the big climb. The trail also reaches the Alpine Lakes Wilderness boundary at this point, noted by a tree sign.

At 1.2 miles, arrive at an intersection with Granite Mountain Trail, which takes a hard right (east). Pratt Lake Trail continues straight ahead toward Pratt and a couple of other lake junctions, so pay attention if you are deep in conversation, or you may miss the turn and end up doing unnecessary mileage.

Once on the Granite Mountain Trail, remind your legs that nobody said this was easy, and start the rocky climb, switching back as you go higher and higher into the hinterlands via the avalanche swales. Vine maples, with their burgundy- and orange-tinged leaves, thrive on these sunny hillsides. The orange leaves and red, round berries of the Sitka mountain ash also add to the gorgeous fall colors on the hillside. This showy deciduous shrub has seven to ten leaves with rounded tips on each stem and can grow three to twelve feet in height. Like many of us, this plant loves sunshine and is often found where full sun and moderate moisture are plentiful. Red elderberry, whose leaves turn red as it prepares for winter, is found here too. This shrub has clusters of small red berries that, when eaten raw, are toxic to humans but, interestingly, not to birds or other mammals.

The switchbacks get tighter and more grueling until, at roughly 3.5 miles, the grade eases and you find yourself high above I-90 in the valley below. Mount Rainier peeks up from the south, and the hillside above you opens up to blankets of fall. A variety of huckleberry bushes, including Cascade mountain and dwarf bilberry, heavily populate these hillsides, tucked into mounds of abundant beargrass. Here

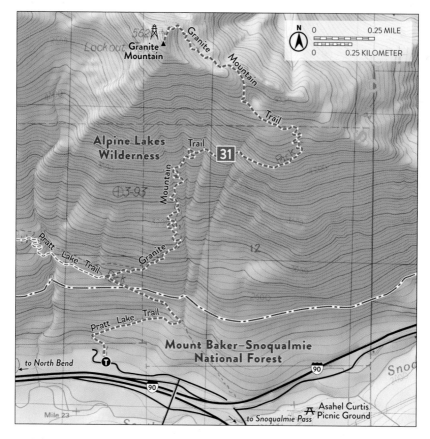

and there, vine maple and Sitka mountain ash as well as the occasional evergreen come to the color festival, which at times feels straight out of a crayon box.

A couple of flattish parkland areas with seasonal tarns are primed for exploration as their quiet waters trickle and drip amidst big boulders. This is the perfect place to rest your worn bod, with plenty of rocks for the plop. Keep your eyes open for bears on neighboring hillsides, especially once you get to the top. You might need binoculars to spot them, but often there are one or two grazing away at the lingering berries in an effort to put on weight before denning.

The final push comes after crossing a relatively gentle meadow to reach a boulder-filled ridgeline and picking your way through talus and scree to the tower at the top. If it's a warm day, you might see guinea-pig-sized pikas in the rocky areas. When predators are near, they sound a verbal alarm, which is more like a

A colorful sight welcomes those who power through the tough climb to the shoulders of Granite Mountain.

dog's squeaky toy than a whistle. These little beauties don't hibernate through winter, so in the fall, they are busy carrying as many dried greens as possible into their burrows. Like us, they seem to relish the warmth of the sun and often will perch or stand guard just outside their homes, soaking in the rays.

What a view and what a place! Below are widespread meadows of autumn foliage with mountains in all directions. Crystal and Tuscohatchie Lakes are nestled in the basins to the north while Mount Stuart stands tall on the distant horizon. For more than one hundred years, the top of this peak has had some sort of structure. The first was a primitive cabin; later, the present L-4 tower was built and is currently maintained by volunteer efforts. If it's staffed, you are welcome inside. Otherwise, consider a visit inside off limits and enjoy its wooden frame instead. When you're done, creak your knees back along the same trail to the parking lot.

32. MASON, RAINBOW, AND ISLAND LAKES

Distance: 10.6 miles
Elevation Gain: 3150 feet
High Point: 4472 feet
Difficulty: Hard
GPS: N 47°25.482', W 121°35.011'
Maps: Green Trails Maps No. 207S: Snoqualmie Pass Gateway
Managing Agency: Mount Baker–Snoqualmie National Forest, Snoqualmie Ranger District

Passes: Northwest Forest Pass or Interagency Pass
Dog-Friendly: Yes, on leash
Kid-Friendly: No
Amenities: Pit toilet at trailhead and backcountry toilet along trail

Notes: The dirt road trail access has occasional potholes. The trail is often muddy and can be slippery in fall months. This hike is very popular and parking can be challenging, especially on weekends. Arrive early or choose a weekday for the most solitude and parking opportunities.

Getting There: Follow I-90 east past North Bend for just over 14.5 miles, take exit 45, and turn left (north). Follow the road as it turns back to the west and becomes dirt and gravel. In roughly 1 mile, stay straight (west) at a fork in the road, marked as Forest Road 9031 (also known as Mason Lake Road) with signage pointing toward Ira Spring Trail.

> This hike description starts at the Ira Spring Trailhead: getting to Mason Lake from there requires a bit of effort with some occasional steep, sustained climbing. Thankfully, in the fall your eyes and your camera will not be able to quit focusing on the brilliant vine maples, which, in colors of yellow, red, orange, and burgundy, make for fantastic reasons to stop, gawk, and catch your breath. While Mason Lake itself isn't bursting with fall colors, the hike to it, and the extended hike to the other lakes beyond, will give you that delicious taste of autumn that you crave.

 Foliage: Cascade huckleberry, fool's huckleberry, oval-leaved huckleberry, rosy spirea, serviceberry, Sitka mountain ash, vine maple

The trail starts with a gentle climb on an old roadbed-turned-trail, allowing your quads to ease into things before kicking into a higher gear. In just over 0.5 mile, the trail passes two waterfalls, one a mere trickle late in the season, the other a bit more impressive and significant enough to warrant a beautiful log bridge across its cascades. Snap your pics, then continue your climb on the roadbed, where trailside alders give you shade and pikas squeaking like dog toys in the occasional talus field divert your attention.

At 1.1 miles, enter the Alpine Lakes Wilderness, announced by a trailside sign to the right. Give your lungs and your legs a pep talk, because the real climb begins 1.5 miles from the trailhead, where the path leaves the lovely cruising grade of the old road and begins a bit of a grueling climb intended to get you into the high country without much mercy. Up you go, eventually reaching some switchbacks that ease your huffing and puffing until you reach a splendid boulder field offering views of Mount Rainier to the south and the ribbon of roadway deep in the valley below you.

Vine maple leaves in vibrant colors set against a brilliant blue sky make for autumn eye candy, while thimbleberry leaves, sadly dying after leading a good life, give a pop of yellow here and there. Vine maples usually prefer a damp forest, and thankfully along this stretch, they grow well because they get a lot of water

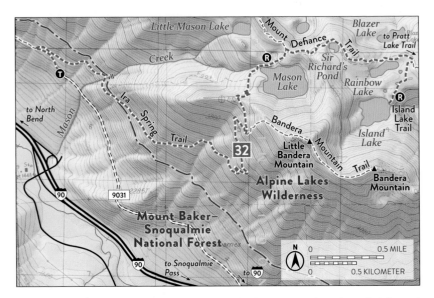

and sunlight. When capturing photos here, try shooting at about knee height and angling the camera slightly toward the sky and trail.

At 2.9 miles the trail arrives at a junction with Bandera Mountain Trail, but we want to stay on Ira Spring Trail, which switchbacks hard to the left (north). If you have time and adequate fitness, you could check out this peak also, or as most do, save it for another day's adventure since it too has splendid fall colors! This area and some of the neighboring peaks were scorched by a fire in 1958, and the barren slopes have yet to recover. Admire the gusto of the tough firefighters who bombed straight up this peak while laden with archaic equipment in the name of protecting the landscapes. For now, continue following the Ira Spring Trail toward Mason Lake, which cruises through fall colors to the western edge of a ridgeline.

From here, it's nearly all downhill to Mason Lake as you drop into the small basin below the ridge and reach the lake's western edge, 3.4 miles from the trailhead. Like most fall hikes, the popularity of the trail and the sheer number of people enjoying the area might seem like a crowd; however, the nooks and crannies amidst large boulders on Mason's edges are plentiful, and solitude is possible, even on weekends. A primitive backcountry toilet is located here on a spur trail, found by following the main trail as it crosses the lake's outlet and starts to wrap around the lake's northwestern shore.

Due to an extensive network of social trails and tenting sites, it's easy to lose the main trail, so those who wish to divert will want to pay close attention as they wander off to snap photos. Thankfully, the kind folks at the Forest Service have put up signs on trees noting the main trail with arrows to help you navigate the

Fall solitude (fall-itude) abounds near the edges of Island Lake, a perfect quiet picnic spot.

maze. For some, a visit to Mason Lake with the beautiful maples guiding the way makes for a full, happy day and they will be content turning around here. Those with liveliness left in their steps may want to continue.

From Mason Lake, follow the signed main trail as it heads northeast, bobbing and weaving through boulders and evergreens. If you mistakenly end up at a tent site, turn back and consult your GPS or map, or simply look for the viscous footprints in gooey mud, which tends to hold sole patterns during the rainy season.

Just 0.3 mile from Mason Lake (3.7 miles from the trailhead), reach a junction marked by a sign on a sturdy conifer. The way you came toward Mason Lake is noted, as is Mount Defiance Trail to the left. If the clock and the quads are happy, you could check out Mount Defiance, yet another trail to a high peak that exhibits fall colors. More likely you'll want to save it for another time and continue on our path, which is signed to Pratt Lake and Island Lake with an arrow to the right. Follow the path to Island Lake east and, ugh, just when you thought you were done climbing, ascend a forested knoll taking you up and over to the other side. Happily, this climb, while steep in a couple places, is short and before you know it, you are on the other side, heading back down toward open meadows and huckleberry utopia.

At 0.5 mile from the trail intersection (0.8 mile after Mason Lake, 4.2 miles from the trailhead) arrive at the first body of water since Mason Lake. Located to the trail's right, the pond is unofficially named Sir Richard's Pond and is shallow with a mucky bottom, but who cares . . . those colors! Mountain ash and rosy spirea with their orange and yellow leaves light up the edges, as do fading orange grasses and burgundy dwarf bilberries. With any luck, a brilliant sky of blue is reflected in the water, creating a scene straight out of a magazine spread.

Next up, to the right in 0.4 mile from Sir Richard's Pond (1.2 miles from Mason Lake, 4.6 miles from the trailhead), is Rainbow Lake, a true lake with more depth and size than the pond. A couple of short side trails will get you to photo-worthy spots. Back on the main trail, continue another 0.2 mile and arrive at a signpost noting Island Lake, down a spur trail, and Rainbow Lake, back the way you came. Head toward Island Lake, passing a couple of lily pad–laden tarns on both the left and the right, as well as a signed spur for a primitive backcountry toilet, before arriving at Island Lake 0.5 mile from the signpost. You've made it! Various trails out to the lake's edges lead to sitting areas, so grab a snack and some photos of the fall colors with all the now-familiar shoreline plants. When you're done, head back the way you came.

EXTENDING YOUR TRIP

If you have two vehicles, you may consider doing a thru-hike and visiting two more lakes by starting at Ira Spring Trailhead and ending at the Talapus Lake Trailhead. To do this, follow the directions above, and after visiting Island Lake, continue on the Island/Rainbow Trail that climbs southeast and arrives at a junction with the Pratt Lake Trail. Bear right on the Pratt Lake Trail until it meets a faint connector to Olallie Lake. Turn right (west) and follow the connector past Olallie Lake, then Talapus Lake, and eventually back out to the trailhead. Hiking the whole trip from the Ira Springs Trailhead to the Talapus Lake Trailhead is 11.8 miles with 3100 feet of elevation gain.

To drive to the Talapus Lake Trailhead, follow the Ira Spring Trailhead directions above, but instead of staying straight (west) at the fork located 1 mile from the exit, turn right (north) and proceed on the signed FR 9030 to the trailhead at the road's end. Of course, you could also go counterclockwise if the mood hits.

33. OXBOW LOOP

Distance: 1.4 miles
Elevation Gain: 65 feet
High Point: 935 feet
Difficulty: Easy
GPS: N 47°31.010', W 121°36.655'
Maps: Green Trails Maps No. 174SX: Middle Fork Snoqualmie

Managing Agency: Washington State Department of Natural Resources
Passes: Discover Pass
Dog-Friendly: Yes, on leash
Kid-Friendly: Yes
Amenities: Pit toilet at trailhead

Notes: Some of the Middle Fork Valley is Department of Natural Resources land, which requires a Discover Pass, and the other part is managed by the Forest Service, which requires a Northwest Forest Pass or Interagency Pass. If you venture farther up the road and decide to stop and picnic or hike somewhere else en route, be prepared with both passes. Park only in designated spots and not along the roadway. While there are two trailheads, this description starts at the beginning of the loop. If you park at the trailhead to the northeast (with the pit toilet), add 0.4 mile roundtrip and 10 feet of elevation gain to the hike.

Getting There: From I-90 near North Bend, head east, take exit 34, and head left (north) on 468th Avenue SE. In 0.6 mile, turn right (east) on SE Middle Fork Road. In 1.5 miles from I-90, at the Y, bear right on the one-way SE Lake Dorothy Road. In 2.8 miles from I-90, the one-way road ends and officially becomes the SE Middle Fork Road (Forest Road 56). Signage here announces you are entering the Middle Fork Snoqualmie River Valley. Stay on the Middle Fork Road, passing trailheads for Mailbox Peak and Granite Creek, until you reach the first Oxbow Trailhead at 8 miles from I-90. If this is full, a second trailhead with a pit toilet is found 0.1 mile farther up the road.

If you are looking for a hike where you can enjoy autumn with the wee ones or perhaps the aging tail-wagger, this one is perfect. Everyone will delight in this forest, where deciduous trees such as bigleaf and vine maples flaunt casts of reds and yellows among the mossy thicket.

What's more, this relatively new hike showing off a former river channel, now turned quiet waterway, has a slightly raised gravel surface to help you avoid muddy shoes. Though some leaves start turning by mid- to late September, the warmer river valley tends to make the leaf-peeping better later in the season. Whenever you go, give an imaginary high-five to the fine folks of the Department of Natural Resources and Mountains to Sound Greenway, who worked hard to put this gorgeous pathway here for us!

 Foliage: Bigleaf maple, black cottonwood, red elderberry, Scouler's willow, vine maple

You can take the loop in either direction, but going to the right (southwest) starts the ball rolling with the maple promenade and opens up the forest to peeks of Russian Butte to the left across the southeastern valley. A handful of steps farther,

Pack up the whole family for this easy, forested walk around the peaceful oxbow of the Middle Fork Snoqualmie.

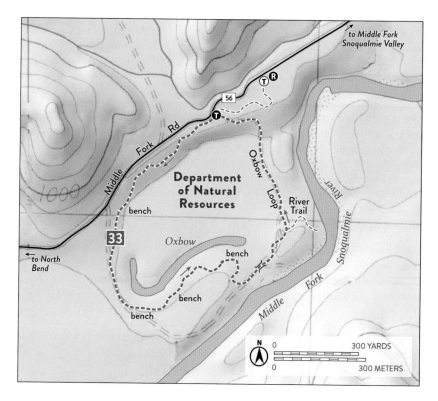

at 0.3 mile, is an official viewpoint complete with the first of four log benches you'll encounter on the hike. During fall, the benches are almost always wet and slippery, so if you intend to sit or picnic, you may want to bring a sit pad.

In another 0.1 mile from the first bench (0.4 mile from the start), look to the left through the foliage and spy one of many evergreens covered in bearded lichen. The effects of the stringy strands, which drop to over three feet in places, make these trees look like they could reach down and grab you—the ultimate creepy Halloween trees! Try telling the kids it's Mother Nature's tinsel instead.

The Oxbow water area is visible through the trees to the left as you walk, so keep your eyes out for waterfowl such as ducks, teals, and geese, which enjoy the calm water. Northern flickers and hairy woodpeckers also call this area home, so task the kids with listening for knocking and their clear, hollow calls.

The hike now exhibits a mossier understory and thicker evergreens as you pass three more benches, all with viewpoints showing off the Oxbow and colorful hillsides of Bootalicious Peak to the northwest; the last bench appears at 0.7 mile from where you started.

The trail takes a hairpin turn at 0.9 mile from the trailhead and then showcases a spectacular nurse tree to the trail's right, where several evergreens have taken advantage of the old stump's nutrients and grown into tall spectacles themselves. Immediately following the nurse tree, cross a wooden bridge over the Oxbow's former outlet.

At 1.1 miles, arrive at a junction where a short, rocky trail heads right (east) down to the banks of the Middle Fork Snoqualmie River. If you choose to visit the river, the out and back from this point will add an additional 0.1 mile roundtrip walk. The loop continues by bearing left (north) at the river trail junction and wandering back under bigleaf maples until reaching the point where you started, 1.4 miles ago. With tired kids, worn-out dogs, and a taste of fall in your camera, head on home or continue to explore the Middle Fork Snoqualmie River Valley.

34. BARE MOUNTAIN

Distance: 8.3 miles
Elevation Gain: 3180 feet
High Point: 5353 feet
Difficulty: Hard
GPS: N 47°38.381', W 121°31.725'
Maps: Green Trails Maps No. 174: Mount Si and No. 175: Skykomish

Managing Agency: Mount Baker–Snoqualmie National Forest, Snoqualmie Ranger District
Passes: Northwest Forest Pass or Interagency Pass
Dog-Friendly: Yes, on leash
Kid-Friendly: No
Amenities: None

Notes: Bring water shoes for crossing Bear Creek if the weather has recently been wet or if you'd prefer to wade instead of cross on logs or rocks. Getting to the trailhead requires following a narrow, bumpy dirt road with potholes, but by going slowly, passenger cars can make it. Allow an extra hour each direction for the rough road. Once you leave the town of North Bend, there are no more services or restrooms.

Getting There: From I-90, take exit 31 in North Bend and take the third roundabout exit, heading toward town (northwest on Bendigo Boulevard S.). In just over 0.9 mile from the freeway, go right (southeast) on W. North Bend Way. Go 0.1 mile farther and turn left (northeast) on Ballarat Avenue N. Stay on Ballarat for the next 4 miles as it winds its way north and changes names to SE 108th Street and 428th Avenue SE and eventually, North Fork Road SE.

At just over 5 miles from the freeway, veer left on the poorly signed North Fork County Road (Forest Road 57, also known as FR 5700). The road is signed "Dead End in 24 miles." In 0.7 mile the pavement ends and the road narrows. Proceed on the rough gravel road for just shy of 17.5 miles, until the road makes a hard left (northeast) and crosses over Lennox Creek. Immediately afterward, take the next right (southeast) and stay on FR 57 for another 3.2 miles until you reach the trailhead to the road's left.

The road leading to this hike is challenging and lengthy. What's more, the first mile and a half of trail is rocky, tough walking. So why go? Simply put, your reward will be worth your effort. This trail is one of the few places where you may actually find some solitude along with splendid fall colors. The top of the hike boasts a barren summit where huckleberries, heather, and Cascade mountain ash make a rug of earth tones fit for a magazine cover while views of distant peaks fill your soul. You might not want to come back down.

 Foliage: Blue elderberry, Cascade huckleberry, Cascade mountain ash, fool's huckleberry, oval-leaved huckleberry, red alder, red elderberry, rosy spirea, vine maple

Once you've filled out your free wilderness permit, begin your climb by carefully picking your steps on the rocky trail. From 1905 to 1934, the trail on which you totter was an old road that carried mined minerals out of the Bear Creek Mine, not far from here. Over the years, the slope has attracted water runoff during spring snowmelt and is now more of a dry creek bed than a road or trail, but at least we don't have to bushwhack.

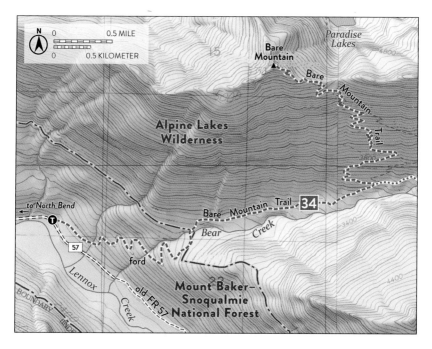

Tolerate the long, bumpy road for the payoff of the view atop Bare Mountain.

At 0.7 mile, the trail reaches a crossing with Bear Creek, which can be high after rains. Most times, it can be crossed on a log or by rock hopping, but that tends to be somewhat precarious and might require more grace than that of a tippy hippo. If you find yourself aflutter, you might prefer to wade across. It's not necessarily deep in the fall, but it can be swift in places so use care.

Thankfully, not long after Bear Creek, the trail tread becomes slightly less rocky and your feet do a little happy dance. Next up, the trail crosses Bear Creek again, only this time, there is a primitive wooden bridge. Here, along the water's shore-line, thimbleberry, salmonberry, and devilsclub are starting their dormancy and are taking on decaying yellow tinges. If your camera offers the option, consider a slow shutter speed for motion-blurred shots of the water framed by the rustic bridge and the greenish-yellow leaves.

Bare Mountain is our hike, yet Bear Creek is the water source. Perhaps this is coincidence, perhaps not. The top of the peak is barren yet filled with berries, which unquestionably attract bears. And the plot thickens.

The trail officially enters the Alpine Lakes Wilderness and an often-overgrown hillside traverse. Thimbleberry, goatsbeard, brackenfern, and other plants in this area are in the process of dying back and, with their weakened stalks, they plop right onto the trail. Whack them if you need to because it's important to watch your feet on this narrow, eroding trail. Vine maple in gorgeous shades of red and orange love the sunshine on the vast hillside.

At 1.9 miles, the trail takes a hard left and begins switchbacking steeply up Bare Mountain. Near this area, you're likely to see an unmaintained boot path leading toward the old mining area and some remaining rusty equipment. It's a fun place to explore if you have good navigational skills, but keep the limited fall daylight hours and navigational challenges in mind. Perhaps save the prospecting adventure for another day.

Continue ascending until views of Rainier to the south show up on a clear day and give you a good excuse to stop, stare, and catch your breath without looking too out of shape. Pro tip: pull out the camera and pretend to snap a photo when you're winded and your in-shape friends will be none the wiser. At your feet, huckleberries show off their burgundy leaves in the midst of the brilliant-green heather and juniper, while Sitka mountain ash comes to the party with orange leaves. Add a little rosy spirea in her gorgeous yellow coloring, and it's as if you've been transported into a Bob Ross painting.

A couple of viewpoints look down on the two Paradise Lakes in the valley below, and before you know it, you are at the top! A classic L-4–style fire tower stood watch on this peak from 1935 to 1973; its rusty metal supports still standing are testament to its existence. In the distance on a clear day, Glacier Peak stands tall on the horizon to the north while jagged molars outline distant ridges of the Alpine Lakes Wilderness. Marinate in the splendor, then head back on the same trail when your tummy growls, reminding you it won't be long until dinner. North Bend has some great options.

Next page: *To find color in the oh-so-green Olympics, head to the river valleys.*

OLYMPIC MOUNTAINS

When folks imagine the Olympics, they often think green trees dripping with moss, not necessarily fall colors. For the most part, that's true, although here and there in the most astounding places, splashes of fall show up and mix beautifully with the evergreens. For this reason, I've added a scenic hike where you can lose your heart and soul amidst goliath evergreen giants and twinges of golden leaves.

35. STAIRCASE RAPIDS LOOP

Distance: 2.3 miles
Elevation Gain: 225 feet
High Point: 1000 feet
Difficulty: Easy
GPS: N 47°30.931', W 123°19.767'
Maps: Green Trails Maps No. 168SX: Olympic Mountains East

Managing Agency: Olympic National Park
Passes: National park entrance fee/annual pass or Interagency Pass
Dog-Friendly: No, not permitted
Kid-Friendly: Yes
Amenities: Pit toilet near parking area

Notes: The trailhead road is occasionally closed during winter. Visit the current road conditions page on the Olympic National Park website, or call Olympic National Park's Wilderness Information Center for updates (see Resources). Trail may be muddy after plentiful rain.

Getting There: From Shelton, head northbound on US Highway 101 for 15 miles to the town of Hoodsport. Turn left (west) onto State Route 119 and follow it for just over 9 miles to a T in the road. Turn left (west) onto Forest Road 24, which eventually turns to gravel, and proceed for 5.5 miles to a junction. Turn right (north) at the junction and continue for 1.2 miles. At the Staircase Ranger Station, turn right on a spur road and locate the parking area to the road's right. To find the trailhead, walk the spur road back to the ranger station and continue walking northwest to locate a large concrete bridge.

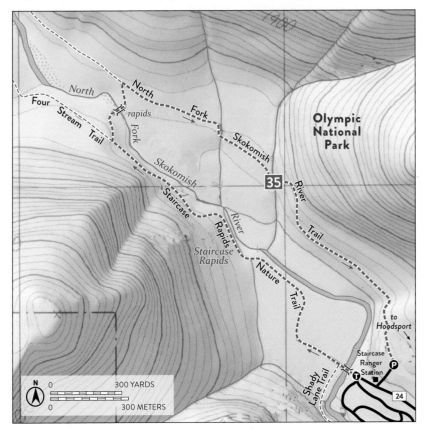

A bigleaf maple leaf hangs out on a boulder by the North Fork Skykomish River waiting for wind or water to move it along to a new home.

This is a perfect hike for kids, the elderly, or those who struggle with mobility. It's short, it's breathtaking, and it's a pleasant walk. Sure, it's not bursting with fall colors, but it will offer enough color and crisp breezes that you'll definitely feel autumn's light touch.

 Foliage: Bigleaf maple, oval-leaved huckleberry, Pacific dogwood, serviceberry, vine maple

Cross the North Fork Skokomish River on a sturdy concrete bridge, then pass a junction with the Shady Lane Trail coming in from the left. If you have more time or want another exploration option, the Shady Lane Trail follows the river downstream and delivers you to Lake Cushman in just shy of 1 mile. For now, proceed straight on the Staircase Rapids Nature Trail/Four Stream Trail. A couple more side trails come in from the left, followed by one signed Big Cedar, which leads to a large, fallen western red cedar. Check it out if time permits; if not, continue on the main trail wandering through the so-green-it-hurts mossy forest of western red cedar, Pacific silver fir, grand fir, Douglas-fir, and western hemlock. Near the trail's edges, occasional groves of devilsclub begin their transition to dormancy, as indicated by the brownish yellow of their huge prickly leaves. Other plants, such as salmonberry, vanilla leaf, bunchberry, and brackenfern, also begin fading, their leaves in shades of tan or light yellow.

Near the water, the occasional vine or bigleaf maple shows up with leaves of burgundy or gold, which, when they are in prime fall colors, look like a Japanese garden against the river's edge. Depending on the recent rains, the river can have many faces. Sometimes, it dances over boulders flowing with playful power and foamy back eddies, and in other spots it crashes in a series of cascades so loud and powerful, it can be tough to carry on a conversation with nearby people.

At 1 mile, arrive at a junction with a new suspension bridge across the river to your right. (The trail you've been following veers left and officially becomes the Four Stream Trail, which carries on with a much more primitive, less used tread—a fun exploration for an out-and-back adventure if time, energy, and agility permit.) Enjoy the steel work-of-art bridge where river views are impressive, and be sure to snap a few pictures from this vantage. The gorgeous bridge was installed in 2013 after its predecessor washed out in the mid-1990s due to high, swift water. Constructed with more height and strength, this one was engineered to avoid the heavy flows and guide hikers across these magnificent cascades for many, many years. Once across, connect with the North Fork Skokomish River Trail, turn right (southeast), and stroll back amidst flourishing evergreens, the occasional Pacific dogwood, and vine maples until you reach the parking area.

Next page: *The eastern side of the Cascades adapts to fall with a distinct variety of more drought-tolerant foliage.*

YAKIMA, SELAH, AND TIETON

When rain prevails on the west side of the Cascades, why not escape to a couple beautiful hikes just over the crest? Both hikes offer popping fall colors and places to meander, with the bonus of quiet canyons and peaceful landscapes.

36. UMTANUM CREEK CANYON

Distance: 6 miles
Elevation Gain: 800 feet
High Point: 1685 feet
Difficulty: Easy
GPS: N 46°51.337', W 120°29.004'
Maps: Washington Department of Fish & Wildlife trail map
Managing Agency: Washington Department of Fish & Wildlife, Wenas Wildlife Area

Passes: Bureau of Land Management parking fee required from May 15 to September 15. Federal Interagency Passes also accepted.
Dog-Friendly: Yes, on leash
Kid-Friendly: Yes
Amenities: Pit toilet at trailhead, campgrounds nearby

Notes: The trail often closes seasonally in winter to protect wildlife, so double-check before you go. Watch for rattlesnakes on warm days.

Getting There: From Ellensburg, drive south on State Route 821 (Canyon Road) into Yakima Canyon. In about 8 miles, find the trailhead and parking area on the road's right (west) near milepost 16. Parking is on the Bureau of Land Management land, while the trail is on the Washington Department of Fish & Wildlife land.

Bring the kids, the dog, and the binoculars for this spectacular fall hike where autumn colors from the many shrubs and trees are showy and wildlife is frequently spotted. If fall comes early to the Cascades, this hike is often snow-free or has just a dusting and is a good alternative to the high country.

 Foliage: Apple, bitter cherry, black cottonwood, black hawthorn, box elder, Douglas maple, English hawthorn, Mackenzie willow, narrowleaf willow, plum, quaking aspen, red-osier dogwood, Scouler's willow, serviceberry, water birch

The trail begins with a wide pedestrian suspension bridge over the swiftly flowing Yakima River. On its banks, willow varieties such as Scouler's and narrowleaf wave in the breeze, introducing you to their fall leaves of gold and offering up photo opportunities in the midmorning sunlight. Once across the bridge, follow the sign with the word *Trail* that points out the path and leads you through an underpass beneath the railroad tracks. After crossing, the trail bobs and weaves through sagebrush until splitting into two trails at an unsigned junction. At this point, continue straight (west) and follow Umtanum Creek, flowing to the trail's right.

Groves of black cottonwood, with their fluffy yellow leaves, shimmy and wiggle with the wind gusts near the creek's shoreline. Aspen thickets show up on both sides of the trail, their golden leaves almost as brilliant and magnificent as their white bark, whose woody knots sometimes look like human eyes. Are we being watched?

In less than 1 mile from the trailhead, cross Umtanum Creek on a makeshift log bridge or by rock hopping. Immediately afterward, follow the creek bed 50 yards upstream to discover a well-built beaver dam, often with the little slappers busy at work. These architects are the largest living rodents in North America, with an adult averaging 40 pounds and living typically to ten to twelve years of age. They mate for life, and kits are often born in the spring. In the fall if it's really cold, beavers might be hiding inside their home located just above the dam, with the only entrance being a tricky waterway. If the weather is warm, you might be lucky enough to see them and their sharp orange incisors chomping at trees, twigs, or plants or dragging freshly harvested wood to their dam.

Back on the trail, look to the right near the creek and see if you can locate the remains of an old homestead. The buildings are gone, but the concrete foundations for the root cellar and front entrance still sit in the meadow. If you had lived here back in the early 1930s, you'd likely be harvesting apples and pears from the nearby trees during this time of year. The trees still produce fruit, despite not being pruned or maintained. If you are inspired, pick a couple and see how they taste.

The trail continues following the creek, with English and black hawthorn landscaping its edges and quaking aspen groves dropping the occasional leaf in the

A trusty bridge ushers hikers over the Yakima River on the way to the Umtanum Creek Canyon.

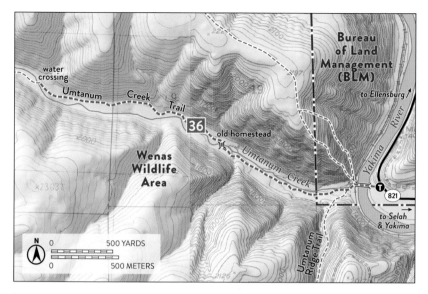

breeze. Stop every once in a while to scan the steeps for deer, elk, or bighorn sheep, all of which are ungulates and mate in the fall in a time known as rut. During rut, bighorn sheep rams (males) compete for ewes (females) by having head-butting contests, where they charge each other at up to 20 miles per hour and smack the tops of their heads so loudly, it can be heard for over a mile away. During fall, elk make an unusual, loud, high-pitched screech sometimes followed by a series of grunts, known as bugling. Be sure to listen when scanning.

At the water crossing around 3 miles from where you started, the trail becomes less and less obvious, so that's where this hike officially ends, but if energy and curiosity are high, feel free to explore farther up the canyon near the steep basalt cliffs until you and the kids have had enough and are ready to head back.

37. TIETON RIVER NATURE TRAIL

Distance: 6.8 miles
Elevation Gain: 220 feet
High Point: 1950 feet
Difficulty: Easy
GPS: N 46°43.173', W 120°49.887'
Maps: Green Trails Maps No. 305: Tieton

Managing Agency: Washington Department of Fish & Wildlife, Oak Creek Wildlife Area
Passes: Discover Pass
Dog-Friendly: Yes, on leash
Kid-Friendly: Yes
Amenities: Pit toilet in Oak Creek Wildlife Area

Notes: This trail has three trailheads, one at each end and one in the middle. You can hike either direction and make it an out-and-back, or bring two vehicles and make it a thru-hike. Trail open to mountain bikes. Watch for rattlesnakes on warm days.

Getting There: Western trailhead: From White Pass summit, travel east on US Highway 12 for almost 30 miles to reach a parking area to the road's right (south).

From Naches, drive west on US 12 for 4.4 miles, then stay left (south) on US 12. Drive for roughly 5 miles and locate a large parking area to the left (south).

If you'd rather try the middle trailhead, that's 1 mile east of the western trailhead on US 12. The eastern trailhead is 3 miles east of the western trailhead in the Oak Creek Wildlife Area. All three trailheads have parking areas.

In the fall, the Tieton River Trail lights up brilliantly with reds from plants like golden currant and serviceberry and yellows and oranges from Scouler's willow, Douglas maple, black cottonwood, and quaking aspen. There are simply so many breathtaking earth tones along the edges of the Tieton River, you'll want to stop often and you might not get anywhere too quickly. But that's okay—this trail is prime for ambling since it's fairly level, mellow, and perfect for a fall stroll.

Foliage: Bitter cherry, black cottonwood, chokecherry, crab apple, Douglas maple, golden currant, narrowleaf willow, Oregon white oak, Pacific willow, pear, quaking aspen, rabbit-brush, red-osier dogwood, Scouler's willow, serviceberry, shinyleaf spirea, Woods' rose

Starting at the western end of this trail gives you plenty of opportunity to see the foliage and make a calorie-burning hike out of it. However, it's not for the faint of heart; the bridge over the river, while level with good tread, is narrow and lacks railings. Watch your step and you'll get across without issues, but if your heart goes pitter-patter too heavily, you may want to go to the middle trailhead and walk either direction or to the eastern trailhead and walk west.

After crossing the bridge and then patting yourself on the back for staying safe, reach the trail junction and go left (east). Wander, watch, and enjoy the ponderosa pines and dormant tan wildflower stalks preparing for winter. Keep your eyes and ears open for Douglas squirrels, who spend this time of year freeing pine cones from tree limbs and allowing them to fall to the forest floor—or on an unsuspecting hiker.

At 0.3 mile, arrive at the first of many trail forks. Over the years, mountain bikers, climbers, sightseers, fisherman, and wildlife have created a lot of options for which way to go, but going in the basic eastbound direction, no matter the boot path, will eventually guide you back to a common path. I prefer the route that heads closer to the river here, since the fall foliage of Oregon white oak, quaking

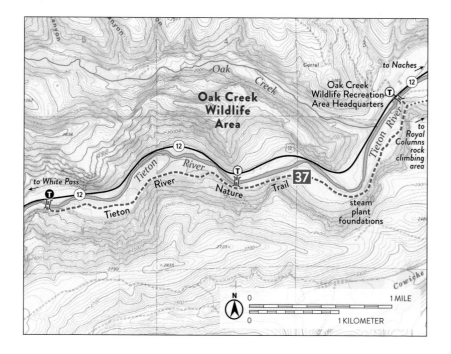

aspen, shinyleaf spirea, Scouler's willow, black cottonwood, and others are lovely in this direction.

One of my favorite trees in this area is the black cottonwood, which thrives in riparian habitats and, due to its lofty heights of 160 feet or more, is frequently home to great blue heron, bald eagle, or osprey nests. While its fluffy cottonseed balls might be a nuisance to allergy sufferers in the springtime, the fall leaves of this upright tree take on a gorgeous yellow hue, and with a stiff breeze they shimmy like a seventies disco ball on Saturday night.

At 1.7 miles, the trail takes you very close to the river and a well-built pedestrian suspension bridge. This is the middle trailhead's connector. Stay right, on the south side of the river, and from here, the trail bobs and weaves from foliage thickets into dormant meadows.

Onward you go, enjoying more fall colors of the desert, a very different set of drought-tolerant and sunshine-loving plants than mountainous environs. Deep-blue Steller's jays, with their black-crested head feathers, squawk from the trees above. In 0.3 mile past the suspension bridge, continue straight to avoid a right fork leading to the Bend rock climbing area. If you brought your binoculars, you can occasionally see golden eagles or their giant nest near the cliffs. In 2002, a 2000-acre fire swept through this area, wiping out a section of trees and shrubs

Color garnishes the Tieton River's edges below barren, rocky knolls.

along the trail, but the recovery is actually quite healthy and thankfully not too much of a buzzkill.

At 2.7 miles from where you started, pass some old concrete foundations that are all that remains of a steam plant that helped create the irrigation canals in the area. If you are comfortable doing so, carefully climb up one of the concrete walls for a better photo opportunity of the steel-blue river, decorated with crimson, gold, and orange near its edges, and the high cliffs up the valley. Fall is alive in this place!

At 3.4 miles, the trail follows an old roadbed to a sign with nothing but an arrow pointing uphill. The arrow is actually a directional sign for climbers who are looking to head up to Royal Columns rock climbing area—not for hikers who are looking to continue ambling. To reach the far eastern trailhead, continue straight (north) on the relatively level trail, then scoot through the small gate on the bottom of the wildlife fence. To the right is a large trailhead sign and to the left, a sturdy, wide bridge leading you to SR 12 and across the street to the Oak Creek Wildlife Area and eastern trailhead. Turn back for the round-trip here.

Next page: *A tapestry of earth-tones adorns the meadow near the Paradise area in Mount Rainier National Park (Hike 43).*

MOUNT RAINIER

It's not hard to fall in love with Mount Rainier in autumn. With diminished crowds, serenity abounds and the trails take on the ambiance of quiet slumber and a vision of unimaginable beauty. Scarlet huckleberry leaves are eye candy when set against the snowy, giant peak or an azure backcountry lake. Wildlife like black bears search out the remaining huckleberries in a last attempt to gain nutrients before a long winter nap, and chilly mountain sunsets meld into late afternoon darkness in colors of sherbet. There is a perfect peace that seeps into your soul in this national park.

38. GOAT PEAK

Distance: 6.4 miles
Elevation Gain: 3210 feet
High Point: 6473 feet
Difficulty: Hard
GPS: N 46°57.896', W 121°15.934'
Maps: Green Trails Maps No. 303S: Goat Rocks, William O. Douglas Wilderness

Managing Agency: Okanogan-Wenatchee National Forest, Naches Ranger District
Passes: None
Dog-Friendly: Yes, on leash
Kid-Friendly: No
Amenities: Pit toilet at campground on southern trailhead

Notes: There are two trailheads for this hike, and both lead to the larch-filled views of the summit. This hike describes the climb from the northern trailhead. In 2021, a hot and destructive fire burned the areas around this hike. This fire, combined with others of recent years, has caused the landscape near here to change rapidly. Use care when hiking in fire zones, especially in high winds.

Getting There: Northern trailhead: From Enumclaw: Follow State Route 410 east for roughly 49.7 miles to Chinook Pass. Continue east on SR 410 for another 17.9 miles (67.6 miles from Enumclaw) to a small, easy-to-miss parking area on the south side of the roadway, across from Hells Crossing Campground. No bathroom facilities. Limited roadway parking.

From Naches: Follow US Highway 12 westbound for nearly 4.5 miles to a junction with SR 410. Continue on SR 410 for 32.7 miles to reach a small, easy-to-miss parking area on the south side of the roadway, across from Hells Crossing Campground.

Southern trailhead: At milepost 88.4 off SR 410, turn south onto Bumping River Road (Forest Road 1800). Follow the paved road for 5.9 miles to a trailhead on the right, across from Cougar Flat Campground. Pit toilet available. Northwest Forest Pass or Interagency Pass required.

> Nobody said getting up to the larch-filled hillsides was easy, and this grueling hike is no exception. But it's worth the labor, as it leads to perfect soil conditions for a tapestry of golden western larches to live harmoniously amongst their evergreen cousins. Shade is an enemy to the western larches, which thrive here on the sunny, often warm eastern side of the Cascade Crest. When they are at their peak, you'll observe speckled carpets of gold as far as the eye can see, save for the fire zones.

 Foliage: arrowleaf buckwheat, grouse whortleberry, sedge, western larch

From the northern trailhead, which also supports the Pleasant Valley Trail, turn left (south) and start your climb toward Goat Peak on Trail 958C. Conifers greet you, as do a smattering of larches—the appetizer for the main course.

At roughly 0.5 mile from the trailhead, not long after entering the William O. Douglas Wilderness, a seasonal creek has you hopping over its trickling flow or, in dry seasons, its rocky bed. This is the only water on this hike, and it can be absent in late season, so be sure to pack plenty.

Continue grinding up the trail, which takes a slightly eastern trajectory before wandering back to the south. Rack up more and more elevation until you reach an open slope with views across to Fifes Peak and, sadly, the remains of the lightning-caused, devastating Norse Peak Fire that burned over 55,000 acres in 2017.

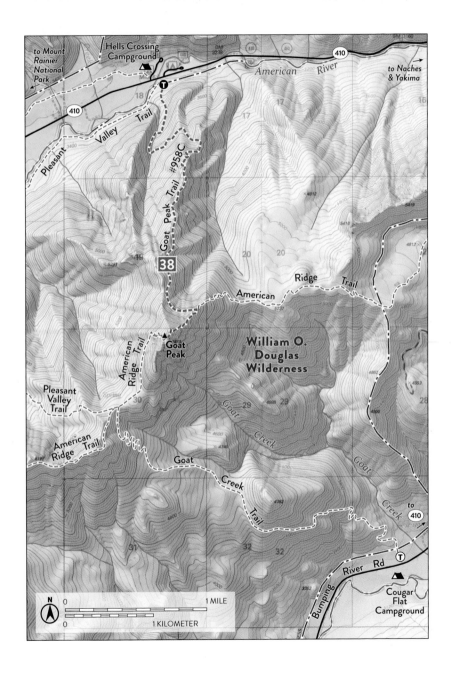

to Mount Rainier National Park

Hells Crossing Campground

410

American River

to Naches & Yakima

410

Valley Trail

Pleasant

Goat Peak Trail #958C

38

American Ridge Trail

17

17

20

20

4912

5418

5416

4812

American

Ridge

Trail

William O. Douglas Wilderness

4862

4953

Goat Peak

American Ridge Trail

Pleasant Valley Trail

30

29

29

4600

28

American Ridge Trail

Goat

Creek

4600

4740

Goat

Creek

Trail

4782

Goat

Creek

to 410

31

32

32

Bumping River Rd

3362

Cougar Flat Campground

N

0   1 MILE

0   1 KILOMETER

Distant larches speckle the hills near Goat Peak while Mount Rainier stands guard in the background.

The larch madness begins in less than 1 mile from where you started. These yellow wonders are happiest in moist north- or east-facing mountain slopes where shade is not found. With thick and sturdy bark, dense wood, and tall tops, they are particularly resistant to fires.

At roughly 1.2 miles, and around 4050 feet elevation, the trail cuts across a sandy slope where it dances in and out of groves of evergreens before it reaches a rocky outcropping. Trail erosion is evident, so watch your footing carefully, especially if there is a dusting of snow or ice.

The trail hops along a ridgeline flirting with both the east and west sides, before the grade eases and you arrive at a junction with the top of American Ridge Trail. From here, turn right (southwest) for the last strenuous push to the summit of Goat Peak, climbing 575 feet in a short 0.5 mile.

Boom—there is the summit! What a view. To the west on the bold horizon is Mount Rainier while Mount Adams shows up to the southwest. You are looking down at the colorful green and yellow evergreen carpets, a unique view for sure. While you might be tempted to pull your camera's lens out to the widest angle for all the pictures, some of the most beautiful shots are simply composed of a zoom of the contrasting trees—backlit if possible. If the sun isn't playing nice the day you visit, point your camera away from the gray, washed-out sky and keep the focus primarily on the trees or the volcanoes.

A southern route up Goat Peak is also possible by following Goat Creek Trail as it climbs through the forest to intersect American Ridge Trail in just under 4 miles. From here, turn right (east) and continue on steep, exposed switchbacks before reaching the summit in 0.9 mile from the junction.

When you are finished, meander back the way you came and keep your eyes open for mountain goats. After all, this is their peak.

39. NACHES PEAK LOOP

Distance: 3.7 miles
Elevation Gain: 690 feet
High Point: 5890 feet
Difficulty: Easy-moderate
GPS: N 46°52.040', W 121°31.108'

Maps: Green Trails Maps No. 269SX
Mount Rainier Wonderland
Managing Agency: Mount Rainier National
Park
Passes: None

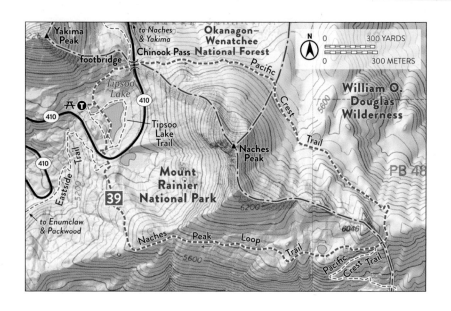

Dog-Friendly: No, not permitted at Tipsoo Lake or the southern side of Naches Peak
Kid-Friendly: Yes

Amenities: Pit toilets and picnic tables at trailhead

Notes: Chinook Pass closes seasonally, so check the park website for updates. This is a fragile alpine environment; stay on designated trails. This loop is very popular—if possible, plan your visit for a weekday or arrive early. If parking at Tipsoo Lake is full, more parking is found by continuing east for 0.3 mile on State Route 410 to a large parking area to the road's left (west). A Northwest Forest Pass or Interagency Pass is required there. From that parking lot, follow the Pacific Crest Trail to the left (east) and across the highway on an overpass with the inscription for the national park.

Getting There: From Enumclaw: Follow SR 410 east for roughly 49.5 miles to just before Chinook Pass. Once at the pass, locate a parking area to the left for Tipsoo Lake (northeast).

From Naches: Follow US Highway 12 westbound for nearly 4.5 miles to a junction with SR 410. Follow SR 410 west for just over 47 miles. Pass Tipsoo Lake and locate the parking area on the lake's western side.

During fall, the open subalpine slopes of this spectacular high country show off fall colors so beautiful that people drive all day just to walk this loop. If you are lucky, you might hear the occasional rutting elk bugling from the valley, watch a sooty grouse foraging along the trail, or observe a black bear on a high hillside eating the last of the berries before her hibernation season. And when Mount Rainier displays its giant snowy glaciers in the southwestern sky, autumn becomes downright captivating here.

Foliage: Cascade huckleberry, grouse whortleberry, mapleleaf currant, oval-leaved huckleberry, rosy spirea, Sitka mountain ash, vine maple

The trail kicks off at the scenic Tipsoo Lake, which in summer has so many wildflowers around its meadow, it's like walking through a fragrant rainbow. This time of year, the lake is still pretty, but the flower stalks near its edges are going dormant, dropping seeds, and coaching their offspring how to carry on their legacy. In Chinook Jargon, a pidgin trading language, the word *Tipsoo* means "grass" or "hair," and it's easy to see why this place was named this, since the meadows around here are plentiful with vegetation. Perhaps the seedpod of the western anemone, which sports a white fluffy hairdo much like an eighties rock star, was also to blame.

The basin below Naches Peak bathed in sunlight and kissed in color is a wondrous feast for the eyes.

Since this is a loop, you can hike it in either direction. I like to hike it clockwise, since Mount Rainier is more visible in this direction and somehow the sections of climbing feel less grueling. For a fun, scenic warm-up, take a 0.5-mile gentle walk around Tipsoo Lake on the various trails. On quiet sunny mornings, Mount Rainier plays peekaboo from the lake's eastern shore while small birds, such as the chest-nut-backed chickadee, flit about searching for sustenance in the changing seasons.

Back near the parking lot, locate a signed trail for Naches Peak Loop heading northeast and (groan) uphill under the shoulders of Yakima Peak. In 0.3 mile, reach a junction where a bridge crosses over SR 410, and continue along the Pacific Crest Trail (PCT) to the east, where you leave Mount Rainier National Park and hop onto national forest land. The William O. Douglas Wilderness welcomes you shortly afterward. Meadows of open hillsides greet you as you traverse along through the Cascade huckleberries, lingering wildflower stalks, and small pockets of subalpine fir trees. In 0.8 mile from crossing the highway (1.1 miles from the trailhead), arrive at an unnamed, twinkling teal pond to the trail's left set in a grassy meadow. The view from the trail makes a breathtaking photo with the crimson huckleberries, the sparkling pond, and the backdrop of Sourdough Gap and rugged peaks in the distance. The pond's small basin has a couple of pleasant places to sit and take a break if you brought the kids or want to marinate in this beauty.

The trail wraps around the meadow-rich shoulders of Naches Peak, which are in full autumn colors with Sitka mountain ash, vine maple, and Cascade huckleberry. In 0.4 mile from the pond (1.5 miles from the trailhead), a viewpoint to the trail's left offers peeks into the Dewey Lake basin, where the PCT continues. Pause, ponder, and photograph! In just a short 0.2 mile from the viewpoint (1.7 miles from the trailhead), reach a trail junction where the PCT makes a hard left and our trail continues onward (westbound). If you are befuddled, just follow the arrow toward Tipsoo Lake. A smaller sign reminds you that no dogs or horses are permitted along the next stretch of trail since you are now headed back into Mount Rainier National Park.

If you haven't been blown away by beauty by now, tighten your laces. The trail climbs a bit, then levels out into some expansive meadows with a scenic tarn sitting right in the middle of the scarlet Cascade mountain and oval-leaved huckleberries and dormant tan stalks of wildflowers. Mount Rainier pops up in the distance while subalpine firs dot the meadow's edges. Wildlife can be anywhere, of course, but this area is a great place to really keep your eyes peeled—especially for black bears, who are somewhat easy to spot against the colorful meadows.

After the tarn, the trail rolls on gently, offering more viewpoints that highlight gorgeous and proud Mount Rainier. The trail begins its descent, and at 1.2 miles from the signed junction with the PCT and Dewey Lake (2.9 miles from the trailhead), another signed junction appears, this time with the Eastside Trail, where you'll want to stay straight (north). This junction may slip by unnoticed since at this point, Tipsoo Lake and the highway are clearly visible. Cross the highway and enjoy Tipsoo Lake once more before meandering back to your waiting ride.

40. UPPER PALISADES LAKE

Distance: 7.2 miles
Elevation Gain: 1720 feet
High Point: 6155 feet
Difficulty: Moderate
GPS: N 46°55.063', W 121°35.254'
Maps: Green Trails Maps No. 269SX: Mount Rainier Wonderland
Managing Agency: Mount Rainier National Park

Passes: National park entrance fee/annual pass or Interagency Pass
Dog-Friendly: No, not permitted
Kid-Friendly: Yes
Amenities: Restrooms at entrance and pit toilets at White River Campground, backcountry toilets along trail

Notes: Sunrise Road is open seasonally most years from late June to mid-October. Concession area and visitor center are open limited daily hours and close for the season shortly after Labor Day. Check road and trail conditions prior to departure. Pets

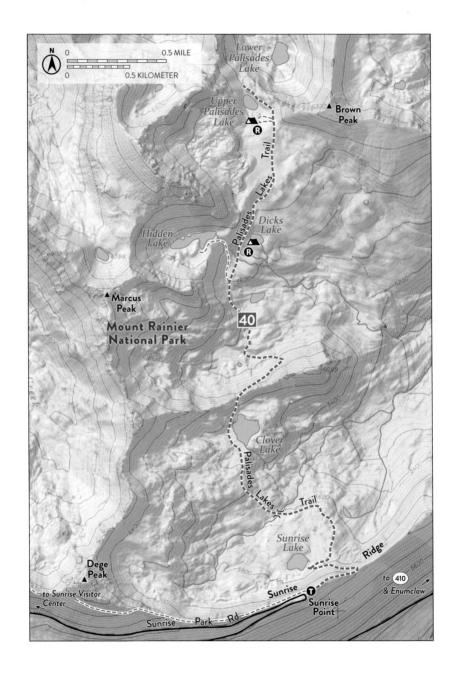

N

0   0.5 MILE

0   0.5 KILOMETER

Lower Palisades Lake

▲ **Brown Peak**

Upper Palisades Lake

R

Palisades Lakes Trail

Dicks Lake

R

Hidden Lake

▲ **Marcus Peak**

Mount Rainier National Park

40

Clover Lake

Palisades Lakes Trail

Sunrise Lake

Ridge

▲ **Dege Peak**

to Sunrise Visitor Center

Sunrise

T **Sunrise Point**

to 410 & Enumclaw

Sunrise — Park — Rd

and pack and saddle animals are prohibited on park trails, with the exception of a few connecting trails where specified. All vehicles are required to carry tire chains when traveling in the park starting on November 1 and must be prepared to use them.

Getting There: From Enumclaw: Follow State Route 410 east for roughly 38 miles to Sunrise/White River Entrance of Mount Rainier National Park. Turn right (southwest) and continue for roughly 12 miles, passing the entrance booth and the turnoff for the White River Campground, until you reach a hairpin turn with a parking area and a viewpoint, known as Sunrise Point. Park here and cross the road to locate the trailhead. Sunrise Lake is visible below.

> One of the great things about this hike is that you'll pass many teaser picturesque lakes before you reach the featured presentation. If you have younger kids or wish for a shorter hike, you could turn back at any of them and still feel like you've reached a worthy destination. You won't find Mount Rainier views on this trail, but rather views of other mountains, framed by azure lakes and fall colors that will spin your head.

 Foliage: Cascade huckleberry, Cascade mountain ash, dwarf bilberry, oval-leaved huckleberry, Sitka mountain ash, vine maple

This hike starts off peculiarly—by going downhill. Switchbacks guide you down talus slopes to the first of four or five lakes (energy and time dependent) that you'll see today. At 0.5 mile, reach a junction with an unmaintained boot path going straight ahead to the shores of Sunrise Lake. To visit it, stay straight (west) and descend a short distance to the water's edge. Back on the main trail, follow a hairpin turn to the right (northeast) at the unsigned boot path and give a look up at Dege Peak west of Sunrise Lake, where mountain goats sometimes hang out.

After the hairpin turn, the trail descends gently through meadows teeming with Cascade huckleberries and dwarf bilberries in the midst of evergreen thickets. Keep your eyes out for wildlife, such as elk or black bears, in the various small meadows, as this area is a popular place for them to feed. At 1.1 miles from the trailhead, cross a short log bridge over the dribbling Sunrise Creek, using caution if it's icy. The trail's grade is gentle, and the cruising easy and mellow.

At 1.5 miles, arrive at Clover Lake, a shallow body of water with forested edges on its far side and quiet meadows on the near side. Scarlet-colored Cascade huckleberries flourish in the open fields to the lake's west, thanks to plenty of light, while the dormant grasses and wildflower stalks offer yellows and tans. The lake twinkles and shines, and a few barren spots near evergreens beg you to stop and enjoy for longer than a minute. If you have the little ones or didn't plan for a long day, this is a perfect turnaround spot.

Otherwise on you go, through thriving berry bushes climbing to a forest ridgeline and then dropping down the other side. This isn't a huge climb—in fact, it's moderate for most trails in the Northwest—but because the path has been so easy until now, it may feel harder than it really is. One foot in front of the other gets you there.

On the other side of the ridgeline, more colorful bushes populate the understory near the forest's edge. Cascade mountain ash as well as several varieties of huckleberries grow near here, and their jewel tones are splendid mixed with the emerald trees and the evergreen shrubs.

The trail passes a couple of creeklets and tarns before it arrives at a signed junction with Hidden Lake Trail to the left at 2.7 miles. Do a quick assessment with your team to see how they are feeling and if you have time and gumption to make a side trip. The roundtrip detour adds 1 mile to your day and an extra 350 feet elevation gain, but it's well worth the effort. Hidden Lake is a gorgeous emerald lake set in a cirque with scree, forest, and meadows lining the edges. Solitude abounds, and peacefulness almost seeps through your pores.

If time is limited, keep going and save Hidden Lake for another visit. In a short distance from the Hidden Lake junction, pass by Dicks Lake to the trail's right

Avoid the busier trails in Mount Rainier National Park by visiting the autumn utopia of the peaceful Upper Palisades Lake.

(east). Dicks Lake Camp is one of the park's many wilderness camps, and if nature is calling, a rustic backcountry toilet is found at the camp. There is also a backcountry toilet at Upper Palisades Lake Camp farther along the trail, so you have options.

Another gradual climb leads to a couple of creeks, or possibly dry creek beds (depending on recent weather), under the stunning ridgeline known as the Palisades because of the protective barrier it offers this basin. Meadows here include some huckleberries, although tan grasses primarily win the color battle.

At 3.5 miles from the trailhead (0.6 mile from Dicks Lake Camp), the trail delivers you to the southeastern edge of Upper Palisades Lake. Depending on the rainfall, the lake might be shallow with a larger shoreline or vice versa. The teal-colored water is a vision underneath a jutting rocky peak, whose shoulders are ablaze in colors from Cascade huckleberry, Sitka and Cascade mountain ash, and vine maple.

Follow the sign to the lake's southern edge where a wilderness camp provides a place to sit, take a load off, and enjoy the views. There is a rustic backcountry toilet here too.

The main trail keeps going north after the camp sign and provides unmaintained access to Lower Palisades Lake, which isn't visited often.

Work your way back on the same trail on which you came after enjoying this colorful and tranquil place.

41. SHRINER PEAK

Distance: 8.4 miles
Elevation Gain: 3440 feet
High Point: 5835 feet
Difficulty: Hard
GPS: N 46°48.135', W 121°33.302'
Maps: Green Trails Maps No. 270: Mount Rainier East

Managing Agency: Mount Rainier National Park
Passes: National park entrance fee/annual pass or Interagency Pass
Dog-Friendly: No, not permitted
Kid-Friendly: No
Amenities: Backcountry toilet along trail

Notes: Cayuse Pass/State Route 123 closes seasonally, so check the park website for updates. During periods of warm weather, this hike can be hot with little shade and no water.

Getting There: From Enumclaw, proceed east on SR 410 for 40.2 miles, passing the Mount Rainier National Park boundary and Sunrise Road to a junction with SR 123. At the fork, stay straight (south) and proceed on SR 123/Cayuse Pass for 7.4 miles to an unsigned pullout on the right (west). The trailhead is marked by a large sign across the road roughly 250 feet to the southeast.

The lookout tower at the top is a noble goal, but the journey, teeming with color, is also enticing.

Not only does this hike lead to one of the four remaining historic fire tower lookouts in Mount Rainier National Park, but it also shows off fall splendor from red vine maple leaves and the variety of huckleberry plants found on its slopes. The views from the hike are outstanding, especially on a sunny day when the mountain is out, but you'll have to work for it. Slow and steady gets you there, and when it does, you'll be grateful you made the climb.

 Foliage: Cascade huckleberry, dwarf bilberry, vine maple

The trail starts off climbing and keeps your heart rate up nearly the whole time. That's okay, though, because there is plenty to see as you get higher and you'll want to stop frequently to take pictures, stare at the magnificent mountain, and

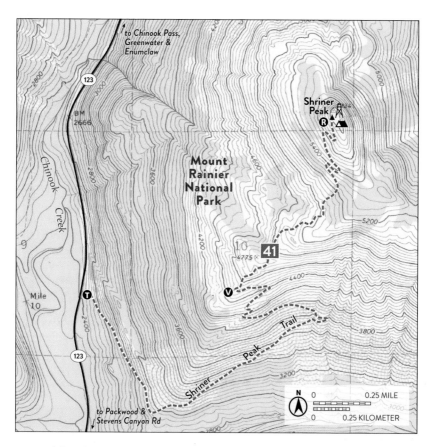

to Chinook Pass,
Greenwater &
Enumclaw

123

BM
2666

Chinook Creek

Mount
Rainier
National
Park

Shriner
Peak

10
4775

41

T

Mile
10

V

123

Shriner Peak Trail

to Packwood &
Stevens Canyon Rd

N   0   0.25 MILE
    0   0.25 KILOMETER

use each break as an excuse to catch your breath. Evergreens, such as Douglas-fir, kick off the hike by shading the path and keeping things chilly.

The trail wraps itself southeast around the lower flanks of an unnamed ridge-line and in 1.7 miles reaches the first official switchback, where the view opens up thanks to an old fire. Vine maples with rust, orange, and burgundy leaves mix with the conifers here as you start your official fall promenade. The path gets slightly less steep now and at 2.6 miles reaches a viewpoint with some well-placed boulders that draw your hindquarters magically toward them. Mount Rainier's Indian Bar basin, with the headwaters of the Ohanapecosh River, is visible from this spot. What a view, but wait, there's more!

Varieties of huckleberries, including Cascade mountain and dwarf, now accentuate the trail's edges, along with more vine maples. Evergreen shrubs, such as white and red mountain heather and beargrass, intermix with the huckleberries, adding some dark green to the scarlet carpets—a fall spectacle!

The trail switches back to the north with outstanding views of the mountain to your left before turning northeast. In summer, wildflowers populate these meadows along with the green leaves of the huckleberries, but this time of year, the huckleberries take over and the wildflowers wither to spread their seeds into the moist soil. This is a perfect place for a photo if you can find a spot where the mountain shows itself in the background between conifer clumps while the red huckleberries make up the foreground. Try bending your knees and changing camera perspective to give the huckleberries more fullness in the bottom part of the frame.

Eventually, the trail turns north for a final, flat push to the tower. What a view and what a place! Mount Rainier, in all its glory, is in full display to the northwest while huckleberry meadows on Shriner and neighboring peaks gloat with fall grandeur. The Shriner Peak lookout, along with so many others in the Pacific Northwest, was built by the Civilian Conservation Corps in the 1930s. Its rustic architecture was standard for national parks at the time and is complete with lower-level storage, upper-level living quarters, full-glass windows for fire spotting, and a surrounding perimeter balcony. Tread lightly on the weathered wood—it takes a beating from the harsh environment.

A wilderness camp with two sites is located here, and camping is available by prearranged backcountry permit. A backcountry toilet is located within the camp if nature calls.

You'll want to stay forever, but what goes up, must come down. Turn back on the same trail when you've taken in the natural bounty of the area.

42. SHEEP LAKE AND SOURDOUGH GAP

Distance: 6 miles
Elevation Gain: 1570 feet
High Point: 6415 feet
Difficulty: Moderate
GPS: N 46°52.522', W 121°31.084'
Maps: Green Trails Maps No. 269SX: Mount Rainier Wonderland

Managing Agency: Mount Baker–Snoqualmie National Forest, Snoqualmie Ranger District
Passes: Northwest Forest Pass or Interagency Pass
Dog-Friendly: Yes, on leash
Kid-Friendly: Yes
Amenities: Pit toilets at trailhead

Notes: Chinook Pass closes seasonally, so check road status before you go.
Getting There: From Enumclaw: Follow State Route 410 east for roughly 50 miles to Chinook Pass. Once at the pass (near Tipsoo Lake) drive 0.3 mile farther and locate a

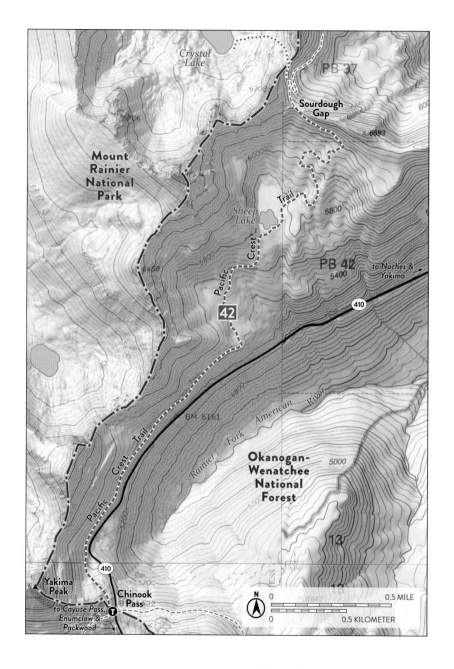

Crystal
Lake

PB 37

Sourdough
Gap

×6593

Mount
Rainier
National
Park

6706

6700

6700

6000

5800

Sheep
Lake

Trail

Crest

5800

Pacific

42

6458

5800

Pacific Crest

PB 42
5400

to Naches &
Yakima

410

4800

Rainier Fork American River

BM 5151

Okanogan-
Wenatchee
National
Forest

5000

5000

Crest Trail

5600

5200

5000

13

Pacific

410

5200

5200

13

Yakima
Peak

Chinook
Pass

to Cayuse Pass,
Enumclaw &
Packwood

T

32

PASS

N

0   0.5 MILE

0   0.5 KILOMETER

large parking area on the left-hand side (west). A signed trailhead connects the parking area with the trail at the lot's northern end.

From Naches: Follow US Highway 12 westbound for nearly 4.5 miles to a junction with SR 410. Follow SR 410 west for just over 47 miles to a large parking area on the right (west).

> Gone are the crowds of day hikers that flock to this place during the busy summer, and in their place, a batch of hardy leafers seek solitude in a color-rich subalpine lake basin. The thru-hikers who started on the Pacific Crest Trail (PCT) at the California-Mexico border are now in a hurry to make it to Canada before winter hides the landscapes in snow. If you see them, give them some encouragement, a fist bump, and some fresh fruit or a special snack if you have extras. Trust me when I say they will appreciate you to no end!

 Foliage: Cascade huckleberry, grouse whortleberry, mapleleaf currant, oval-leaved huckleberry, pearly everlasting, rosy spirea, Sitka mountain ash, vine maple

This portion of the PCT begins by heading northeast across a hillside traverse where vegetation abounds. You might catch a few stalks of pearly everlasting, a tall, perennial, white wildflower that is one of the last lingering species to retain its blooms before winter. Vine maples and Sitka mountain ash also grow here with the abundant sunlight on the boulder-strewn hill. For a stretch, the trail is parallel to the highway, but the noisy cars and civilization are soon forgotten as you turn northwest and duck into the evergreens.

Back and forth you go through evergreens and meadow pockets, climbing steeply at times, until at 1.8 miles, you arrive at Sheep Lake. What a vision this basin is! The shallow emerald lake is set underneath the jagged Chinook Peak and its impressive rocky ridgeline with high buttresses. In fall, the landscape lights up with the orange and yellow tones of Sitka mountain ash and the red and burgundy clusters of Cascade huckleberry leaves. The tones of taupe from dormant grasses and wildflower stalks add to the earth tones as Mother Nature does her best to impress visitors.

One of the best photo locations, depending on the lighting, is from the eastern side near a trickling outlet stream. Shooting back to the west, Chinook Peak and the mountain ridgeline frame the sky while the colorful bushes and tranquil lake stand out in the foreground.

If you are feeling sufficiently tired from the climb to the lake, the campsites around the lake's edges make good places to stretch out, have a nibble, and maybe take a snooze before heading back. But if energy and motivation are on your side, continue walking along the PCT as it climbs out of the lake's basin, high above the northeastern side, where viewpoints show off Goat Rocks to the south as well as

Shallow Sheep Lake basin is a marvelous fall playground and an obtainable destination for most.

the giant ice-cream cone of Mount Adams. Most of Mount Rainier is still hidden from view due to the ridgeline, but its very top peeks out as if playfully spying.

At 1.2 miles from Sheep Lake (3 miles from the trailhead), arrive at a pass known as Sourdough Gap, which was named for the prospectors who mined near here and carried sourdough bread starter from claim to claim. Freshly baked bread in this gorgeous country? Priorities in line! The views here are outstanding and worthy of camera snaps, although it's hard to capture the vastness. This makes a good turnaround spot.

EXTENDING YOUR TRIP

Feel like exploring a little more? Continue walking another 0.1 mile north on the PCT to discover a boot-beaten, unsigned spur that crosses a scree field and connects to the Crystal Lakes Trail in Mount Rainier at the top of the ridge. If you have two cars, you could even make a thru-hike with one car parked at the Crystal Lakes Trailhead and one at the parking area for Sheep Lake. Starting at the Sheep Lake parking area and ending at Crystal Lakes Trailhead would be about 7 miles total and roughly the same elevation gain.

No matter where you stop the hike, you're sure to have a gorgeous day full of soul-refreshing moments when you backtrack to your vehicle.

43. MYRTLE FALLS AND GOLDEN GATE LOOP

Distance: 4.1 miles
Elevation Gain: 1210 feet
High Point: 6400 feet
Difficulty: Moderate
GPS: N 46°47.102', W 121°44.498'
Maps: Green Trails Maps No. 269SX: Mount Rainier Wonderland

Managing Agency: Mount Rainier National Park
Passes: National park entrance fee/annual pass or Interagency Pass
Dog-Friendly: No, not permitted
Kid-Friendly: Yes
Amenities: Restrooms, visitor center, snack bars, gift shop, and lodging

Notes: Watch for sudden changes in weather. Arrive early, as parking can be challenging, especially on weekends. Stock and pets prohibited on park trails. All vehicles are required to carry tire chains when traveling in the park starting on November 1, and you must be prepared to use them.

Getting There: From Ashford, drive 6.3 miles east on State Route 706 to the Nisqually Entrance of Mount Rainier National Park. Enter the park through the entrance booth and proceed 18 miles, passing the Longmire area, and bear left (northwest) at Stevens Canyon Road to remain on Longmire-Paradise Road. Park at one of the parking lots or on the side of the one-way Paradise Valley Road east of Paradise Inn.

The Paradise area in Mount Rainier is one of the most popular places to hike in the fall—and for good reason. But in the fall, when the brilliant Cascade huckleberries, rosy spirea, and Sitka mountain ash line the walkways and the giant volcano is in your face, it's a particularly impressive sight. Because a portion of this trail is paved, those with limited mobility may also be able to enjoy the views.

 Foliage: Cascade huckleberry, dwarf bilberry, pearly everlasting, rosy spirea, Sitka mountain ash

Locate the steps inscribed with the words of John Muir, just outside of the Henry M. Jackson Visitor Center. Hop up them, then turn right (northeast) on the Skyline Trail, which in this section is paved. Leisurely wander through breathtaking burgundy Cascade huckleberry, yellow and orange rosy spirea, and Sitka mountain ash, keeping your eyes open for Columbian black-tailed deer, golden-mantled ground squirrels, and hoary marmots who are getting some delicious foliage bites before winter arrives.

Mount Rainier's showy summit sticks up in the distance as the trail gently ascends and, in 0.5 mile, drops at an easy-to-miss-if-your-eyes-are-on-the-mountain junction to the right (east), to Myrtle Falls. The short, steep descent to the falls viewpoint is the perfect spot for the quintessential Mount Rainier photo with the falls, the mountain, the bridge, the fall foliage, and maybe even a hiker or two. Lighting can be tricky this time of year because of the shadows, but do your best and perhaps try to lighten the shadows with your post-editing tools. Those with tiny tykes or mobility issues might be content to turn back at this spot, while others will want to keep exploring.

Back on Skyline Trail, cross the bridge over Edith Creek, still steeped in gorgeous views and fall foliage until at 0.1 mile from the Myrtle Falls junction (0.6 mile from the trailhead) you reach the Golden Gate Trail to your left (northeast). Sigh, gulp, gag. Yes, those switchbacks are where we are going, but don't fret with

Watch for hoary marmots feeding on lingering berries as you hike along the Golden Gate Trail.

sweat—it's not as bad as it looks. Soothing creeklets bounce playfully nearby, marmots spread out like putty in the sun, and dwarf bilberry intermixes with the deep-green heather and yellowing stalks of dormant wildflowers. Hoary marmots live on this hillside and hibernate deep in their burrows during the cold winter. During fall, they are easy to photograph as they fatten up and gather as much weight as possible to sustain them as the seasons change. With any luck, you might get a cute snap of their little whiskers, white snouts, and buckteeth working their way through berry patches. Even if you don't see any, you'll be sure to hear their loud whistle that sounds straight out of a referee's mouth. As you climb higher, the Tatoosh Range to the south shows up with a ridgeline like shark teeth, and before you know it, you are at a trail junction 0.9 mile from turning off the Skyline Trail (1.5 miles from the trailhead). Here the trail rejoins Skyline Trail, making Golden Gate Trail a welcomingly beautiful shortcut.

At this point you have options. You could turn left (north) and wander higher on the ridge. But instead, go right (south) and begin descending, completing the loop as described here. Alpine scenery takes over, and for a short while, the fall

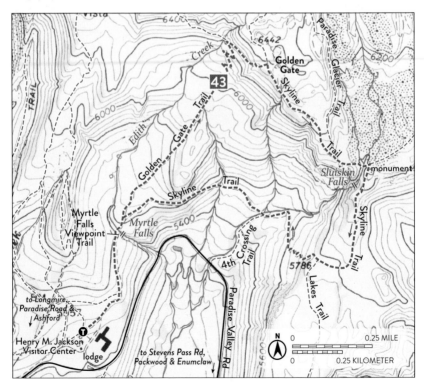

colors are replaced with glacial deposits and small swamps harboring mosses and grasses preparing for winter.

In 0.6 mile from rejoining the Skyline Trail (2.1 miles from the trailhead), arrive at the signed Paradise Glacier Trail heading off to the left (northeast). If time allows, wander down this trail for more alpine landscapes, or make a note to come back another day. For our planned hike, stay straight (southeast), and almost immediately after the junction, arrive at a monument placed at this location in 1921 by The Mountaineers and Mazamas hiking clubs in honor of the first men to reach the summit of Mount Rainier. The stone-and-concrete bench is now over a hundred years old, and with the harsh mountain weather, it's amazing it's still in good shape!

With history spinning in your head, press onward, following the Skyline Trail as it travels through meadows of Cascade huckleberry, Sitka mountain ash, pearly everlasting, rosy spirea, and evergreen shrubs. Pass junctions for the Lakes Trail (2.5 miles from the trailhead), then drop down a small ravine and give a nod to the 4th Crossing Trail junction (2.9 miles from the trailhead) at the bottom. A little effort takes you up the other side of the ravine, then once again pass the junctions with the Golden Gate Trail at 3.5 miles and Myrtle Falls Viewpoint shortly thereafter, until you end up back where you started. Well done! Perhaps some hot chocolate from the visitor center is in order?

Next page: *The relatively gentle trails along the colorful assortment of huckleberry bushes make fall a perfect time to visit Indian Heaven Wilderness.*

INDIAN HEAVEN WILDERNESS

Because of their challenging location, the South Cascades don't see quite the traffic that the North and Central Cascades do, and they make a great mini-getaway, even if you're fortunate enough to already live here. The tiny hamlet of Trout Lake touts a couple of cute lodging options along with a restaurant and coffee shop, making it the perfect base camp to enjoy a romp in this area in style. You only get one lap around life's track—make it count!

44. EAST CRATER LAKES LOOP

Distance: 10.3 miles
Elevation Gain: 1540 feet
High Point: 5015 feet
Difficulty: Moderate
GPS: N 45°58.879', W 121°45.477'
Maps: Green Trails Maps No. 365S: Indian Heaven

Managing Agency: Gifford Pinchot National Forest, Mount Adams Ranger District
Passes: None
Dog-Friendly: Yes, on leash
Kid-Friendly: Yes
Amenities: None

Notes: The road to the trailhead can be washboarded and rough; high-clearance vehicles highly recommended. Muddy conditions on the trail in the fall are common.

Getting There: From the town of Trout Lake, head west on State Route 141 (although the road is signed north, it goes west). After 5.4 miles enter the Gifford Pinchot National Forest, and the road now becomes Forest Road 24. At 7.9 miles, near Peterson Prairie, go straight onto FR 60. In another 1.7 miles (at 9.6 miles from Trout Lake), veer slightly right toward Goose Lake/Carson to remain on FR 60. Continue another 1.7 miles (11.3 miles from Trout Lake) before turning right (northwest) onto FR 6030 toward Forlorn Lakes/East Crater. Continue 4.2 miles (15.5 miles from Trout Lake) on FR 6030, which becomes FR 6035, to reach a parking lot to the right. The trailhead is across the road to the left (west).

Indian Heaven Wilderness is known for its alluring autumn colors, thanks to the abundance of meadows containing oval-leaved and Cascade huckleberry bushes. In fact, people come from near and far in the late summer to secure permits in Gifford Pinchot National Forest for commercial huckleberry harvesting. You might find a few straggler berries on your visit, but in the fall, it's more about color than nibbles.

Foliage: Black cottonwood, Cascade huckleberry, Cascade mountain ash, fool's huckleberry, Oregon ash, oval-leaved huckleberry, red elderberry, rosy spirea, Scouler's willow, serviceberry, shinyleaf spirea, Sitka mountain ash, vine maple

East Crater Trail starts out gaining gentle elevation under a canopy of evergreens mixed with an understory of Cascade huckleberry and wilting stalks of lingering grasses and wildflowers left over from a sunny summer. In just under 0.5 mile, the trail crosses into Indian Heaven Wilderness and continues its climb, crossing seasonal creeks and wetlands on small footbridges.

In the very dry early September of 2017, a fire known as the East Crater Fire started near here, and evidence of it is still very present as you walk through loamy soils. But in just a few short years, the area is starting to rejuvenate, proof of new life after struggles.

At just shy of 1.5 miles, the path levels out, and quiet, shallow ponds show up on either side of the trail where colorful Cascade huckleberry, rosy spirea, and oval-leaved huckleberry landscape the shorelines. In the early summer, this place is swarming with mosquitoes, so count your blessings you are visiting in autumn and able to enjoy it without having pests buzzing by your noggin.

At 2.6 miles, Junction Lake shows up to the trail's right. Near its edges, the orange leaves and red berries of Cascade mountain ash pop up along with Cascade mountain and oval-leaved huckleberry, giving color and energy to the shallow,

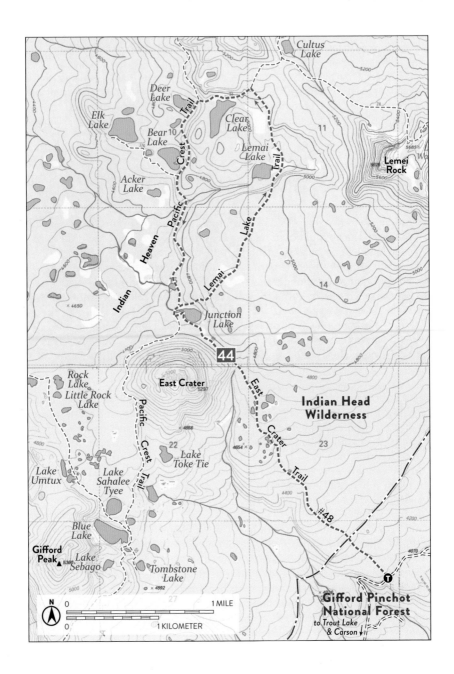

Cultus
Lake

Deer
Lake

Elk
Lake

Bear
Lake

Clear
Lake

Lemai
Lake

Lemei
Rock

Crest Trail

Acker
Lake

11

10

5000

5600

Pacific

Indian

Heaven

Lake

Trail

Lemai

14

× 4650

Junction
Lake

44

East Crater
5297

Rock
Lake

Little Rock
Lake

East

Crater

Indian Head
Wilderness

Pacific

Crest

4800

× 4868

22

Lake
Toke Tie

4654 ×

23

Trail

Lake
Umtux

Lake
Sahalee
Tyee

Trail

#48

4200

Blue
Lake

Gifford
Peak

Lake
Sebago

Tombstone
Lake

4070

5000

27

× 4592

T

**Gifford Pinchot
National Forest**

*to Trout Lake
& Carson*

N

0   1 MILE

0   1 KILOMETER

The hushed waters of Junction Lake take on a tranquil feeling during autumn.

reflective water. Thick groves of fir trees populate the lake's northern shoreline, while the southern is mostly meadows. Turn right (north) on the Pacific Crest Trail (PCT) when the trail you've been following, East Crater 48, dead-ends. In a short distance, turn right (east) again at the west corner of Junction Lake onto Lemei Lake Trail. People with young kiddos or those limited on time might decide this is the end of their day and snap a few pictures before turning back, while others may choose to keep going.

Walk past the northern edge of Junction Lake before ducking into the forest and climbing gently through the woods. Meadows laden with fall colors show up while in the distance Lemei Rock—standing at 5925 feet, the highest point in Indian Heaven Wilderness—is visible to the east. The trail gives you a little reprieve from climbing when it descends into Lemei Lake basin, where the fabulous fall-chromatic-meadow march continues. This time of year, shadows can be tricky with photography, so do your best and perhaps lighten them in the post-editing.

From here the trail climbs 165 feet through the forest to reach a junction with Indian Heaven Trail, located 4.8 miles from where you started.

Turn left (west) and pass the large blue Clear Lake before descending to reach the PCT again where the loop continues. Turn left (south) on the PCT, passing several unnamed shallow lakes and tarns before arriving at a junction with Elk Lake Trail to the trail's right (west) at 5.4 miles. That trail goes to Bear and Elk Lakes and is a worthy 0.8-mile, 55-feet-elevation-gain roundtrip detour, since these are two of the largest, most tranquil forested lakes in this wilderness. Sit by the shoreline for a moment and crack open that thermos you brought if the mood hits.

If a visit with Bear and Elk Lakes is not in the cards, continue southbound in wooded terrain on the PCT, crossing several creeklets or dry stream beds (weather dependent) before arriving back at Junction Lake and East Crater Trail. Stop and enjoy the place once more—you've earned it after 7.7 miles of hiking so far!

Retrace your steps back down East Crater Trail before arriving at the trailhead tired but happy.

45. THOMAS, BLUE, AND TOMBSTONE LAKES

Distance: 7 miles
Elevation Gain: 1020 feet
High Point: 4150 feet
Difficulty: Moderate
GPS: N 46°00.344', W 121°50.347'
Maps: Green Trails Maps No. 365S: Indian Heaven

Managing Agency: Gifford Pinchot National Forest, Mount Adams Ranger District
Passes: Northwest Forest Pass or Interagency Pass
Dog-Friendly: Yes, on leash
Kid-Friendly: Yes
Amenities: Pit toilet at trailhead

Notes: High-clearance vehicle required to get to the trailhead, or park near the washout and add roughly 4.4 miles roundtrip to the hike. Very muddy conditions on the trail are common in the fall. Distance varies depending on how many lakes you visit; trail description here includes the main trail all the way to Tombstone Lake and back. This trail is very popular on weekends, and parking can be full. Arrive early and use caution if parking on road's edges.

Getting There: From the town of Trout Lake, head west on State Route 141 (although the road is signed north, it actually goes west). After 5.4 miles, enter the Gifford Pinchot National Forest, and the road now becomes Forest Road 24. At 7.9 miles, near Peterson Prairie, go straight onto FR 60. In another 1.7 miles (9.6 miles from Trout Lake), veer slightly right toward Goose Lake/Carson to remain on FR 60. Continue another 10.2 miles (19.8 miles from Trout Lake) before coming to a four-way intersection known as Four Corners. Turn right (northwest) here onto FR 65 and drive for 1.9 miles to a Y (21.7 miles from Trout Lake). Veer right (north) and go another roughly 4.5 miles (26.2 miles from Trout Lake) to a large washout in the road. High-clearance vehicles and a driver with moxie can clear this without issue, but passenger cars likely will not. If your vehicle can

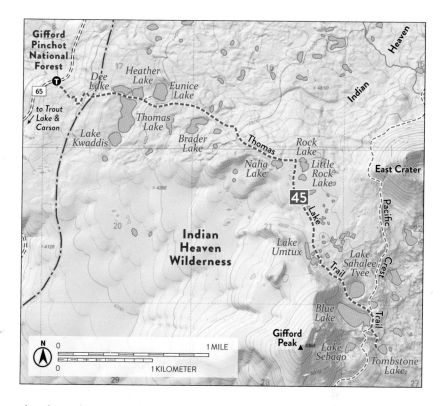

clear the washout, proceed 2.2 miles farther (northeast) and locate the trailhead on the road's right (east). If you have a passenger car, park near the washout and walk the 2.2 miles farther up the road to the trailhead on the right, located 28.4 miles from Trout Lake.

Another option if you can't clear the washout is to approach this hike from the community of Stabler by following the Wind River Road/Wind River Highway northbound for just over 20 miles, during which its name changes to Meadow Creek Road. Turn right (southeast) on FR 6507 and proceed 4.2 miles; turn left (northeast) on FR 65. The trailhead is on your right in 0.5 mile.

Despite this area being somewhat remote, it gets a lot of use and can be busy and, also, wet and muddy. So why go? When fall color is in its prime, the meadows in this area are tapestries of reds, oranges, tans, and yellows—a wonderful place to rest the eyes and restore the soul. Throw a few shallow lakes into the mix and it's a grand place to enjoy a backcountry outing before the snow falls.

Wind ripples the water of Blue Lake while fog engulfs the sky.

Foliage: Cascade huckleberry, Cascade mountain ash, fool's huckleberry, oval-leaved huckleberry, red elderberry, rosy spirea, Scouler's willow, serviceberry, shinyleaf spirea, Sitka mountain ash, vine maple

Kick off your hike by following the trail eastbound, through an old clear-cut. Mother Nature has done a great job taking over with oval-leaved huckleberry, fool's huckleberry, and Sitka mountain ash along with grasses, saplings, and much larger evergreens. It's a first taste of a smattering of fall colors to whet your appetite.

A gentle climb gains 210 feet under a forest canopy before arriving at Dee and Heather Lakes to the left and Thomas Lake to the right, at 0.7 mile. Just beyond Thomas Lake, the trail splits. Straight ahead would take you down a small spur trail to Eunice Lake, while right (southeast) takes you toward Blue Lake, one of our destinations.

A little climbing follows, eventually leveling out in a grassy, broad meadow, where Cascade huckleberry, oval-leaved huckleberry, rosy spirea, and other shrubs carpet the ground with burgundy, tan, green, and orange. You'll see more meadows up ahead, with more of the same colorful foliage, so snap a few shots and continue. The area is dotted with swampy areas, tarns, and small, shallow lakes, and you can count your blessings that you are visiting in autumn when the mosquitoes are mostly gone. This area can swarm!

East Crater Peak is visible through the trees, giving you a slight perspective of height in this flat, open landscape while the shallow Naha Lake, which is more like a pond, shows up to the trail's right. The shoreline of Naha Lake can be quite colorful, and waterfowl such as buffleheads and mallards are often seen skimming for food—a gorgeous photo if the lighting is in your favor.

The kaleidoscope of colorful meadows continues, and at 2 miles, the trail gets confusing and seems to dead-end at Rock Lake and Little Rock Lake. The two lakes are more like delicate, shallow ponds set in meadows populated with groves of firs, and are visions in fall. Stop and snap pictures, then double-check your bearings. The official trail makes a hard right (south) here and has befuddled many a hiker.

Pick your way through more gorgeous, multicolored meadows and the often muddy and swampy trail before arriving at Lake Sahalee Tyee to the trail's left at 3 miles. While it looks like a pretty body of water, it holds a little secret. It's actually the crater of an ancient volcano! American Indians spent a lot of time in this area building trenches for slow-burning fires, which helped with berry preservation. The lake's name, translated from Chinook Jargon, a pidgin trading language, means "the chief's high, heavenly ground."

Very shortly after passing Lake Sahalee Tyee, the forest escorts you to the beautiful, large, and deep Blue Lake to the trail's right, where camps in the area make fine places to open up the thermos and have a picnic. The lake's southwestern shoreline has a few vine maples tucked into the scree field, colorful backdrops to the teal lake.

At 3.5 miles, the trail meets up with the Pacific Crest Trail, where you might meet a few effervescent thru-hikers who are cruising as fast as possible to get to Canada before the snow flies. Greet them with fist bumps or, better yet, a banana and watch their faces light up. These hardy souls have likely walked here from Mexico and have been on this trail for months; fresh fruit is akin to currency.

If time, energy, and curiosity are still on your side, turn right (south) and look for a short spur trail that heads left (southeast) a short 0.5 mile (1 mile roundtrip if you go all the way to the spur's end) to Tombstone Lake. Don't get the creeps; Tombstone was named for a rock that sticks out of the lake, not a burial site. Whew, so that's good. Now, off you go, backtracking to where you left your car.

Opposite: *Vine maples burst into shades of yellow along the White Pass Byway Loop (Scenic Drive 7).*

SCENIC DRIVES

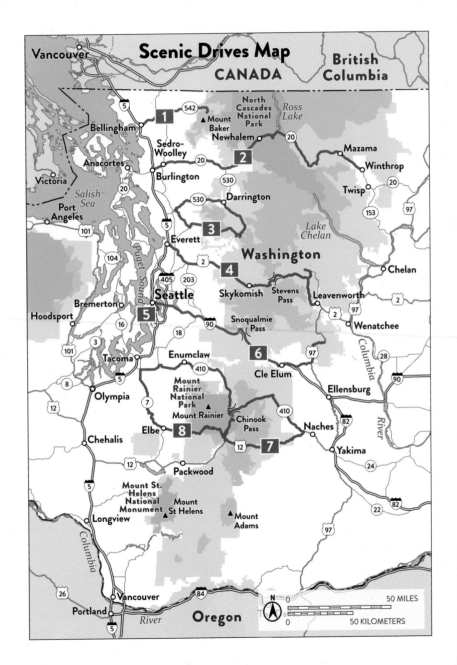

Scenic Drives Map

Vancouver

CANADA

British Columbia

5

1 542 ▲ Mount Baker

North Cascades National Park

Ross Lake

Bellingham

Sedro-Woolley

Newhalem 20

Mazama

Winthrop

Anacortes

20

Burlington

20

2

Victoria

Salish Sea

20 530

530 **Darrington**

Twisp 20

153 97

Port Angeles

101

5 **Everett**

3

Lake Chelan

104

2

Washington

Chelan

105

405 203

Seattle

4

Skykomish

Stevens Pass

Leavenworth

2 97

Bremerton

5

90 **Snoqualmie Pass**

2 **Wenatchee**

Hoodsport

101

16

18

3

Puget Sound

97 **6**

28

Columbia

90

Tacoma

5

Enumclaw

410

Cle Elum

Ellensburg

82

8

Olympia

7

Mount Rainier National Park

▲ **Mount Rainier**

410 **6**

Chinook Pass

Naches

River

12 101

Elbe

8

12 **7**

Yakima

Chehalis

24

12

Packwood

Mount St. Helens National Monument

▲ **Mount St Helens**

▲ **Mount Adams**

82

22

97

5

26

Longview

Columbia

84

N

0 **50 MILES**

Vancouver

Portland

River

5

Oregon

0 **50 KILOMETERS**

SCENIC DRIVES

Washington showcases autumn in glamorous ways throughout the backcountry. However, I'd be remiss not to recognize the incredible places you can enjoy the changing colors, vistas, and wayside pullouts via your wheels! Pack your thermos, snacks, and camera, and fuel up for a full day of eye-popping scenery.

1. ARTIST POINT AND MOUNT BAKER

Roundtrip Distance from Bellingham: 120 miles
Estimated Trip Duration: Half day
Communities with Services: Bellingham, Deming, Kendall, Maple Falls, Glacier
Attractions: Fall colors, volcano, mountain views, small towns, farmlands
Passes for Stops or Entrances: None
Notes: Double-check road conditions at the Washington State Department of Transportation website, as area closes seasonally with the first significant snowfall.

The drive to Artist Point is unquestionably one of the most scenic in the state during the summer, but in the fall, one might argue it's the absolute best. If you happen to get a sunny day, or at least one with high clouds, you'll not only get to see the rugged Mount Shuksan, but you'll also find that beneath the peak, shrubs burst with all the colors of the season, making drive-by photography easy and plentiful. This area is very popular and for good reason. Plan your trip on a weekday if possible.

 Foliage: Bigleaf maple, black alpine sedge, Cascade huckleberry, Cascade mountain ash, oval-leaved huckleberry, rosy spirea, sedge, Sitka mountain ash, vine maple

From I-5 in Bellingham, take exit 255 for State Route 542/E. Sunset Drive. Head east and merge onto Mount Baker Highway (SR 542). Follow the highway past the stoplights in Bellingham, cruising through verdant farmlands as you make your way northeast.

In roughly 21 miles, reach the hamlet of Deming, where you might make note of the North Fork Brewery to the road's left; it's a great place to stop for a nibble and a libation on the way back home. Most cellular phones have limited reception from this point until you get up higher near Mount Baker Ski Area, so be sure you take care of any necessary phone needs while you can.

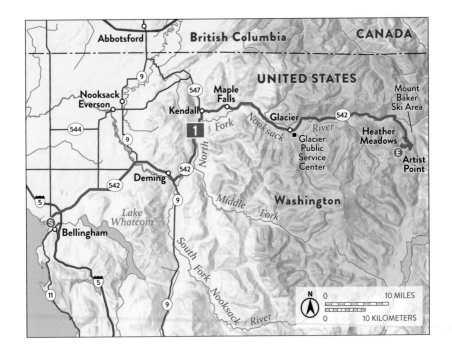

Remain on SR 542, and at roughly 23.5 miles from turning off I-5, take the first right at the roundabout to stay on SR 542. The area you are in is known locally as Kendall, part of the Maple Falls community. Services, such as gas stations and small grocers or mini marts, are located both here and farther east, in the center of Maple Falls. If you need fuel, these two areas are your last opportunities before the road ends near Artist Point.

Onward you go, now heading directly east and winding your way past more services until you reach the small borough of Maple Falls, a sleepy foothills community. After Maple Falls, the roadway feels enclosed in evergreens until it finds its way to the North Fork of the Nooksack River, where it opens up under a golden canopy of bigleaf maple trees. When the leaves are in full color, it's tempting to stop and grab a photo; however, this single-lane highway has limited shoulders, so photography can be tricky. There are more opportunities ahead, so don't fret.

At 34 miles (7.5 miles from Maple Falls), pass the quiet community of Glacier. If timing works out and you need a pick-me-up, there are a couple places to grab a bite or a cup of coffee.

Travel another 0.5 mile from Glacier and note the Glacier Public Service Center to your right, a worthy stop. This building is staffed jointly by the United States Forest Service (USFS) and national park rangers, and it offers exhibits and information on hiking, climbing, and camping in the vicinity. A stop at the service center will also allow you to photograph the bigleaf maples along the highway.

From here, the highway winds around and climbs to eye-popping views of various distant peaks. Please use extreme caution when gawking, since roadways are narrow and winding with occasional drop-offs. Turnoff spots are in short supply, but sometimes you can get lucky.

Just shy of 21 miles beyond the Glacier Public Service Center (55.5 miles from Bellingham) and past Mount Baker Ski Area, arrive at a one-way loop, where you'll go right (west/southwest). This area is called Heather Meadows and is simply breathtaking with autumn colors and two picturesque lakes. Pull the car off in one of the base area parking lots, or in a safe roadside spot, and take a short stroll to the lakes. Cascade huckleberry, rosy spirea, and Sitka mountain ash add to the colorful shorelines and hillsides while Mount Shuksan stands prominently to the southeast. The Forest Service has worked hard at restoring delicate vegetation damaged by footpaths, so please stay on established trails and respect the restoration areas. When composing photos, if lighting, weather, and wind are in your favor, it is possible to get a reflection of Mount Shuksan in the water, but you'll also

Shots like this one near Heather Meadows are possible just a few steps away from your car.

need to be lucky—fingers crossed! Even if you can't, the giant distant peak is still a vision to use as a backdrop to the fall colors. The hillsides near here are often good places to see black bears, so keep a keen eye out.

Back on the road, continue following SR 542 past the lakes until you reach Austin Pass picnic area to the road's right (northwest). If you brought a sack lunch and need a place to stop, this is a fantastic location. A small lake near here has several spur trails to quiet, private picnic table sites that offer great views of Table Mountain high above the valley. The seasonally open Heather Meadows Visitor Center is located in this area and worth checking out if it's operating. Be sure to snap a few pictures from the Bagley Lakes viewpoint area, just down the hill from the visitor center, and plan time to come back and hike at some point (Hike 2, Chain Lakes Loop).

In 23.5 miles from Glacier Public Service Center (roughly 58 miles from Bellingham), the road ends in the Artist Point parking lot, where a pit toilet is available. Short trails near here offer various opportunities to stretch your legs and take in spectacular mountain views, but most of the fall-colored foliage is a little lower in elevation from this point. This is the end of the road, so turn back when you've seen the beauty and follow the same route homeward.

2. NORTH CASCADES HIGHWAY

Roundtrip Distance from Burlington: 270 miles
Estimated Trip Duration: Full day
Communities with Services: Burlington, Sedro-Woolley, Concrete, Rockport, Marblemount, Mazama, Winthrop
Attractions: Small towns (see Resources for a walking map of Newhalem), mountains, viewpoints, North Cascades National Park.
Passes for Stops or Entrances: None
Notes: This highway closes seasonally with snow; check on its status before you go (see Resources).

When you have the whole day and you want to bombard your eyes with mountain views and gorgeous scenery, this is the drive for you. It's not quite as autumn-ish as some, but it gives you the opportunity to see larch trees without having to do much work. What's more, the jagged "alps" of this area will burn up your camera, especially as they get a slight snow dusting in late season.

 Foliage: Bigleaf maple, black cottonwood, subalpine larch, western larch

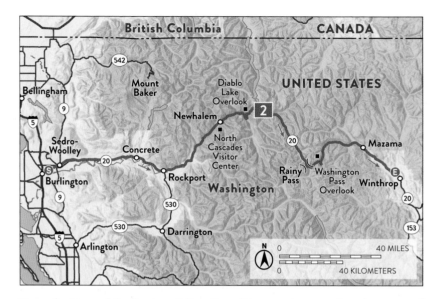

From the town of Burlington, follow State Route 20 east, passing the towns of Sedro-Woolley and Concrete, to arrive in the tiny community of Rockport in about 37 miles.

To the right side of the road, the mighty Skagit River ebbs and flows, providing lush shoreline for black cottonwood and red alder to display their turning leaves.

This diverse ecosystem is one of the only rivers to have all five salmon species (pink, chinook, chum, coho, sockeye) consistently returning to spawn, and because of that, it has the highest concentration of eagles during the salmon spawn in the lower 48 states. The eagles usually start arriving in late November, but a few eager ones always show up early, so watch high in the limbs as you travel.

The town of Marblemount is up next, located about 5 miles east of Rockport. The last of the services, such as gas and food, are found here before heading into the rugged North Cascades Mountains, so fill up.

At about 15 miles beyond the town of Marblemount (57 miles from Burlington), the North Cascades Visitor Center is a great place to stop and learn more about the area. Open seasonally until the end of September, its exhibits, displays, and videos offer education about wildlife, forest management, and local history.

The community of Newhalem arrives next, owned by Seattle City Light and populated entirely by employees of the Skagit River Hydroelectric Project. The old locomotive that ran here, known as *Old Number Six*, played a key part in the hydroelectric project and is on display for all to see. If time permits, download a walking map of the historic town and wander through the 1-mile-roundtrip Trail

The first snowfall of the season crowns the spires and valleys as seen from Washington Pass Overlook.

of the Cedars nature walk, located at the suspension bridge in Newhalem. It parallels the banks of the Skagit River and shows off a few gorgeous bigleaf maples amongst the western red cedars.

From here onward, you will be gawking in all directions at waterfalls, jagged mountains, and photo-worthy sights. As you drive through the mossy forests, you'll cross the Thunder Arm branch of Diablo Lake. In 13.4 miles from Newhalem (72 miles from Burlington), stop by the Diablo Lake Overlook to the road's left (north) and enjoy sweeping views of the gorgeous jade Diablo and Ross Lakes and their many coves, sheltered by the giant mountain fortresses. Some call the North Cascades the Alps of America, and here you'll see why. This area has a lot of green and is not the best representation of autumn, save for the dusting of snow in higher peaks, but just wait! Ahead is the highlight of the drive!

There are plenty of gorgeous mountains, such as Whistler to the road's left (north), to fix your gaze on as you traverse Rainy Pass and start down the other side. This book includes several recommended hikes in this area, if time and oomph are available (see the North Cascades section). At 102 miles from Burlington (41.8 miles from Newhalem), arrive at the Washington Pass Overlook to the road's left (north). What a place and what a sight! You may want to get out and follow the paved pathway to a series of railings atop rocky outcrops with panoramic views of the highway along with sheer cliffs below rugged peaks, such as Kangaroo Ridge, Early Winter Spires, and Liberty Bell Mountain. Larches, with their yellow needles, dot the slopes under the ridges, providing a true burst of autumn in the North Cascades. The pathway around the overlook continues but climbs some precarious steps and uneven surfaces as it loops back to the car, a round-trip of 0.25 mile. Those with mobility challenges will likely opt to follow the paved path back the way they came, knowing that they've seen what they came for.

From here, follow the North Cascades Highway (SR 20) farther east, passing the little community of Mazama to the western-themed town of Winthrop, 30 miles beyond the overlook (132 miles from Burlington). This quaint town is the perfect place to end the drive, with plenty of lodging, dining, and shopping before heading back the way you came.

EXTENDING YOUR TRIP

For a much longer drive, make a giant loop by following SR 20 south, then continuing straight on SR 153. At the town of Pateros, hop onto I-97 and follow it to Wenatchee, where it turns into US Highway 2. From here, head west on US 2, past the towns of Cashmere, Dryden, and eventually Leavenworth. Continue on US 2 as it passes the beautiful Tumwater Canyon and Stevens Pass areas before eventually arriving back on I-5 at Everett. Northbound heads back to Burlington; south takes you to Seattle and beyond. This way adds about 260 miles to your trip but eliminates having to backtrack over the North Cascades Highway. If you do the big loop you'll be cruising approximately 400 miles in total.

3. MOUNTAIN LOOP HIGHWAY

Roundtrip Distance from Granite Falls: 133 miles
Estimated Trip Duration: Full day
Communities with Services: Lake Stevens, Granite Falls, Darrington, Arlington, Marysville
Attractions: Small towns, rivers, mountain vistas, maple trees
Passes for Stops or Entrances: Northwest Forest Pass or Interagency Pass

The Mountain Loop Highway has a primitive feeling as it winds its way near river valleys and flirts with mountain views. Steeped in mining and logging history, today the drive offers places to picnic, enjoy changing maple leaves, and spend some time absorbing the backcountry right from the car interior. A portion of this drive is on unpaved roads, but passenger cars can make it. Pack a lunch or find some delicious eats on either end—Granite Falls or Darrington—and enjoy the day!

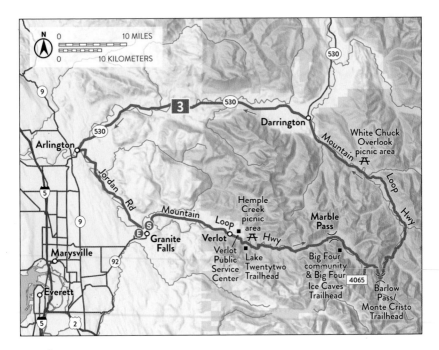

 Foliage: Bigleaf maple, vine maple

From the town of Granite Falls, follow State Route 92 east for 0.3 mile until you reach N. Alder Avenue, also signed for Darrington and Monte Cristo. Turn left (north) on Alder and proceed for a short distance until the road becomes the Mountain Loop Highway. Follow the Mountain Loop Highway under a canopy of evergreens and past small-town homesteads until it enters the Mount Baker–Snoqualmie National Forest and reaches the Verlot Public Service Center to the road's left (northeast) in 10.9 miles.

The Verlot Public Service Center was built by the Civilian Conservation Corps (CCC) in the mid-1930s as a headquarters for the Monte Cristo Ranger District. These days, it serves as a visitor information center offering exhibits and details on hiking, camping, and other recreational opportunities in the area. During fall, hours are limited to 8:00 AM to 3:30 PM on weekends; check it out if your timing allows.

From here, the road begins passing popular trailheads such as Heather Lake and Lake Twentytwo (Hike 14), which are lovely adventures for another day, or perhaps a combined jaunt. In 0.1 mile beyond the signed Lake Twentytwo Trailhead (13.1

miles from Granite Falls), Hemple Creek picnic area is a pleasant place to stop with a sack lunch or to check out the South Fork Stillaguamish River. A few bigleaf maple trees adorn the adjacent banks near here, although photo buffs might find the lighting tricky since the shady valley isn't always cooperative.

Several pullouts offer river views on the opposite side of the road, complete with gorgeous vine and bigleaf maples, which shimmy in the wind near the river's edge. Photo opportunities abound—just use extreme caution when crossing the road and standing on its edges, since cars come whipping around corners.

The road passes Marble Pass, the site of a yesteryear aerial mining tram and the little community known as Silverton, which was lively in the late 1800s and early 1900s as mining boomed in Monte Cristo. These days a few cabins remain as a quiet reminder of the bustling past, but you'll probably zip by them without much thought to history.

At 26 miles from Granite Falls, the Big Four community appears on the road's right and is worth a visit. In the 1920s, a lavish hotel known as the Big Four Inn was built in this area and was known far and wide as a wealthy vacationer's retreat for enjoying the wilderness experience with all the luxuries of extravagant conveniences, including tennis courts and a nine-hole golf course. But as so often happened in those days, the place burned to the ground in September 1949. Today you can visit the Big Four picnic area and see the remaining foundations and chimney of the inn, letting your mind drift back to a different time. The picnic area is a good place to pull out the thermos of coffee and enjoy the valley.

Big Four Ice Caves Trail is located here and, at just over 2 miles roundtrip, is a good one for leg stretches, if it's accessible. (In 2019 the bridge over the river washed out and the road to the trail, as well as the trail itself, has been closed, although it's rumored to reopen soon.) If you are able to visit, do not go into the caves, as they are unstable and have sadly claimed a life in recent years.

Back on the road, you'll find that campgrounds in these areas are usually closed and abandoned by early autumn, and the quietness as you pass them seems to fit the mood of the changing season. Nearly 4 miles from the Big Four turnout, Forest Road 4065 to the road's right (south) is a good detour for leaf-peeping vine and bigleaf maples, especially as it crosses various creeks.

The Mountain Loop Highway continues until it reaches Barlow Pass, 30.5 miles from Granite Falls. A trail in this area (8 miles roundtrip) leads to the abandoned ghost town of Monte Cristo, a large former mining camp where a thousand people lived in the late 1800s. Mining operations came to a halt in 1907, when geologists and seasoned miners discovered that they'd misjudged the depth of the minerals and most were only surface deposits. Very few structures remain, but it's still quite popular to explore here.

At 30.8 miles from Granite Falls, the pavement you've been following ends, and for the next 14 miles the road is gravel, narrow, and poor quality at times. Potholes slow your progress substantially, but taking your time both saves your car and allows you to enjoy the forested scenery. At 2.3 miles from the pavement-to-gravel transition, a scenic pond and marsh on both sides of the road offer interesting views.

The evergreens continue, but as you get closer to Darrington, they mix with some bigleaf maples and a smattering of forest understory plants such as thimbleberry, which, in their dormancy, start producing yellow and brown tones.

Just prior to the gravel's end, a pullout goes to White Chuck Overlook, a picnic area, and a pit toilet, which thankfully is usually open, even in fall. The overlook contains a scenic viewpoint along with an interpretive sign noting the days of timber harvest that took place here from the 1920s through the 1950s.

Eventually, the gravel road turns back to pavement and guides you beyond the Mount Baker–Snoqualmie National Forest and into the quaint town of Darrington, roughly 53 miles from Granite Falls. If time and tummy warrant, there are a couple places to grab a nibble or a cup of joe.

When you've finished enjoying Darrington, you have options. To return to Granite Falls and close the loop, turn left on SR 530 westbound and continue for

Bigleaf maple leaves dance in the sunshine along a rustic stretch of the Mountain Loop Highway.

almost 27 miles, then turn left (east) onto Arlington Heights Road for 0.9 mile. Turn right (south) onto Jordan Road and arrive in Granite Falls after another 11.3 miles. If you want a more direct route to I-5 from Darrington, turn left on SR 530 west and continue for 32.2 miles to where you can pick up I-5 and head north toward Bellingham or south toward Seattle.

4. STEVENS PASS, TUMWATER CANYON, AND LEAVENWORTH

Roundtrip Distance from Everett: 220 miles
Estimated Trip Duration: Full day
Communities with Services: Monroe, Sultan, Startup, Gold Bar, Index, Skykomish, Stevens Pass Ski Area, Leavenworth
Attractions: Fall colors, mountains, small towns, farms
Passes for Stops or Entrances: Discover Pass for Wallace Falls and Lake Wenatchee State Parks, Northwest Forest Pass or Interagency Pass for Lake Valhalla

When the crisp fall air rolls in on the breeze and the first snowfalls grace the tippy tops of high peaks—to the mountains you go! This drive showcases life in small towns outlined by the rugged peaks of the Central Cascades, which are ignited with chromatic spectrums of colors. The roaring Wenatchee River, engorged with the rainfalls of autumn storms, guides you through colorful Tumwater Canyon to the Bavarian-themed town of Leavenworth, which is an attraction all in itself. This drive is truly a fantastic way to celebrate the season.

 Foliage: Bigleaf maple, black cottonwood, Cascade huckleberry, Cascade mountain ash, Scouler's willow, shinyleaf spirea, vine maple, western larch

From the city of Everett, drive east on US Highway 2 for 15 miles to the city of Monroe, a good place to get fuel and snacks before heading off again. The smaller mountain towns ahead will also have services, but this is the last decent-sized community before you get to Leavenworth.

The busy US 2 continues east next to the Skykomish River, where a keen eye can often spot birds of prey such as bald eagles or red-tailed hawks sitting high in the black cottonwood trees. Yellow leaves abound when the trees are in prime season.

Next, the highway passes through the small towns of Sultan and Startup before reaching the town of Gold Bar, whose name, like so many in the area, came from mineral prospectors. If time, energy, and gumption permit, a visit to Wallace Falls State Park near here offers 12 miles of forested trails, including its main feature,

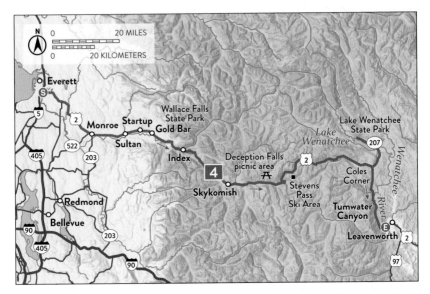

the 265-foot waterfall. If it's only the waterfall that you seek, a moderate roundtrip hike of 5.6 miles gets you there and back and perhaps eases some of your preemptive guilt for the bratwurst gnashing you might be planning to do in Leavenworth.

After Gold Bar, pass the itty-bitty community of Index, named after Mount Index, a popular area for rock climbing. The Espresso Chalet, located at milepost 36 to the road's right (south), is a fun stop. The snacks, pastries, coffee, and ice cream are delicious, and the Bigfoot theme is just plain fun. A small gift shop sells Bigfoot souvenirs, even "Bigfoot hair," since the area was used as an actual filming location for the 1987 movie *Harry and the Hendersons*. A snap of you posing next to the 14-foot-tall wood carving of Bigfoot Harry makes a delightfully ridiculous picture.

The town of Skykomish is next, up off the main road to the right (south). Roughly 8.5 miles east of Skykomish near milepost 56 (57.5 miles from Everett), you'll find Deception Falls picnic area on the north side of the highway. It closes seasonally, usually after Labor Day, but it's occasionally open later in the year. If it's open, stroll the 0.5-mile loop around the thundering cascades; the path is easy enough that most folks, even those with limited mobility, will be able to enjoy most, if not all, of it. The parking lot contains a pit toilet and a picnic area.

From here all the way to Stevens Pass Ski Area, the fall colors pop! The majority of color is thanks to its abundance of vine maples in reds, oranges, and yellows that mingle with the evergreen trees and shrubs to create a mosaic of colors that will make you want to slow down. Use extreme caution when slowing or stopping, though, since this highway is winding, fast, and busy.

The Stevens Pass Ski Area, located nearly 65 miles from Everett, is a good place to stop, stretch the legs, snap some pictures, and use the pit toilet in the parking area if nature is calling. Stevens Pass has limited services in fall, but it does offer some snack bar and dining options, depending on the day and time. Make a mental note to come back to this area and hike to Lake Valhalla (Hike 22) another day.

For now, onward and eastward! After you leave Stevens Pass, the scenery changes, and it becomes quite obvious that you are now on the drier side of the Cascades. Pine trees of several varieties show up, as do more sun-loving vine maples. At just over 20 miles from Stevens Pass (85 miles from Everett), arrive at what is known as Coles Corner, with a few services as well as signs pointing left (northeast) to Lake Wenatchee State Park. If you have time, turn left on SR 207 and follow it for 4 miles to Cedar Brae Road. Go left (west) and proceed to the park's entrance. With

Fall is showcased in brilliant colors as you drive through the Tumwater Canyon.

492 acres and a 5-mile-long lake, there is plenty to see. Leaf-peepers will enjoy the shimmering black cottonwood trees, the Scouler's willow, the shinyleaf spirea, and the Cascade mountain ash from the shorelines and the walking paths.

When you've enjoyed Lake Wenatchee sufficiently, trace your path back to Coles Corner and continue on US 2 (south), beginning your descent into what is known as Tumwater Canyon, one of the most popular fall foliage viewing areas in the state. The twisting and winding road hugs Wenatchee River tightly, so use extreme caution when gawking. Several pullouts offer better views. In late July of 1994, wildfire swept across this landscape, burning fast and extremely hot, but thankfully, shrubs and trees have come back to give life to this otherwise black-and-white area. The show stealer, as it was on Stevens Pass, is the lively vine maple that tucks itself onto the burned hillsides and around the rushing water's edges. Bigleaf maple, black cottonwood, and western larch show up too, with yellow and gold colors. As you get even closer to Leavenworth, Douglas maple, Nootka rose, quaking aspen, Scouler's willow, and red elderberry grow on fire-scalded hillsides and dry canyon walls.

In 15 miles from Coles Corner (35 miles from Stevens Pass; 100 miles from Everett), arrive in the cozy, Bavarian-themed town of Leavenworth. Bratwurst, pretzels, and sauerkraut await, along with plenty of other dining and shopping options. In the fall, Leavenworth hosts the Autumn Leaf Festival, which features live music, food booths, and a grand parade, all to honor the changing season.

Walk off the bursting belly by checking out Leavenworth's Waterfront Park, with easy, flat riverside trails and plenty of birding opportunities. You can walk from downtown or find closer parking. To get there, follow 9th Street southeast (turn right off US 2, going eastbound), and then go right on Commercial Street (southwest). In a block and a half, look for a parking area to the road's left (south). Stroll to your heart's content amidst black cottonwoods, willows, and vine maples. Alternatively, you could continue eastbound onto US 97 and catch Blewett Pass (Drive 6) southbound for a big loop through Cle Elum and North Bend to I-5. Whatever you do, drive safely and enjoy your continuing romp with fall.

5. SEWARD PARK AND WASHINGTON PARK ARBORETUM

Driving Distance from I-90 near Rainier Avenue S.: 15 miles
Estimated Trip Duration: Half day
Communities with Services: Seattle
Attractions: Lake Washington views, Mount Rainier views, fall colors, urban landscapes
Passes for Stops or Entrances: Fee required for Seattle Japanese Garden

When you are in the mood for a scenic drive and also feel like taking a trip to the city, or perhaps you already live in Seattle, look no further than a meandering road from park to park, complete with gorgeous marine views, fall foliage, and plenty of places to stretch your legs and snap pictures to your heart's content.

 Foliage: Bigleaf maple, black cottonwood, cherry trees, fool's huckleberry, Garry oak, Japanese maples, Oregon ash, Pacific dogwood, red elderberry, red-osier dogwood, Scouler's willow, vine maple

From near I-90 in Seattle, follow Rainier Avenue south for just over 3 miles until you reach S. Orcas Street. Turn left (east) and follow S. Orcas Street for 0.9 mile to its end, where you'll find Seward Park. In the early 1900s, the City of Seattle purchased this chunk of land, which includes 50 feet of shoreline and 300 acres of forested landscapes, and created one of the finest urban recreation areas in the city. You'll want to enjoy the walking paths, which guide you under fluffy, yellow bigleaf maples, black cottonwood, and the occasional Pacific dogwood, red-osier dogwood, or Oregon ash. The understory here is made up of a number of colorful fall shrubs, such as vine maple, red elderberry, fool's huckleberry, Scouler's willow, and others.

The main path in Seward Park is the paved Perimeter Loop, which wanders 2.4 miles around the water's edge and showcases Mount Rainier if it's a clear day. Birding in Seward Park is very popular since the mix of forest and waterway attracts a wide variety of waterfowl, as well as owls, gulls, and, oddly, even mitred parakeets, which you'll likely hear before you see. The Seward Park Audubon Center, located in a building near the entrance, offers programming if you wish to learn more. If you don't have time for a walk, make a loop around the park in your car.

From Seward Park, travel north on Lake Washington Boulevard while admiring the bustling waterfront scene of active Seattleites working on their fitness goals as the road winds its way up the lake's edge. Garry oak trees and cherry trees are planted along the drive, and if you happen to hit it when the leaves are in their prime, they can be quite beautiful.

Follow Lake Washington Boulevard, passing several other great parks, including Genesee Park, Stan Sayres Memorial Park, Mount Baker Park, and Colman Park. If time permits, stop and check out the views and walking paths, or save that for another outing if today is all about the window seat. The road continues under the I-90 bridge and passes well-manicured estates and lake views.

In 3.9 miles from Seward Park (8.2 miles from where you started), bear right (north) on Lakeside Avenue S., and shortly afterward, pass the Leschi

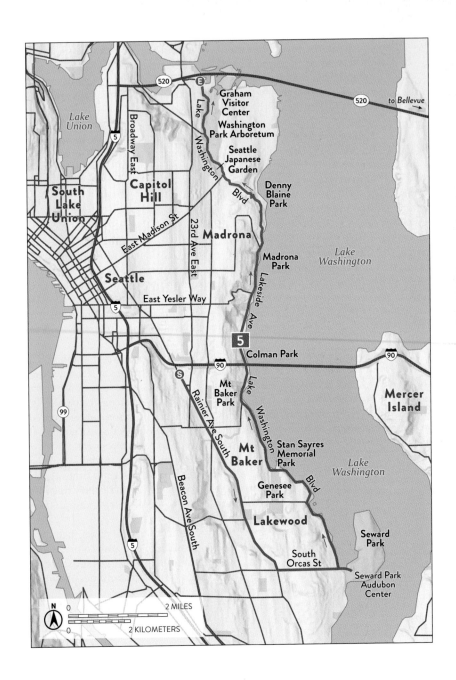

520

E

Graham
Visitor
Center

Washington
Park Arboretum

520

to Bellevue →

*Lake
Union*

5

Broadway East

Seattle
Japanese
Garden

Lake Washington Blvd

**Capitol
Hill**

Denny
Blaine
Park

**South
Lake
Union**

East Madison St

23rd Ave East

Madrona

Madrona
Park

*Lake
Washington*

Seattle

East Yesler Way

Lakeside Ave

5

5

99

5

90

Colman Park

S

Rainier Ave South

Mt
Baker
Park

Lake Washington

90

**Mercer
Island**

**Mt
Baker**

Stan Sayres
Memorial
Park

*Lake
Washington*

Beacon Ave South

Genesee
Park

Blvd

Lakewood

**Seward
Park**

South
Orcas St

Seward Park
Audubon
Center

N

0   2 MILES

0   2 KILOMETERS

A rustic, ornate bridge shelters cars under its arches in the Washington Park Arboretum.

neighborhood, complete with a waterfront park and a quaint downtown. If you need a lunch, a snack, or a cup of coffee, you may want to stop here briefly. Madrona Park shows up next, complete with a beachfront walking path if you need to stretch your legs. A few golden bigleaf maples in the area remind you of the season.

Immediately after Madrona Park, bear slightly right (north) to stay on what is now Lake Washington Boulevard again. Pass Denny Blaine Park, then wind up a series of S curves to a mildly confusing intersection, 6 miles from Seward Park. Bear slightly left (northwest) on Lake Washington Boulevard, ignoring signs for Lake Washington Loop, and continue the journey.

At 6.4 miles from Seward Park (10.7 miles from the start of the drive), cross E. Madison Street, and immediately afterward, enter Seattle's Washington Park Arboretum. Almost every trail in the area leads to a variety of vibrant fall colors, but one of the most popular destinations is the Japanese maple groves located not far from the Graham Visitor Center. Park in one of the many lots and wander one of the paved pathways (see Resources for maps), or continue your drive, which is also impressive.

Just 0.2 mile after entering the arboretum, reach the Japanese garden to the road's left (northwest), where you'll want to stop if the timing lines up. This 3.5-acre sanctuary features water, lanterns, bridges, cobblestone pathways, and bright Japanese maples that are manicured so beautifully, you'll feel like you are in a painting. It's a grand place for fall photo buffs! If that's you, the lighting tends to be better earlier in the day, so get there before or shortly after noon if possible. Unlike the other trails and visitor areas in the arboretum, the Japanese garden comes with a fee for admission. Check price and hours before you go at www.seattlejapanesegarden.org.

Parking lots beyond the gardens offer places to stop and gawk, or park and walk, a popular activity especially in good weather in the first few weeks of October. You may have to wait for a spot or circle several different lots.

At 7.6 miles from Seward Park (11.7 miles from the start), roughly 1 mile after entering the arboretum, arrive at a junction. A right (east) onto E. Foster Island Road leads to the Graham Visitor Center, well worth a visit if you have the time. A left at the junction puts you on Lake Washington Boulevard which connects to the 520 Bridge, the floating toll bridge. West on the bridge allows you to loop back to the start of the drive; east carries you toward Bellevue and the Cascade foothills. However you end the day, you'll have stories to share of nature in the city.

6. SNOQUALMIE PASS, TEANAWAY ROAD, AND BLEWETT PASS

Roundtrip Distance from Seattle: 230 miles
Estimated Trip Duration: Full day
Communities with Services: Seattle, North Bend, Snoqualmie Pass, Easton, Cle Elum
Attractions: Fall colors, mountains, small towns, farms
Passes for Stops or Entrances: Northwest Forest Service or Interagency Pass

> If you are looking for a weekend jaunt to an area where beauty abounds and you have plenty of time to enjoy the sights, consider heading over to the far side of the Cascade Crest, where larch populations are visible from your car window and peaceful country farms, complete with grazing horses, bring a tranquility to the season.

 Foliage: Cascade huckleberry, cottonwood, vine maple, western larch

From Seattle, follow I-90 east for roughly 54 miles to Snoqualmie Pass. Be sure to take in the beauty of the rocky summit of Mount Si to the north near the town of North Bend and, farther east just past exit 47, a jagged peak tucked back into the hills known as The Tooth, a popular alpine rock climbing route. From the freeway, you'll see the vibrant colors of red and yellow vine maples brightening the scree-filled hillsides where avalanche swaths have allowed the sunlight to flourish. During fall, the peaks near Snoqualmie Pass summit occasionally get a dusting of snow on their tippy tops, making the scene even more breathtaking.

Once you reach the pass, if you feel the need to stretch your legs, check out the paved loop trail at Gold Creek Pond. To reach it, take exit 54, just east of the summit, and turn left. Head back under the interstate to the north 0.1 mile, then turn right (southeast) onto Forest Road 4832. Follow this road, paralleling the freeway for 1 mile, then turn left (north) onto Gold Creek Road/FR 142. From here, continue 0.3 mile and then turn left (east) into the Gold Creek Pond parking lot, where a pit toilet can be found. You'll need a Northwest Forest Pass or Interagency Pass to park here. The paved, ADA-accessible loop around the pond is only 1 mile, with nearly no elevation gain, so it's perfect for kids, pets, and those with physical disabilities. Foliage such as rosy spirea, Cascade mountain ash, and cottonwood trees add splashes of fall color to the walk, while mountains reflected in the still water provide picture-perfect views.

On the road again, continue driving east from Snoqualmie Pass for nearly 31 miles, noting the yellow cottonwoods near the town of Easton and also where the Yakima River nears the interstate.

Take exit 85 and at the stop sign, go left (north) and cross back over the interstate. In a short distance, arrive at a T and go right (southeast) on State Route 10, yielding onto SR 970 shortly thereafter. Follow SR 970 for nearly 7 miles from the

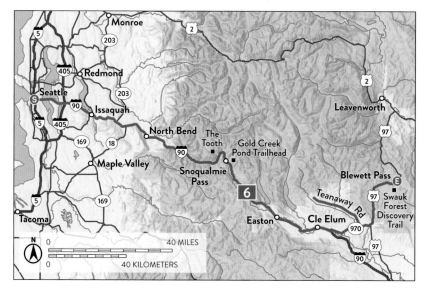

All the warmth of fall is on display along with a peaceful sample of rural countryside as you savor this drive.

interstate until you see Teanaway Road to the left (north). If you have time, drive down this road to see quiet farming communities and peekaboo views of the Teanaway River and the magnificent colors from the cottonwoods and maples on its shoreline. A few larches are scattered among the evergreens on distant hillsides. Turn back when you've enjoyed this beautiful sample of rural America.

Continue north on SR 970 and, nearly 10 miles from I-90, the road officially becomes US Highway 97. Get ready, the larches are about to show up on both sides of the road and nearby slopes! At roughly 25 miles since turning off I-90, arrive at the summit of US 97, known as Blewett Pass, with snow park areas on both sides of the road. Larches are brilliant around here, and you'll want to pull off and snap roadside pics.

If you are comfortable driving on a narrow dirt road with the occasional deep pothole, you might consider following FR 9716 to the right (south) of the highway for a half mile until you reach a large parking area with a pit toilet to the road's right. Swauk Forest Discovery Trail is located here but gets little maintenance, so unless you are up for some navigational challenges and perhaps climbing over downed trees, you may choose to skip it, or journey only a little bit along this 3-mile loop. Regardless, larches with their brilliant golden needles are along the road and parking area, so you'll be able to get up close and personal right from the start.

Once you've enjoyed Blewett Pass, head back the way you came.

EXTENDING YOUR TRIP

If you'd rather make this journey a loop, you could continue driving north on US 97 for 21 miles to intersect US 2. From there, head west on US 2 and in 5 miles reach the town of Leavenworth, where a stop for a soft pretzel and some cider is almost as mandatory as seeing the fall colors. With full bellies, continue west on US 2, and in a couple miles pass what is known as Tumwater Canyon, also famous for its brilliant fall colors (Drive 4). Just shy of 100 miles past Leavenworth, US 2 intersects I-5 at Everett. Head south toward Seattle for the full loop.

7. WHITE PASS BYWAY LOOP

Roundtrip Distance from Enumclaw: 220 miles
Estimated Trip Duration: Full day
Communities with Services: Enumclaw, Greenwater, White Pass, Cliffdell
Attractions: Fall colors, waterfalls, mountain lakes, volcano viewpoints
Passes for Stops or Entrances: National park entrance fee, annual pass, or Interagency Pass for Mount Rainier National Park entrances; Northwest Forest Service or Interagency Pass for Boulder Cave or Sheep Lake Trailhead
Notes: Cayuse Pass (State Route 123) and Chinook Pass (SR 410) close seasonally with the first significant snowfall in October. Double-check the Mount Rainier National Park website (see Resources) to ensure they're open before setting out.

Where can you go to see western larch trees up close and personal without having to do much backcountry hiking? This scenic drive! Not only will you get to see the stunning golden deciduous trees in their full display, but you'll also be treated to mountain lakes, a waterfall, rugged peaks, and even a glimpse of Mount Rainier—an unforgettable drive.

 Foliage: Bigleaf maple, black cottonwood, Cascade huckleberry, Pacific dogwood, rosy spirea, vine maple, western larch

Because this is a loop, you can start in any number of places. You could take Tacoma through Stevens Canyon (Drive 8) and connect with SR 123, or catch US

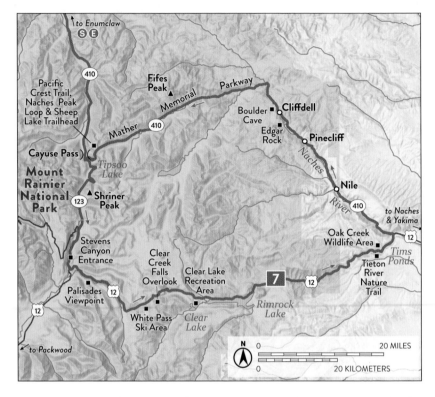

Highway 12 south of Napavine off I-5, then connect with SR 410 near Naches for the return loop. This drive description starts in Enumclaw.

From the last stoplight in Enumclaw (284th Avenue SE/Farman Street N. and Roosevelt Avenue E.) on SR 410 eastbound, proceed on SR 410 for 40.2 miles, passing the town of Greenwater, the Mount Rainier National Park boundary, and Sunrise Road, to a junction with SR 123 (Cayuse Pass). Prior to reaching this, look for a couple of turnoffs to the road's right where, on a clear day, Mount Rainier can be seen in full glory above the White River valley. If you pull off, use extreme caution on the narrow shoulders and when reentering the highway.

Proceed straight (south) at Cayuse Pass to stay on SR 123, noting the high country and a few Cascade huckleberries and vine maples, which are just starting to show themselves. The roadway begins curving gently downhill to follow the contours of the lower flanks of Seymour and Shriner Peaks. Double Peak to the road's right (west) shoots skyward, while under its summit, the hillsides turn shades of orange and red thanks to vine maples.

In the 1930s, many of the park's roadways were created, and the rustic stone "park-itecture" still seen on bridges and guardrails along this stretch is like a walk back in time. Bigleaf maple, black cottonwood, vine maple, and Pacific dogwood provide gorgeous fall colors in a canopy over the roadway with pullouts sprinkled about for quick snaps. As the road continues, the Ohanapecosh River peeks out from the forest—a tranquil setting where elk like to roam, so keep your eyes peeled.

In 11 miles from Cayuse Pass, reach Mount Rainier's Stevens Canyon (Drive 8) Entrance, and just after that, the Ohanapecosh Visitor Center and Campground. At roughly 16 miles from Cayuse Pass, turn left (south/southeast) at the junction with US Highway 12 to continue the adventure. As a side note, if your stomach is rumbling or you need fuel, the little hamlet of Packwood is located just 7 miles to the right (southwest) of this junction. Should you choose to visit, you'll want to do it as a detour and return to this spot when both belly and gas tank are full.

US 12 heads east now, climbing narrowly in the mountains and, in places, hugging tight corners. In 2.4 miles, the Palisades Viewpoint appears on the right (south) side of the highway, a worthy stop to ogle at the volcanic columnar basalt rock across the valley. This site has a picnic area and restrooms.

As you continue onward, give a look to the right to see the Goat Rocks area. The rocky steeps are the remains of what once was an ancient stratovolcano that stood much like Mount Rainier, at a height of 12,000 feet. They no longer represent one giant volcano, but the independent mountains standing tall and proud are still impressive.

In just over 8 miles from the junction with US 12, arrive at White Pass Ski Area, complete with a gas station and a small store full of snacks. Don't be surprised if you stop there and see a gaggle of weary, malodorous hikers piled up inside the store near its deli, taking advantage of the tables and chairs. The Pacific Crest Trail (PCT), which runs from Mexico to Canada, is very near this area, and almost all hikers stop here to resupply along their pilgrimage. Give them a fist bump for their efforts—most have likely been on the trail since spring and are within a few weeks of reaching their goal. If you are interested in their journey or would like to hike the Washington leg of the PCT at some point, check out my book *Hiking the Pacific Crest Trail: Washington*.

A couple miles beyond White Pass summit, Dog Lake shows up to the road's left (north), along with a healthy population of golden western larch trees mixed with the evergreens. And the larch madness begins! Western larch trees are often taller and have more of a compact, triangular shape than their more petite and outstretched subalpine larch cousins. What's more, their growing elevation is lower, and while they both prefer similar habitat, western larches tend to be found farther west of the Cascade Crest than subalpine larches.

Almost immediately after Dog Lake, a pullout to the road's right (south) showcases Clear Creek Falls Overlook, a worthy stop to view the powerful,

228-foot-high waterfall plunging through the stony canyon. Western larch trees populate the area, including distant hillsides, and interpretive signage guides you along the vistas. A pit toilet is found here too.

The road twists and turns along narrow shoulders with a few spots to pull off (take care in doing so) when the waterfall you just visited makes an appearance to the west. Larch trees dot the evergreen landscape, and the whole scene is breathtaking with a sprinkle of autumn. Clear Lake and its recreation area are up next, followed by Rimrock Lake, which is controlled by dams and often has interesting layers of mud along its banks.

At 30 miles beyond White Pass summit, the western trailhead for the Tieton River Nature Trail (Hike 37) shows up to the road's right (south), followed by the middle and finally the eastern trailhead near Oak Creek Wildlife Area. If you want to get out of the car for a bit and have time, this hike offers a prime opportunity to take a break, with plenty of pleasant fall colors for your eyes and your camera.

In 0.8 mile from Oak Creek Wildlife Area (30.8 miles beyond White Pass), pass a couple of picturesque small ponds, called Tims Ponds, to the right. Osprey often sit in neighboring trees scanning for their next meal, and fishermen dream of a good catch here as well.

At 2 miles beyond the Oak Creek Wildlife Area the road reaches a junction with US 12 and SR 410. Turn left (west) onto SR 410 and proceed, now on the upper half of the driving loop. Bighorn sheep are often seen in this area, roaming around the geological lava formations that helped form this region, so keep your eyes sharp when looking at the hillsides. The sheep blend in well!

The road follows the Naches River, which babbles scenically to the left (south/southwest) as it makes its way from the rugged mountains to the flat scrublands. Small, blink-and-you'll-miss-them communities such as Nile and Pinecliff come and go, along with the official start of the Mather Memorial Parkway. Named after Stephen Mather, the first director of the National Park Service, the commemorative roadway you are about to follow passes from Okanogan-Wenatchee National Forest into portions of the Mount Baker–Snoqualmie National Forest and, of course, into and through Mount Rainier National Park. Built as a wagon road in 1897, it is one of the oldest roads in Washington State and is certainly one of the most scenic.

As you drive, give a look off to the left (south/southwest) to catch a glimpse of Edgar Rock, a monolith that used to house a fire lookout.

The small community of Cliffdell shows up in just over 20 miles from the US 12/SR 410 junction. If hunger kicks in, Whistlin' Jack's Outpost Lodge and restaurant is visible from the roadway and is a good place for some eats.

Boulder Cave, found near here, is a fascinating lesson in geology and worth the 1.4-mile roundtrip hike, if luck is on your side. This weird COVID world has made management difficult for the Naches Ranger District, and the cave has been closed for a couple years, though rumor has it, guided tours may be in its future.

Clear Creek Falls drops into the valley below as larches keep watch from their lofty perches.

Regardless, it usually closes in late fall to protect a small, very rare population of Townsend's big-eared bats. Check the Naches Ranger District/Okanogan-Wenatchee National Forest website before you go (see Resources).

The transition from scrubland to a more mountainous climate takes this drive in a gorgeous trajectory, and before long, you'll be back in a sea of western larches mixed with evergreens. The rugged mountains here near the American River valley stand tall and proud, and you'll want to hop out of your car at safe roadside pullouts to snap a few pictures. At roughly 14 miles past Cliffdell, give a look off to the road's right (north) to see if you can spy the tall columnar andesite lava spires of Fifes Peak, the remains of an extinct caldera that exploded 25 million years ago. In August of 2017, the Norse Peak Fire hit the north side of this road and burned over 55,000 acres of wilderness. Sadly, the charred remains are now part of the drive, but thankfully, Mount Rainier and most of the William O. Douglas Wilderness were spared.

The landscapes are impressive as you continue onward, reaching a large parking area to the road's right (north) for the Pacific Crest Trail/Naches Peak Loop/Sheep Lake Trailhead (Hikes 39 and 42) in just over 26 miles from Cliffdell. Pit toilets are here, but they are often in rough shape, so it's best to hold it unless it's an emergency. Immediately after the parking area, the road crosses into Mount Rainier National Park and arrives at Tipsoo Lake—a vision! More desirable pit toilets are usually found here as well as picnic tables. If time permits, do a quick stroll around the lake to check out the reflection of Mount Rainier on the eastern side, especially if you get lucky enough for a sunset. Rosy spirea, Cascade huckleberries, and tan stalks of dormant wildflowers can add a little foreground interest to photos.

From here, the road descends by twisting and turning sharply to reach Cayuse Pass and the junction with SR 123 again, completing the loop. Bear right (north) at the junction, following SR 410 all the way back to Enumclaw, having celebrated autumn in a gorgeous way.

8. STEVENS CANYON ROAD TO PARADISE

Roundtrip Distance from Enumclaw: 145 miles
Estimated Trip Duration: Full day
Communities with Services: Enumclaw, Greenwater, Longmire, Elbe, Eatonville, Buckley
Attractions: Fall colors, small towns, volcano views, mountain lakes
Passes for Stops or Entrances: Mount Rainier entrance fee/annual pass or Interagency Pass

Notes: Stevens Canyon Road and Cayuse Pass (State Route 123) close seasonally with the first significant snowfall in October. Double-check the Mount Rainier National Park website (see Resources) to ensure it's open before setting out.

In autumn, the 19-mile Stevens Canyon Road lights up with splendid views of Mount Rainier and the rugged peaks near its perimeter. Colorful vine maples coat the hillsides in a smattering of earth tones, and on a clear day, you may even get double vision with the mountain reflecting in the appropriately named Reflection Lakes. The drive to Stevens Canyon Road is also scenic, with bigleaf maple trees and occasional peeks of the Ohanapecosh River. What's more, the opportunities to take a hike on one of many park trails are countless if you desire more than a day in the car. Then again, the window seat is perfectly relaxing and extremely scenic. You choose!

 Foliage: Bigleaf maple, black cottonwood, Cascade huckleberry, Pacific dogwood, rosy spirea, Sitka mountain ash, vine maple

There are several ways to get to Stevens Canyon Road. You can approach it from Tacoma via SR 7 or from Packwood via US Highway 12 and SR 123. The route described here is a loop starting from the city of Enumclaw, which is generally accessible from major metropolitan areas. Those living on the east side of the Cascades might find catching Stevens Canyon Road from US 12/SR 123 a better option, which offers the double bonus of seeing the White Pass Byway Loop (Drive 7) too. It's a lot of window time but makes for a big, beautiful day.

From the last stoplight in Enumclaw (284th Avenue SE/Farman Street N. and Roosevelt Avenue E.) on SR 410 eastbound, proceed on SR 410 for 40.2 miles, passing the town of Greenwater, the Mount Rainier National Park boundary, and Sunrise Road to a junction with SR 123 (Cayuse Pass). Just before Cayuse Pass a couple of narrow pullouts offer magnificent Mount Rainier views if the mountain is not shrouded in clouds. Use caution on the narrow shoulders and when reentering the roadway.

At the top of Cayuse Pass, arrive at a fork and stay straight (south). Proceed on SR 123/Cayuse Pass, where a few Cascade huckleberries and vine maples start to show up on neighboring hillsides. The next 11 miles of roadway are interesting as you wind your way down the narrow, twisting road under the broad shoulders of Seymour and Shriner Peaks. To the road's right (west) is Double Peak, an impressive sight with its two summits shooting skyward and its shoulders adorned with clumps of vine maple.

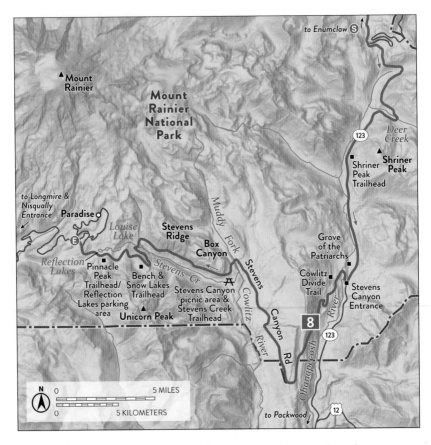

Most of this road was constructed in the 1930s with tunnels and rustic stone guardrails and bridges, such as the one over Deer Creek, still holding strong and providing a glimpse into a different era. Along the roadsides, bigleaf maple, black cottonwood, vine maple, and Pacific dogwood make up most of the colors mixed with their woodland friends, the evergreens. At 7.4 miles past the Cayuse Pass junction, the Shriner Peak Trailhead (Hike 41) stealthily shows up to the road's left. The trailhead is hidden in the evergreens across from a large pullout to the road's right. Make a note to come back and hike it another day, since it's a doozy and daylight is most likely limited.

After Shriner Peak Trailhead, the road delivers you to the Ohanapecosh River basin, where you'll want to keep your eyes peeled for elk as they wander the forest. The Ohanapecosh River to the road's right (west) plays peekaboo with passing cars, and the vine maples near its edges explode in color. Several pullouts offer opportunities to stop and grab the camera.

At 11 miles past the Cayuse Pass (SR 123) junction, the well-signed Stevens Canyon Road and Stevens Canyon park entrance appears on the road's right. Turn right (west), pay your park entrance fees, and proceed 0.2 mile to the Grove of the Patriarchs feature. If you need a restroom or a break from driving, this is a good place for it. If time, gumption, and drive line up, you might want to check out this hike—a round-trip of 1.3 miles to a grove of behemoth trees. Kids will particularly enjoy the swinging bridge across the river, which takes you to the giant evergreens.

Stevens Canyon Road winds in tight, twisty corners, where you'll pass the unassuming Cowlitz Divide Trailhead to the right and wind your way past evergreens and the occasional vine maple grove until you reach Box Canyon, 10.3 miles past the entrance booth. This is another great place to stop, stretch, and sightsee. Across the road from the parking area, a short walk delivers you to a bridge where the Muddy Fork Cowlitz River enters a narrow slot canyon that funnels water through a tight space with furious speed and force. The sound and power of the water are impressive, although it's hard to capture in a picture; video might be a better choice. A few rosy spirea plants in this area offer colors, as do the thick yellowish-tan mosses on the rocks—a testament to the copious amount of rain this area receives.

Immediately after Box Canyon, the road crosses under an overpass for the Wonderland Trail and enters Stevens Canyon picnic area and Stevens Creek Trail to the road's left (south). The picnic area is tranquil under the forest canopy and a good stop if you want a nibble. The Stevens Creek Trail here descends steeply for 0.7 mile to enter Stevens Creek Canyon, revealing a series of cascades and eventually waterfalls. Seeing all the waterfalls will slow you down even though it's only an 8-mile roundtrip journey, so perhaps save it for another day.

The narrow road traverses under Stevens Ridge and opens up views to the south of talus-laden hillsides sprinkled with vine maples. Stevens Canyon is far below to the left (south) as the road climbs, making an S turn over the bubbling Stevens Creek, which drops in from the mountain high above. Subalpine landscapes start coming more into view now, showing off Cascade huckleberries and dormant wildflower stalks.

The road you are on was the final road created in the park, in 1957, and was a key connecting point between the east and west sides of Mount Rainier National Park. Construction was started in the late 1930s but was put on hold thanks to World War II for nearly a decade. Besides being a leisurely drive, the road also makes it easier for those with disabilities and physical challenges to enjoy the high country from a window seat.

To the left, 16.2 miles from the Stevens Canyon Entrance, a trailhead with a small parking lot takes off to Snow and Bench Lakes. If time, energy, and parking allow, this moderate hike is a pleasant one at 2.8 miles roundtrip to a pair of lakes in the

On a clear day, a drive through Stevens Canyon Road is the perfect place to marinate in fall colors and enjoy the charm of Washington's highest mountain.

Tatoosh Range. The second lake, Snow Lake, is the main feature, as it sits under the pointy Unicorn Peak with a shoreline fringed with colorful leaves of Sitka mountain ash and Cascade huckleberries.

Just after that trailhead, Louise Lake to the right (north) is seen in a small basin below the road, followed by Reflection Lakes immediately to the road's right. Be sure to park at Reflection Lakes and check out the Mount Rainier views and, if the mood hits, the surrounding trails near the lake.

To the road's left (south) from the parking area of Reflection Lakes is Pinnacle Peak Trail, a more difficult climb of 1050 feet and 2.6 roundtrip miles. If this hike and all the others in the park are on your bucket list, I have a book on that too: *Day Hiking Mount Rainier.*

At 1.5 miles after Reflection Lakes, Stevens Canyon Road ends at Longmire-Paradise Road. Going right here will take you to the Paradise area—a worthy visit if you have time.

When you've had your fill, head back the way you came. Alternatively, you could continue on Longmire-Paradise Road to Elbe, where the name changes to SR 7. Proceed on SR 7 westbound, which eventually winds its way back to I-5 in just over 100 miles, or follow your GPS back to wherever you call home.

ACKNOWLEDGMENTS

So many wonderful people have helped me in my work, behind the scenes and in front of them.

Foremost, I wish to thank my husband, Vilnis, who supported me as I trotted off to spend chilly autumn weeks researching and developing content for this guide to the finest fall hikes in Washington. Once again, his boundless love, patience, and support have allowed me to live my dreams as he stayed home with our sweet collie and kept the home fires burning.

Special thanks to my family and friends who believed in me and pushed me hard to continue the things that seemed impossible at times. You guys are my rocks.

To the forest and park rangers who have been patient with my questions, queries, and curiosities, thank you. You have a tough job, but you don't show it with your welcoming generosity and endless patience.

Lastly, I wish to acknowledge my readers. You, like me, have a heart for the wild places and won't stop until you've seen all corners of this big, beautiful planet. May you find, amongst these pages, places that will make you smile long after winter arrives in the high country and Mother Nature takes her slumber. Sharing these places with you is the reason I write. May your soul be filled with the bounty of autumn.

Finding myself along trails like this one, near Clover Lake (Hike 40), makes me feel over-whelmingly grateful for public lands and open spaces to soak my soul in natural grandeur.

RESOURCES

LAND MANAGEMENT AGENCIES

See relevant national forest website for links to specific districts.

Gifford Pinchot National Forest
fs.usda.gov/giffordpinchot

Mount Adams Ranger District
509-395-3400

Mount Baker–Snoqualmie National Forest
fs.usda.gov/mbs

Darrington Ranger District
360-436-1155

Mount Baker Ranger District
360-854-2553

Skykomish Ranger District
360-677-2414

Snoqualmie Ranger District
425-888-1421

Okanogan-Wenatchee National Forest
fs.usda.gov/okawen

Cle Elum Ranger District
509-852-1100

Methow Valley Ranger District
509-996-4000

Naches Ranger District
509-653-1401

Wenatchee River Ranger District
509-548-6977

Mount Rainier National Park
nps.gov/mora/index.htm
360-569-2211

Olympic National Park
Wilderness Information Center
nps.gov/olym/index.htm
360-565-3130

Washington Department of Fish & Wildlife
wdfw.wa.gov
Maps at: wdfw.wa.gov/about/wdfw-lands/green-dot#print

Oak Creek Wildlife Area
509-653-2390

Wenas Wildlife Area
509-457-9308

Washington State Department of Natural Resources
dnr.wa.gov
360-825-1631

Washington State Parks
parks.state.wa.us

Riverside State Park
509-465-5064

Wallace Falls State Park
360-793-0420

Spokane County Parks
spokanecounty.org
509-477-4730

City of Spokane, Parks and Recreation/Urban Forestry
my.spokanecity.org/parksrec
509-625-6200

ROAD CONDITIONS

Washington State Department of Transportation
Travel Info Phone Number: 511
wsdot.com/traffic/trafficalerts

PASSES

Discover Pass
discoverpass.wa.gov

Every Kid Outdoors
everykidoutdoors.gov/index.htm

Interagency Pass
nps.gov/planyourvisit/passes.htm

National Park Passes
yourpassnow.com

Northwest Forest Pass
fs.usda.gov/main/r6/passes-permits/recreation

ADDITIONAL MAPS

Dishman Hills Conservation Area (Spokane)
dishmanhills.org/maps/

Finch Arboretum (Spokane)
my.spokanecity.org/urbanforestry/programs/finch-arboretum

Historic Newhalem walking tour (Newhalem)
seattle.gov/light/DamTours/Newhalem_ flyer.pdf

Riverside State Park (Spokane)
parks.state.wa.us/DocumentCenter/ View/1935/Riverside-State-Park—-over-view-PDF

Washington Park Arboretum (Seattle)
botanicgardens.uw.edu/washington-park-arboretum/visit/maps-trails

BOOKS

Arno, Stephen and Ramona Hammerly. *Northwest Trees*, 2nd Edition. Seattle: Mountaineers Books, 2007.

Asars, Tami. *Day Hiking Mount Rainier*, 2nd Edition. Seattle: Mountaineers Books, 2018.

Asars, Tami. *Hiking the Pacific Crest Trail: Washington*. Seattle: Mountaineers Books, 2016.

Whitney, Stephen R. and Rob Sandelin. *Field Guide to the Cascades and Olympics*, 2nd Edition, Seattle: Mountaineers Books, 2004.

INDEX

A

Alpental Ski Area 132–33, 136

Alpine Lakes Wilderness 76,79,110–111,113–114, 120, 123,129,132,136, 140–141, 143–144,151, 153

Alta Mountain 23, 128–29, 131

amenities 33

America the Beautiful Pass 12

Arlington 203, 205, 209

Artist Point 43–44, 199–202

B

Bare Mountain 150–53

Bear Lake 192

bears 21–24

Bench Lake 227

Big Four Ice Caves 207

Blewett Pass 125, 212, 216–19

Blue Lake 69–72, 190, 192–95

Boulder Cave 219–20, 222

Bowl and Pitcher Loop 85–87

Box Canyon Creek 128, 130, 226–27

Burlington 54–55, 202–05

C

Carne Mountain 10, 15, 94–97, 100

Cayuse Pass 177, 181, 219–21, 224–26

Chain Lakes Loop 18, 38, 42–45, 202

Chinook Pass 167, 171, 179–81, 219

City of Spokane Parks & Recreation Urban Forestry 88, 234–35

Clara Lake 116–18

Cle Elum Ranger District 119,124, 127, 233

Clear Creek Falls Overlook 220–21

Clear Lake 190–92

Cliffdell 219, 222, 224

Clover Lake 174–75, 230

Colchuck Lake 112–15

Coles Corner 95–96, 98–99, 210, 212

Concrete 202–203

Crater Lakes 75–79

Cutthroat Lake 61–63, 65–67

Cutthroat Pass 63–67

D

Damfino Lakes 50–52

Darrington 81, 83, 205–06, 208–09

Darrington Ranger District 81, 223

Deer Creek 225–26

Dege Peak 174–75

Denny Creek 135–38

Dick Lake 174, 176–77

difficulty 31–32

Dishman Hills Conserva-tion Area 91–92

distance 31

Dog Lake 221

dog-friendly 33

Double Peak 220, 225

E

Eagle Lakes 75–81

East Crater Lakes Loop 188–92

East Crater Peak 195

Easy Pass 20, 67–69

elevation gain 31

elk 24–25

Elk Lake 192

Enumclaw 167, 170–71, 174–75, 177, 179–81, 185, 219–20, 224, 225

Evergreen Mountain Look-out 104–06

Excelsior Peak 50–53

F

Finch Arboretum 88–89

Franklin Falls Trailhead 135, 137

G

Gem Lake 132, 134–35

getting there 35

Glacier Public Service Center 39, 43, 47, 50, 200–02, 206

Goat Peak 166–170

Gold Bar 209–10

Golden Gate Loop 184–87

GPS 32

Granite Falls 81, 83, 205–09

Granite Mountain 139–42
Grasshopper Pass 57–60
Greenwater 219–20, 224–25

H
Heather Meadows 44,
47–48, 200–01, 206
Hemlock Pass 136
Hibox Mountain 129–130
Hidden Lake 174, 176
high point 31
Hope Lake 110–12

I
Iller Creek 91–93
Index 210
Indian Heaven Wilderness
188–196
Interagency Pass 12–13
Ira Spring Trail 143–47
Iron Bear 124–27
Island Lake 142–46

J
Junction Lake 189– 92

K
Keekwulee Falls 136–37
kid-friendly 33

L
Lake Ann 47–49, 73–75
Lake Ingalls 19, 26, 119–23
Lake Sahalee Tyee 190,
193, 195
Lake Stevens 205
Lake Twentytwo 81–84, 207
Lake Valhalla 107–09, 209,
212
Leave No Trace 17–21
Leavenworth 94, 117–18,
205, 209–12, 219

Lila Lake 128–31
Little Giant Pass 12, 97–101
Longmire-Paradise Road
184–85, 224–26, 228

M
managing agency 33
Maple Falls 199–200
Maple Pass Loop/Lake Ann
72–75
maps 15, 17
Marblemount 61, 64–73,
203
Marion Lake 116–118
Mason Lake 32, 142–46
Mather Memorial Parkway
222
Mazama 58–59, 202–03,
205
Melakwa Lake 135–39
Methow Valley 57
Methow Valley Ranger
District 233
Mig Lake 110–12
Mission Ridge Ski Area 116
Monroe 209–10
Mount Adams Ranger
District 188, 192, 233
Mount Baker 38, 233
Mount Baker Wilderness
40, 42, 44, 47–48, 51, 55,
104–05, 107–08, 110–11, 132,
136, 141, 144, 151, 180, 205
Mount Rainier 166–87, 234
Mount Rainier National
Park 13, 166–87, 198,
219–20, 222, 224–27, 234
Mount Shuksan 39, 42, 44,
46–49, 53, 199, 201
mountain goats 18–19,
25–26, 68, 70, 121–23, 175
mountain lions 26

Mountain Loop Highway
57–84, 205–09
Myrtle Falls 184–87

N
Naches Peak Loop 22,
170–73, 224
Naches Ranger District
166, 222–24
Newhalem 202–04
North Bend 119–153, 212,
216–217
North Cascades 57–84,
202–205,
notes 35

O
Oak Creek Wildlife Area
162–65, 220, 222, 234
Ohanapecosh River 179,
221, 225–226
Olallie Lake 147
Olympic Mountains 154–57
Olympic National Park 13,
154–155

P
Pacific Crest Trail 60–65,
107–08, 110–11, 170–72,
181–82, 190–93, 195,
220–21, 224
Palisades Lake 173–77
Paradise 184–85, 224–28
Park Butte 53–56
parking 1 1, 13–14, 18, 33
passes 11–13, 33, 35
permits 11–13, 17–18, 33, 35
photography 27–30
pika, 46, 118, 133, 133,
142–143
Pinnacle Peak Trail 228

R

Rachel Lake 127–31
Rainbow Lake 142–46
Rampart Lakes 128–31
Rampart Ridge 127–31
rattlesnakes 159, 162
Reflection Lakes 225–28
Rimrock Lake 222
Riverside Park 85–88
Rockport 202–03

S

safety 16–17, 21
salmon 203
scenic drives 11, 35, 199–228
Seattle 213–19
Selah 158–64
Seward Park 212–16
Seymour Peak 220, 225
Sheep Lake 180–83, 219,
    224
Shriner Peak 177–80, 220,
    225–26
Skykomish 101–07, 110,
    209–10
Snoqualmie Pass 119–52,
    216–19
Snow Lake 131–35

Sourdough Gap 180–83
Spokane 85–93
Staircase Rapids Loop
    154–57
Startup 209–10
Stevens Canyon Road
    224–28
Stevens Pass 94–118, 209–12
Sultan 209–10
Sunrise Creek 175
Sunrise Lake 174–75
Syncline Mountain 59–60

T

Talapus Lake 146–47
Tatie Peak 57–60
Teanaway 119–52, 216–18
Teanaway Ridge 124–27
Teanaway Road 121, 216–18
Tieton 158–65, 220, 222
Tieton River Nature Trail
    161–65
Tims Ponds 222
Tipsoo Lake 170–73, 180,
    220, 224
Tombstone Lake 192–96
Tumwater Canyon 117, 205,
    209–12, 219

U

Umtanum Creek Canyon
    158–61
Upper Palisades Lake
    173–77

W

Wallace Falls State Park
    209–10,
Washington Park Arbore-
    tum 213–16
Washington Pass Overlook
    204
Washington State Parks 12
Wenas Wildlife Area 158–61
West Cady Ridge 101–03
White Pass Byway 34,
    219–24, 225
Winthrop 59, 61, 64–65,
    67–68, 70, 72–73, 76, 79,
    198, 202–05

Y

Yakima 158–165, 220
Yakima Peak 172, 181
Yakima River 159160, 281
Yellow Aster Butte 39–42

ABOUT THE AUTHOR

Tami Asars is the author of several trail and hiking guides, including *Hiking the Pacific Crest Trail: Washington*, *Hiking the Wonderland Trail*, *Day Hiking Mount Rainier*, 2nd edition, and *Day Hiking Mount Adams and Goat Rocks*. She is also an avid thru-hiker and has hiked the Pacific Crest Trail (PCT), Continental Divide Trail (CDT), Colorado Trail (CT), Arizona Trail (AZT), Wonderland Trail, and West Coast Trail, among others. Tami has served as a backpacking guide in Mount Rainier National Park and has explored nearly every corner of Washington State, from the dense coastline to the Cascade Mountains and beyond. For more information, or to drop her a line, please visit www.tamiasars.com.

MOUNTAINEERS BOOKS
SKIPSTONE BRAIDED RIVER

recreation · lifestyle · conservation

MOUNTAINEERS BOOKS is a leading publisher of mountaineering literature and guides—including our flagship title, Mountaineering: The Freedom of the Hills—as well as adventure narratives, natural history, and general outdoor recreation. Through our two imprints, Skipstone and Braided River, we also publish titles on sustainability and conservation. We are committed to supporting the environmental and educational goals of our organization by providing expert information on human-powered adventure, sustainable practices at home and on the trail, and preservation of wilderness.

The Mountaineers, founded in 1906, is a 501(c)(3) nonprofit outdoor recreation and conservation organization whose mission is to enrich lives and communities by helping people "explore, conserve, learn about, and enjoy the lands and waters of the Pacific Northwest and beyond." One of the largest such organizations in the United States, it sponsors classes and year-round outdoor activities throughout the Pacific Northwest, including climbing, hiking, backcountry skiing, snowshoeing, camping, kayaking, sailing, and more. The Mountaineers also supports its mission through its publishing division, Mountaineers Books, and promotes environmental education and citizen engagement. For more information, visit The Mountaineers Program Center, 7700 Sand Point Way NE, Seattle, WA 98115-3996; phone 206-521-6001; www.mountaineers.org; or email info@mountaineers.org.

Our publications are made possible through the generosity of donors and through sales of 700 titles on outdoor recreation, sustainable lifestyle, and conservation. To donate, purchase books, or learn more, visit us online: Mountaineers Books is proud to support the Leave No Trace Center for Outdoor Ethics, whose mission is to promote and inspire responsible outdoor recreation through education, research, and partnerships. The Leave No Trace program is focused specifically on human-powered (nonmotorized) recreation. For more information, visit www.lnt.org.

MOUNTAINEERS BOOKS
1001 SW Klickitat Way, Suite 201 • Seattle, WA 98134 •
800-553-4453 • mbooks@mountaineersbooks.org • www.mountaineersbooks.org

An independent nonprofit publisher since 1960

Mountaineers Books is proud to support the Leave No Trace Center for Outdoor Ethics, whose mission is to promote and inspire responsible outdoor recreation through education, research, and partnerships. The Leave No Trace program is focused specifically on human-powered (nonmotorized) recreation. For more information, visit www.lnt.org.

OTHER TITLES YOU MIGHT ENJOY FROM MOUNTAINEERS BOOKS

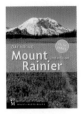

Day Hiking Mount Rainier, 2nd edition
Tami Asars
Full color guide to 80 hikes in or close to
Mount Rainier National Park

Hiking the Pacific Crest Trail: Washington
Tami Asars
Section hikes ranging from four to ten days in the
Washington State portion of the PCT

Washington Wildflower Hikes
Nathan Barnes and Jeremy Barnes
Colorful guide to 50 hikes that feature
gorgeous seasonal wildflowers

Hiking Washington's Fire Lookouts
Amber Casall
A guide to hiking to Washington State's
accessible and still-standing 44 fire lookouts

Trees of the West: An Artist's Guide
Molly Hashimoto
A lavishly illustrated tribute to dozens of
beloved tree species of the West

www.mountaineersbooks.org